Reclaiming migration

MANCHESTER
1824

Manchester University Press

Reclaiming migration

Voices from Europe's 'migrant crisis'

Vicki Squire, Nina Perkowski,
Dallal Stevens and
Nick Vaughan-Williams

Manchester University Press

Published by Manchester University Press
Altrincham Street, Manchester M1 7JA

www.manchesteruniversitypress.co.uk

British Library Cataloguing-in-Publication Data
A catalogue record for this book is available from the British Library

ISBN   978 1 5261 4481 2   hardback

ISBN   978 1 5261 4483 6   paperback

First published 2021

Typeset by New Best-set Typesetters Ltd

Contents

Acknowledgements

First and foremost, we would like to extend our sincere thanks to all those people who have generously and courageously shared their stories and struggles with us as part of this research. This book is dedicated to all of those who continue to experience the effects of crisis politics today.

A warm thanks also to our friends and colleagues, Angeliki Dimitriadi and Maria Pisani, whose incredible work has been vital to the research on which this publication is based. We also extend our sincere appreciation to Vasiliki Touhouliotis for her excellent research during the second phase of the project (Athens and Istanbul), along with Skerlida Agoli (Kos), Emanuela Dal Zotto (Sicily), Alba Cauchi, Sarah Mallia and Mario Gerada (Malta) for their impressive efforts during the first phase of the project. In addition, we would like to sincerely thank all the translators who enabled us to speak to people on the move in different languages, as well as everyone who generously helped us obtain access to reception centres and informal camps across the various research sites.

This project has benefitted from the important insights and feedback of multiple audiences at various workshops and conferences, for which we are grateful. We would like to offer particular thanks to members of our Advisory Board, including Anne Bathily, Veronika Bilger, Paolo Cuttitta, Edward Albert Hall, Suzan Ilcan, Pia Oberoi and Federico Soda. Thanks also to Marie-Louise Coleiro-Preca for support with

Acknowledgements

research in Malta, to Aine Bennett for editorial assistance with Chapters 1 and 3, and to the anonymous reviewer for their helpful suggestions on an earlier draft of the text.

The research on which this book is based was funded by the UK Economic and Social Research Council Mediterranean Migration Research Programme, Urgent Research Grant ES/N013646/1. The findings were published in a co-authored report freely accessible at www.warwick.ac.uk/crossingthemed, and parts of Chapter 6 have been published as part of a journal article in *Environment and Planning C: Politics and Space*.

All royalties from the sale of this book will be donated to NGOs directly supporting people arriving to the EU under precarious conditions.

Introduction
Reclaiming migration: voices from Europe's 'migrant crisis'

You can go round and ask the people and find more and more information. You can go round ... for even someone on the street and he passed this way he can tell you his history, history of suffering.

(ROM2.01, man from Mauretania, Rome)[1]

... you have to understand asylum-seekers' problems here. They are people who have fallen in a hole and cannot get out of the hole. You have to understand this and you have to get the information and after that you can make a sound and transfer our voices to the decision-makers and policymakers of European countries.

(IST2.14, man from Afghanistan, Istanbul)

These excerpts are taken from testimonies of people who had made – or were contemplating making – the dangerous journey across the Mediterranean Sea by boat during 2015 and 2016. They point both to the challenges that people faced at that time in Rome, Istanbul and elsewhere, as well as to the additional difficulty of making such challenges known. In other words, the testimonies above point to the processes of *silencing* experienced by people on the move as the European Union (EU) engaged migration as a 'crisis'. It is this politics of crisis, as well as the experiences of voicelessness involved, that *Reclaiming Migration* seeks to challenge. It does so by directly engaging the largely unheard voices of people on the move. The book rejects both the silencing of people migrating in precarious conditions, as well as the crisis-oriented intensification of a preventative policy agenda across the EU. Specifically, we suggest that processes of silencing were integral to a problematic form of crisis politics advanced by the EU in 2015–16, which was not simply narrated as an emergency at the external borders but also as a humanitarian emergency demanding the 'immediate imperative' to 'protect those in need' (European Commission, 2015a: 2). By focusing attention on the multiple ways through which people on the move contest these narratives of crisis, we highlight the importance of engaging a counter-archive of the testimonies of people on the move in challenging 'official truths' about the situation in the Mediterranean during 2015 and 2016. Far from a benign response to a situation of human tragedy, we argue, a preventative policy agenda grounded in a politics of crisis both produces and embeds experiences of precarity such as those highlighted in the quotes that open this chapter. Speaking to the '*histor[ies] of suffering*' that people on the move continue to endure on arriving to the EU (ROM2.01) and to the '*holes*' that people can so easily fall into throughout various stages of the migratory experience (IST2.14), the demand to ensure that '*our voices*' reach '*the decision-makers and policymakers of European countries*' continues to resonate well beyond 2015 and 2016.

Setting the scene

Reclaiming Migration argues that a form of crisis politics demanding swift and decisive action by governing authorities has played a key role in silencing people on the move. In April 2015 around 1,200 people died in a series of shipwrecks across the central Mediterranean. While these deaths were by no means new or novel, they drew increased attention to the precarious journeys that many people made at the time in the hope of creating a life of peace and safety. The European Commission sought to respond to this situation with haste. On 20 April 2015, a 'Ten-point action plan on migration' (European Commission, 2015a) was presented as an immediate response to the loss of life. This was followed on 13 May 2015 by the Commission's launch of *A European Agenda on Migration* (hereafter the '2015 *Agenda*') as a

Introduction

communication to the European Parliament, the Council, the European Economic and Social Committee and the Committee of the Regions. Addressing migration as a complex phenomenon with a long history, and stressing the importance of a longer-term response to the issue (European Commission, 2015b: 2), the 2015 *Agenda* built on the 'Ten-point action plan on migration' through advancing a series of immediate actions as well as a four-pillar approach to 'manage migration better' (European Commission, 2015b: 6). In focusing both on the need to address 'those who exploit migrants' and the 'root causes of migration', it directly called for an approach upholding the EU's 'international commitments and values while securing our borders' (European Commission, 2015b: 2). Although it was acknowledged by the Commission that 'the situation in the Mediterranean is not a new nor a passing reality' (European Commission, 2015a), the spring of 2015 was also represented by the *Agenda* as a critical juncture. Specifically, it was narrated as a moment highlighting 'serious doubts about whether our migration policy is equal to the pressure of thousands of migrants, to the need to integrate migrants in our societies, or to the economic demands of a Europe in demographic decline' (European Commission, 2015b: 2). This claim about large numbers of people arriving in the EU, combined with an understanding of 2015 as a critical moment in addressing migratory 'pressures', invoked a form of crisis politics that we argue eclipsed the demands of people on the move.

Data on sea arrivals and deaths are notoriously troublesome, reflecting assumptions about mobile populations, the inconsistent use of value-laden administrative categories, and often severe methodological limitations (IOM, 2014). According to Frontex (2016) – whose datasets have been criticised and do not escape these problems[2] – there were 60,200 arrivals by boat via the central (4,500) and eastern Mediterranean (55,700) routes in 2010. In 2014 this total increased to 221,590 (170,760 on the central route; 50,830 on the eastern route), and in 2015 it rose to 1,039,332 (153,946 central; 885,386 eastern). Between 2014 and 2016, arrivals in Italy were primarily via the central route across the Mediterranean Sea from North Africa, and in 2015 arrivals in Greece came through the eastern route (usually via the Aegean Sea). Despite fluctuations in death rates at sea, which do not strictly correlate with known arrival data, the International Organization for Migration's (IOM) 'Missing Migrants Project' documented 3,279 deaths in 2014, rising to 3,784 in 2015 and 5,098 in 2016 (IOM, 2017); in 2010 there were twenty known deaths according to the UNHCR (2017). By April 2015, the European Commission (2015a) had started to narrate increased sea arrivals and deaths as a 'migration crisis' facing the EU as a whole, a narrative that has since been adopted and used widely – albeit in various ways and by diverse actors – in order to refer to the events described above (see Chapter 1). Critically, a focus on increased arrivals and increased deaths at sea closed down any room for disagreement surrounding the need for decisive action. Moreover, it also situated people on the move as border transgressors and/or as victims in need of protection, rather than people with a voice within wider political and policy debates.

While the claim that the EU is under 'pressure from thousands of migrants' might initially appear to be correct on consideration of the arrival statistics during 2015, this belies a much more complex situation and is underpinned by a problematic form of crisis politics that this book rejects. Certainly, 2015 will be remembered as a year in which there was a dramatic increase in new arrivals along the eastern route via Turkey, many of whom went on to travel along the 'Balkan route' to Germany and elsewhere following initial entrance to Greece. Those fleeing civil war in Syria made up many of these arrivals, although Afghans, Iraqis, Iranians and others also travelled along the eastern route.[3] Nevertheless, it is important to note that the 2015 *Agenda* effectively emerged in the context of the increased visibility of deaths along the central route via North Africa, where arrival numbers actually dropped marginally in 2015 and where the number of deaths remained consistent with those during 2014. Migration across the central Mediterranean had become increasingly prominent since 2011, with increased arrivals in the EU associated with 'Arab Spring' states such as Tunisia,

Introduction

Libya and Egypt. Yet arrival figures fluctuated during the early 2010s, until a rapid increase to unprecedented levels was sustained from 2014 throughout Europe's so-called crisis period during 2015 and 2016. Increasing instability in Libya was particularly significant at this time, with many sub-Saharan Africans who had escaped to Libya being forced to flee from situations of further exploitation and violence. Although deaths at sea along this route, as well as across the western Mediterranean, were by no means a new phenomenon, in the spring of 2015 it became ever more apparent that these were consistently high and on the rise. Also apparent was that the routes to the EU were changing, with a relative decrease in arrivals along the western route to Spain, contrasting with an increase in arrivals along the eastern route via Greece at that time.[4] As well as a humanitarian 'crisis' represented by mounting deaths at sea, the situation was thus also narrated as a 'crisis' of increasing arrivals. The spring of 2015 was in this regard an optimal moment for the European Commission to advance a more long-standing preventative agenda with greater ferocity than ever.

A preventative policy agenda

So how did the European Commission advance a preventative policy agenda during 2015, in which people on the move were silenced as either victims or perpetrators of Europe's increasing migratory 'pressures'? It is worth noting that *A European Agenda on Migration* was not a radically new framework, but rather served to pull together a range of more long-standing policies as part of a 'coherent and comprehensive approach to reap the benefits and address the challenges deriving from migration' (European Commission, 2015b: 2). In particular, the 2015 *Agenda* stressed the importance of using 'the EU's global role and a wide range of tools to address the root causes of migration' (European Commission, 2015b: 2). This reflects earlier developments under the EU's Global Approach to Migration and Mobility (GAMM), which from 2005 operated as the 'overarching framework for the EU external migration and asylum policy' (European Commission, 2019). The 2015 *Agenda* provided both short- and medium-term solutions designed to address pressing priorities, as well as a framework for the development of a longer-term approach grounded in a Common European Asylum System, shared management of the European border and a new model of legal migration (European Commission, 2015b: 17). Comprised of four pillars understood as 'four levels of action for an EU migration policy which is fair, robust and realistic' (European Commission, 2015b: 7), it included:

- **Reducing the incentives for irregular migration:** Pillar 1 included actions designed to address the root causes of irregular and forced displacement in third countries; actions to combat smugglers and traffickers; and actions to ensure the effective return of irregular migrants.
- **Border management – saving lives and securing external borders:** Pillar 2 included actions to strengthen the role of Frontex, the European Agency for the Management of Operational Cooperation at the External Borders (subsequently relaunched as the European Border and Coast Guard Agency in October 2016), and to ensure standardised border management across the EU; actions to coordinate coastguard functions and further develop 'Smart Borders' proposals; and actions to strengthen the capacity of third countries to manage their borders.
- **Europe's duty to protect: a strong common asylum policy:** Pillar 3 included actions to ensure coherent implementation of the Common European Asylum System; and actions to ensure greater sharing of responsibility across member states through revisions to the Dublin system.
- **A new policy on legal migration:** Pillar 4 included actions towards a well-managed regular migration and visa policy; actions to ensure effective integration; and actions to maximise development benefits for countries of origin.

Introduction

Three implementation packages were advanced in 2015, which built on key areas outlined in the 2015 *Agenda*. These included a Europe-wide relocation scheme designed to foster solidarity across the EU in hosting new arrivals, and an EU Action Plan Against Migrant Smuggling as part of a first implementation package on 27 May 2015 (European Commission, 2015c). An extended relocation programme, as well as an Action Plan on Return and setting up a Trust Fund for Africa, formed part of a second implementation package on 9 September 2015 (European Commission, 2015d). In addition, a series of actions towards revising European border security were advanced as part of a third implementation package on 15 December 2015 (European Commission, 2015e). Indeed, as policy initiatives were developed over time, many aspects that were introduced or discussed in the 2015 *Agenda* were implemented and further substantiated across a series of concrete sites. Notable during 2015–16 were developments regarding EU–Turkey joint action on preventing migration to the EU (March 2016), the development of a 'hotspot approach' in which EU agencies worked with 'front-line' states to identify new arrivals to the EU (from September 2015), and efforts to revise the Common European Asylum System (ongoing). Significant is that the *Agenda* has retained its relevance over time, because it has 'guided the EU's response to immediate challenges' (European Commission, 2020).

Reclaiming Migration does not seek to develop a comprehensive analysis of the 2015 *Agenda* or of EU policy developments directly. Rather, it engages a counter-archive of migratory testimonies in order to assess some of the key dimensions of the framework as this was advanced by the European Commission during 2015–16. We understand the 2015 *Agenda* to be a complex and contested approach, which nevertheless reflects a broader and more long-standing tendency across the EU (and beyond) to prevent precarious forms of migration. This preventative or deterrent approach can be understood both in terms of the rolling out of border security and migration control to a range of 'third countries' outside the EU, and in the creation of various 'hostile environments' within the EU. For instance, a preventative approach is implicated in development and aid policies overseas, including bilateral agreements and programmes to train border security and coastguard authorities. Moreover, it is also implicated in identification and reception programmes and asylum processes that leave people separated from family members and waiting for extended periods of time without adequate legal and financial resources. Rather than developing an assessment of the preventative policy agenda directly, however, this book considers how people on the move in precarious conditions assess the impacts of policy developments based on their own experiences of the migratory journey and of arriving to the EU. Such an analysis is imperfect in the sense that we cannot straightforwardly make direct causal links between policy developments and lived experiences. Nevertheless, consideration of how the people who are migrating interpret, engage with and speak back to the preventative policy agenda is critical in assessing an approach that is otherwise skewed towards dominant perceptions regarding the interests and preferences of more settled EU populations. It is thus to the contested politics of testimony that this book turns.

The contested politics of testimony

Reclaiming Migration undertakes a critique of the EU's preventative policy agenda on the basis of a detailed qualitative analysis of the testimonies of people on the move across the Mediterranean Sea by boat (see Squire et al., 2017). More than simply engaging these testimonies in order to undertake an analysis of migratory journeys and experiences in all their complexity (e.g. Crawley et al., 2017), it focuses on the *political claims or demands* that such journeys and experiences give rise to. Such a focus draws inspiration from a broader body of work across the fields of migration and citizenship studies, which emphasises the claiming of rights, or a 'right to have rights', as an integral dimension of political subjectivity (Isin and Nielsen, 2008). The book, in this regard, considers how people on the move speak

Introduction

and act 'in the name of equality' precisely where relations of *inequality* are otherwise presupposed (Rancière, 2004). It engages people on the move as experiential 'experts' and theorists in the field of migration, to develop an approach to the politics of knowledge production in which those who are usually discounted in policy debates are approached as those with the authority to speak (Johnson, 2016; Squire, 2018; see also Vaughan-Williams and Stevens, 2016; Jarvis, 2018). The aim here is not to advance an objectivist analysis of testimony as an expression of authenticity and proof of the truth of the situation in the Mediterranean during 2015 and 2016. Certainly, our testimonies shed light on lived experiences of migration and on the tangible and embodied effects of policy developments, but they do not produce knowledge about a singular truth or uncontestable reality. Yet, neither does the book seek to advance a subjectivist analysis that focuses solely on the personal experiences and perceptions of people on the move. Instead, we engage migratory testimonies in terms that firmly reject the way the constitution of knowledge about the 'migrant crisis' of 2015–16 is shaped by the official archive, and show how knowledge production in the field of migration is *politically contested* (see Chapter 2). Intervening in a situation marked by dynamic and conflictual relations between policy developments and migratory dynamics (Squire, 2011), the book thus focuses on engaging a counter-archive that is oriented specifically towards assessing policy developments from the perspective of those whom policy in the field of migration affects most directly: people on the move themselves.

Addressing the contested politics of testimony and engaging a counter-archive produced with people on the move demands a distinctive terminology that runs throughout this book. We distance ourselves from the framing of precarious migration as 'illegal' or 'irregular' here, based on an understanding of irregularity not as a status or objective 'problem', but as a 'condition that is *produced* through various processes of (ir)regularisation' (Squire, 2011: 5). This emphasis on denaturalising governmental categories is also reflected in our avoidance of terms such as 'migrant', 'refugee' and 'asylum seeker'. Instead, we refer to 'people on the move in precarious conditions', 'people migrating' and 'precarious migration' in order to draw attention to precarity as a lived experience. Such terminology reflects analytical appreciation of the complexity of migratory journeys and experiences, an ethical appreciation of the importance of avoiding the judgement of people based on their legal status, and a political appreciation of the problems of governmental categories that divide people on the move between forced and voluntary, or political and economic migration (see Scheel and Squire, 2014). Nevertheless, there are also problems with this language as it implies that people 'on the move' are inherently mobile, when situations of immobility are also prevalent (see Hage, 2005). In an attempt to disrupt this assumption, we also move away from the terminology of 'countries of origin', 'transit' and 'destination' that assumes a linear and progressive movement from one place to another. Such terms underpin a Eurocentric account of migratory journeys, which advances a preventative policy agenda in order both to deter people prior to their arrival to EU territory and to judge the need for protection in reductive terms. By contrast, we seek to develop a new terminology surrounding 'intersecting drivers and conditions of flight', which fosters appreciation of the fluid and fragmented journeys of many people on the move, and the cumulative experiences of precarity over time (see Chapter 4). Rather than using a governmental language of Europe's 'migrant crisis', we thus seek to engage a critical language that rejects the assumptions on which such narratives of crisis rely.

Engaging a counter-archive and addressing the contested politics of testimony from the perspective of people on the move enables a distinctive position both surrounding what we call crisis politics (see also Squire, 2020a), as well as surrounding the preventative policy agenda that has been advanced with increased intensity since 2015. Highlighting the complementarity between crisis politics and a preventative or deterrent agenda, we show the importance of moving beyond a debate about the specific nature of the 'crisis' that emerged during 2015–16. By contrast, we adopt an 'anti-crisis' perspective that more

Introduction

fundamentally rejects the narrative of crisis. In Chapter 1 we show how this is not simply based on a critical analysis of conceptual work into crisis politics, but emerges from our sustained engagement with the testimonies of people on the move, through which crisis narratives are contested along various lines. These lines of critical analysis are subsequently carried through into our empirical chapters (Chapters 3–6). For example, in Chapter 3 we draw attention to the physical as well as epistemic forms of violence experienced by people on the move in the context of the EU's deterrent approach, casting doubt on the suggestion that migration poses a 'threat' *to* European populations. In Chapter 4, we highlight the limits of assumptions about the need to provide people on the move with humanitarian succour, drawing attention to the multiplicity of demands for peace and safety that are advanced on the basis of cumulative experiences of precarity. Chapter 5 focuses on the ways in which our migratory testimonies pose a more far-reaching challenge to Europe's self-proclaimed image as a place of peace and safety. Drawing out the claims to justice on which such a critique rests, Chapter 6 suggests that our counter-archive involves a collective rejection of long-standing legacies of colonial injustice within which the politics of crisis and a preventative policy agenda are embedded.

Reclaiming Migration contributes to an emergent 'postcolonial turn' in critical border and migration studies (Tudor, 2018), specifically by emphasising the ways in which people on the move play a central role as producers of knowledge and as protagonists of counter-narratives of the so-called crisis. Driven by a close engagement with the testimonies from our counter-archive, we point to racialised forms of violence and ongoing colonial trajectories that continue to infuse the experiences of people migrating across the Mediterranean today. The book neither aims to provide a comprehensive postcolonial analysis of contemporary migration nor of the policies advanced by EU states, but rather it seeks to foster sensitivity to the ways migratory testimonies explicitly and implicitly point to racialised experiences of migration in the context of what we call Europe's 'postcolonial present' (see Bhambra, 2016).

It does so on the basis of a distinctive politico-methodological approach, which is grounded in a commitment to recognising people on the move as experts and theorists in the field of migration (Chapter 2). *Reclaiming Migration* thus marks an important departure from existing works that simply document the journeys and experiences of people migrating across the Mediterranean in the midst of Europe's so-called crisis. By engaging a counter-archive of the testimonies of people on the move during 2015 and 2016, it provides an analysis of the various ways deterrence, asylum and even Europe itself is questioned and contested. In so doing, it engages in broader debates about the relationship between elite and non-elite knowledge production (Chapter 1), the concept of the counter-archive and questions of voice (Chapter 2), the problems of a deterrent approach to migration (Chapter 3), the limits of asylum and international protection (Chapter 4), the failings of Europe's rights-based framework (Chapter 5), and the relationship between migration and postcolonialism (Chapter 6). Far from being limited to an examination of the situation in the Mediterranean during 2015 and 2016, *Reclaiming Migration* thus provides an empirically substantiated conceptual intervention that is of broader significance across multiple contexts.

Chapter overview

Reclaiming Migration draws on a large-scale qualitative research project, which involved over 250 interviews with people on the move across the Mediterranean during 2015 and 2016 (see Chapter 2). Chapter 1 locates the study in the context of dominant narratives of Europe's 'migrant crisis' as advanced by elites, especially since 2015, to characterise population displacements and their effects in the Mediterranean region and the EU as a whole. It shows how some policy-makers drew on the securitised language of crisis to argue for tougher deterrent measures with reference to perceptions of the scale of new arrivals, loss of control over land and sea borders, and threats to European societal and economic security. It also shows how other actors harnessed

Introduction

the crisis discourse as a strategy to draw public attention to increasing deaths at sea, the humanitarian needs of those on the move and the failure of the international response to provide adequate protection. The chapter demonstrates how at times these apparently contending narratives were mobilised simultaneously by governmental actors – including the European Commission and its agencies – thus creating a highly ambiguous and confusing policy-making environment. What unites these otherwise diverging narratives of crisis, however, is that they all conflate a complex series of geographically and historically situated events, experiences and responses *as if* they were a singular occurrence across multiple contexts. In repeating the language of crisis uncritically, some academic commentary also runs the risk of reproducing this frame, which we argue is problematic both empirically and politically. Instead of accepting the totalising frame – one that obfuscates the heterogeneous and fragmented realities of crossing the Mediterranean Sea by boat – we argue for an alternative starting point. Informed by the testimonies of those on the move, the chapter develops a postcolonial critique of the narrative of Europe's 'migrant crisis' as one that silences the experiences of those on the move, ignores the political claims and demands of those in flight and downplays the continued violent impacts of colonial legacies. By contrast, we adopt an explicitly 'anti-crisis' position – one that rejects the politics of crisis and reorients the analytical frame to prioritise the contested politics of testimony, in order to address more fundamental questions relating to increased arrivals and deaths at sea.

Chapter 2 reflects on the politico-methodological contribution of the research in further detail, focusing in particular on questions of positionality and voice while drawing attention to the political significance of producing a 'counter-archive' based on the testimonies of people on the move. Creating this counter-archive, the chapter argues, is important in enabling an appreciation of the diverse narratives, practices and projects of migration that are rendered invisible where a singular conception of the European 'migrant crisis' pre-dominates. The research on which *Reclaiming Migration* is based is critical in this regard, because it seeks to contribute to a wider set of documentary practices that collectively work to counter the 'control bias' of knowledge production in the field of migration. Nevertheless, the process of producing a counter-archive in such terms is by no means straightforward. The chapter shows how questions of positionality, in particular the uneven power dynamics between researchers and research participants, present an issue that haunts the research and remains irresolvable despite the commitment of the research team to embedding the principles of participation, respect and equality in the project design at all stages. Chapter 2 explores this issue in relation to the question of voice, more specifically by drawing attention to the problems of 'giving voice' and by reflecting on some of the silences that this potentially produces. By contrast, the chapter also emphasises the importance of moments in the research process in which people on the move 'take voice' in ways that undermine the very grounds on which the research is based. These moments, it argues, are critical dimensions of a counter-archive that seeks to unsettle the predominance of a singular account of Europe's so-called migrant crisis, along with the power dynamics within which such forms of knowledge production are grounded.

Chapter 3 focuses attention on people's experiences en route in order to highlight the ineffectiveness of the deterrence paradigm. In particular, it challenges claims that intensified border policing, the limitation of rights and increased deportations function as an effective deterrent to migration. Contributing to conceptual debates on the limits of the deterrence paradigm and its application to migration management, the chapter situates such policies in long-standing histories of racialised violence and argues that deterrent measures are ineffective on two primary grounds. First, in order to be effective, deterrence presupposes *knowledge* of deterrent measures among those whom authorities seek to deter. Second, in reflecting the elite assumptions of a postcolonial crisis frame, a deterrent approach fails to understand *why* people migrate in the first place. Examining anti-smuggling as a key measure of deterrence, Chapter 3 also contests the dominant policy framing of smugglers as the 'problem' at hand, highlighting the drivers that necessitate movement as well as the wider conditions that make smuggling the only viable option for escape. Presenting nuanced accounts of the relationships and encounters of people on the move with smugglers, it problematises the dangers of the anti-smuggling approach to present a damning critique of the EU's preventative policy agenda. Although it is clear that deterrent border security measures are ineffective on their own terms, the experiences of those on the move are paramount in any assessment of the deterrent approach – and yet they are often neglected. Emphasising the lived experiences of deterrent bordering practices, the chapter proceeds to argue that deterrent measures increase the risk of racialised violence and abuse that individuals face on their journeys, at times far beyond the EU's territorial borders and independent of whether the intended destination is Europe. Indeed, we show how people on the move face a continuum of border-related violence when travelling towards and across the EU, in their encounters with border guards, police, smugglers and the material environment.

Chapter 4 also examines experiences en route as well as experiences of arrival to the EU, emphasising in particular the limitations of European asylum and protection policies. It draws attention to the complexity of migratory journeys and explores how the struggle to find peace and safety often involves a seemingly unending search by people on the move. By pointing to the longevity of many journeys outside EU territory, their fragmented nature and what we call varied and 'intersecting drivers and conditions of flight', the chapter shows how people on the move often face cumulative experiences of precarity, in which the racialised forms of violence highlighted in Chapter 3 forms only a part. Testimonies suggest the significance of colonial histories that bind states and that are manifest in the racialised exclusions of the EU protection regime – histories that were not only ignored in the 2015 *Agenda*, but which are also silenced in European asylum and refugee policies more generally. Notably, the idea of a 'duty to protect' does not extend to assisting people as they traverse complicated land routes, instead remaining largely territorially bounded to only those who reach Europe and who can meet stringent legal requirements. As such, the provision of protection in 2015–16 remained focused on harms suffered in the first country of departure and ignored experiences of ill-treatment during complex, disrupted and traumatic journeys. Indeed, our counter-archive reveals the racialised violence of an asylum system that necessitates cross-border travel irrespective of the difficulties and risks that this imposes. It shows how some people were aware and actively seeking asylum on arrival to the EU, while others were more generally seeking peace and safety. Nevertheless, in contesting the cumulative experiences of precarity faced both before and after arrival to the EU, people on the move advanced a multiplicity of claims and demands, importantly drawing attention to the limits of assumptions about the need to provide them with humanitarian succour.

Chapter 5 extends the analysis of arrival given in Chapter 4 by engaging critically with the perception that Europe forms a desirable destination from the perspective of those seeking protection. It highlights specific challenges across different sites of arrival and emphasises the frustration of many people on the move about their experiences in the EU. Drawing on the testimonies from our counter-archive, the chapter questions the received wisdom of Europe as place of human rights, humanitarianism, peace and safety, pointing to the tensions between the outward image projected by Europe – in particular by the European Union – and the lived experiences of those arriving to the EU. Contrasting people's expectations prior to arrival with the conditions experienced in different member states, the chapter chronicles sub-standard living conditions, a lack of information on asylum and reception procedures, long periods of uncertainty due to opaque bureaucratic systems, and delays and administrative hurdles to family reunification. Instances of 'reverse smuggling' (i.e. the facilitated return to unsafe third countries or countries of origin) point to the deep disappointment with reception conditions, in particular those related to the prolonged separation from family members elsewhere. The

Introduction

testimonies highlight the continuity of violence and precarity many people on the move face across fluid and fragmented migratory journeys, and challenge the temporal and spatial borders of the 'migration crisis' as commonly narrated. They also open up the question of Europe itself, which is inseparably linked to how the EU relates to its 'others', especially people on the move in precarious conditions. Indeed, Chapter 5 argues that our counter-archive presents a challenge to the colonial legacies of the European project, through demands on the EU to honour its own values and commitments. In so doing, it suggests that testimonies of people on the move reveal a Europe that is unable to address its postcolonial present.

Chapter 6 deepens the analysis of the challenge posed by people on the move to Europe and the EU, specifically by exploring those claims and demands that bring to bear a deeper critique of the role of the European policy agenda in *producing* the drivers and conditions of flight. The analysis draws attention to two key ways in which such a challenge occurs, which largely correspond with movements along the eastern and central Mediterranean routes respectively. The first line of critique, most evident in testimonies of those following the eastern route, points to the significance of the involvement of EU member states – or lack thereof – in regional wars that drive people's movement, and questions the assumption that closing borders is an effective response to concerns surrounding migration as a security 'threat'. The second line of critique, most evident in testimonies from people following the central route, points more directly to the ongoing significance of colonial legacies to the migratory journey, and highlights the effects of failing aid initiatives and unequal visa policies. Chapter 6 argues that an approach that engages the testimonies of people on the move as a form of knowledge produced by experts and theorists of migration highlights the importance, limitations and problematic impacts of a policy focus *beyond* EU borders. While a concern with addressing 'root causes' has become increasingly significant to the policy agenda over recent years, the long-standing failure of such an approach is evident in the ways that people on the move speak to the importance of addressing issues in the regions they have escaped from. Far from a request simply for aid, the chapter shows how such testimonies involve a demand for equality and justice, thus opening up ways for rethinking or *reclaiming* migration in alternative terms. Specifically, the chapter argues that the testimonies from our counter-archive suggest that migration can be understood as a postcolonial or anti-colonial movement, whereby migration is reclaimed through the enactment of claims to justice that reject the unequal right to free movement embedded in the EU's preventative policy framework.

The concluding chapter summarises the key arguments of the book, reflecting on three key themes that emerge from the analysis: precarity, justice and postcoloniality. First, it emphasises precarity as a multidimensional condition, which is manifest not only in the lived experiences of those who escape to the EU but also in the experiences of those who refuse or are unable to flee. Second, it highlights how claims to justice are not simply orientated towards movement, but also need to be appreciated as claims to settlement that reject Europe's positionality as 'host' to newly arriving migrants. Finally, the Conclusion draws attention to the recurring colonial dynamics of the contemporary policy agenda, to suggest that the voices of people on the move who speak out against a postcolonial present can no longer be ignored.

Notes

1 Interviews are coded throughout this book based on the interview location (ATH – Athens; BER – Berlin; IST – Istanbul; KOS – Kos; MAL – Malta; ROM – Rome, SIC – Sicily), the research phase (1 – autumn 2015; 2 – summer 2016), and interview number for that location. For example, the interview ROM2.01 was carried out in Rome during the summer of 2016, and it was the first interview carried out in that location.

2 Frontex notes on its website that 'illegal border-crossings at the external borders may be attempted several times by the same person'. The use of Frontex data has been the subject of controversy on these grounds. We use Frontex data in this case over UNHCR (Operational Portal – Mediterranean) data, because the latter includes some minor inconsistencies and limitations.

3 For more details about the migratory context along each route and about the sample this book draws on, please see Squire et al. (2017a).

4 See the UNHCR data portal (https://data2.unhcr.org/en/situations) for monthly arrival statistics along the three main Mediterranean routes. Further fluctuations followed after Europe's so-called 'crisis' was over, with arrivals dropping along the central route from 2017 and subsequently increasing along the western route to Spain. Far from a straightforward picture of migratory 'pressure' on the EU, fluctuations in migratory dynamics suggest a much more complex situation in which people on the move are forced to negotiate various barriers to their movement – not least policy initiatives seeking to prevent arrivals to the EU.

1

Narratives of 'crisis'

Constantly, every time you open the news, the refugee crisis, the refugee crisis. The refugee crisis is in all the countries of the world whether they are European or Arab. We Syrians became the crisis of the world? Why are we a crisis?
(ATH2.24, man from Syria, Athens)

Introduction

This chapter undertakes a critical analysis of how the narrative of Europe's so-called migration crisis came to frame dominant understandings of and policy responses to increased arrivals and deaths at sea. As will be made clear, however, we do not posit a linear causal relationship between event and response in this context. The book as a whole argues that the narrative of 'crisis' has had a transformational effect on the social realities that it claims merely to describe. That is to say, the crisis narrative must be seen as a political intervention that actively came to shape – and not merely respond to – the course of events in 2015; its impact continues to set the context in which political and legal challenges associated with migration are framed in the EU. In this endeavour, we are guided by two broad conceptual and methodological orientations. First, the concept of *narrative* is central to our analysis. Far from neutral devices, narratives are always embedded within and serve to reinforce particular relations of power and knowledge. As White argues, social events do not present themselves in an unmediated way and are not imbued with meaning outside of their representation; the role of narratives, understood broadly as discursive attempts at producing an order of meaning, is to offer a plot, a sequence and a sense of coherence in the absence thereof (White 1987: 11). Because all narratives inescapably entail 'ontological and epistemic choices with distinct ideological and ... specifically political implications', they performatively produce the reality that those using them often purport only to observe (White, 1987: ix). Second, there is a specificity to *crisis narratives* as a particular genre of political narrative, which take a given issue out of the normal realm of politics and relocate it with reference to the politics of emergency (Schmitt, 2005 [1922]). As such, narratives of crisis do not have 'objective' standing, but rather should be thought of as instruments that set up social reality in ways that enable non-routinised responses to a set of circumstances. On this twinned basis, any attempt to unpack the dominant framing of increased sea arrivals and deaths as a 'crisis' facing Europe needs to examine how this narrative has been propagated, by whom, on what basis and with what implications.

The following analysis begins by mapping how seemingly divergent narratives of Europe's 'migration crisis' have been mobilised by diverse governmental and non-governmental actors. Some politicians drew on the securitised language of crisis in order to argue *for* tougher deterrent measures, with reference to perceptions of the scale of new arrivals, loss of control over land and sea borders, and/or threats to European societal and economic security. Other interlocutors in public policy debates, particularly those representing non-governmental organisations (NGOs), harnessed the crisis narrative as a political strategy in order to draw public attention to increasing deaths at sea, make demands in support of the humanitarian needs of those on the move and critique what they saw as the failure of the international governmental response to provide adequate protection for them. At times these apparently contending narratives were mobilised simultane- ously by the same governmental actors, thus creating a highly ambiguous and confusing policy-making environment. What unites these otherwise diverging narratives of crisis, which were often reproduced uncritically and with sensationalising effect in mainstream media sources, is that they tend to conflate a complex series of geographically and historically situated events, experiences and responses *as if* they were a singular and homogeneous 'event' across multiple contexts. Such simplification is not only empirically problematic; the decontextualisation involved in many crisis narratives also has significant political and ethical ramifications. In focusing on the 'here and now', narratives of Europe's 'migration crisis' produce subjectivities that are outside of history and politics, which enables interventions that focus narrowly on managing the lives of people on the move rather than recognising their life histories and responding to their political claims. The simple and yet profound question posed by the Syrian man interviewed in Athens and quoted above – *'Why are we a crisis?'* – thus urgently requires unpacking. Another common denominator is that, in perpetuating the notion that the 'crisis' is geographically, historically and politically exogenous to Europe, many crisis narratives reproduce a Eurocentric and ultimately violent postcolonial imaginary of 'us' and 'them'. In embracing the narrative of crisis uncritically, academic analysis also runs the risk of reproducing these problems and forestalling the effort to find alternative grounds for response. For this reason, we argue for the need to abandon the crisis frame and, in recovering the otherwise silenced voices of those on the move, adopt an explicitly 'anti-crisis' perspective (Roitman, 2014).

Narrating Europe's 'migrant crisis'

The first official use of the term 'crisis' by the European Commission to refer to events in 2015 came in April that year (see Introduction). Following a shipwreck on 18 April in which approximately 650 passengers were killed, then Vice-President Federica Mogherini and former Commissioner Dimitris Avramopoulos spoke of the emerging 'crisis situation in the Mediterranean' when outlining the 'Ten-point action plan on migration' (European Commission, 2015a). One month later, reflecting concerns about a rapid increase in sea arrivals and deaths, the European Commission announced a new framework for EU border security and migration management in the form of 'A European Agenda on Migration' (hereafter the '2015 *Agenda*'). On the one hand, unlike the more measured language of the 2011 'Global Approach to Migration and Mobility' (GAMM) framework that it replaced, the 2015 *Agenda* was infused with the vocabulary of 'emergency', 'urgency', 'pressure', 'influx' and 'exceptionalism', and referred directly for the first time to 'the migration crisis in the Mediterranean' (European Commission, 2015b: 6). On the other hand, while the 2015 *Agenda* adopted this new 'crisis' footing, it also perpetuated the older dual narrative of *both* 'securing borders' *and* 'saving lives' that had already been established in the 2011 GAMM (European Commission, 2011). With its focus on deterring 'would-be' arrivals from leaving for the EU in order to reduce deaths at sea, this confusing blend of securitised-humanitarianism became the defining hallmark of the European Commission's narrated response to the 'crisis' (see Chapter 3). This was typified by Operation Sophia, part of the EUNAVFOR MED military task force which, from June 2015, was deployed in order to *both* 'identify, capture, and dispose of vessels' that are 'used or suspected of being used by migrant smugglers or traffickers' *and* 'to prevent the further loss of life at sea' (EUNAVFOR MED, 2019; see also Chapter 3). In its initial evaluation of how the 2015 *Agenda* had been implemented, the Commission praised Frontex for having already 'saved over 122,000 lives' while at the same time reaffirming its commitment to 'strong border control' in order to 'support Member States managing exceptional numbers of refugees on their territory' (European Commission, 2015f: 4). Thus, the European Commission's framing of increased arrivals and deaths combined two ostensibly divergent narratives of crisis that are discernible in wider public policy debates concerning the situation in the Mediterranean: a securitising narrative that sees those on the move as threats to European identities, economies and societies, and prioritises the interests of sovereign nation states and their citizens; and a humanitarian narrative that operates via a continuum that positions the same people as helpless victims in need of saving by

Reclaiming migration

Europe at one end and as the bearers of rights at the other (see Chapter 6).

Securitising narratives of crisis

Securitising narratives of crisis have been notably pursued in a number of EU-level policy responses. References to a 'surge' in human mobility (European Commission, 2016b) and 'uncontrolled flows' (European Council, 2016a) dramatically portrayed a loss of control of Europe's external borders. Frontex, latterly known as the European Border and Coast Guard Agency, enthusiastically embraced the 'migration crisis' narrative in its representation of events in 2015. Its 2016 Annual Risk Analysis Report revealed the Agency's working assumptions about the core features of Europe's so-called migration crisis: the cause was unambiguously framed in terms of transnational flows of people heading towards the European continent (Frontex, 2016: 6); the scale of arrivals was presented as 'immense' and historically unprecedented (Frontex, 2016: 4); people on the move were referred to in catch-all terms as 'illegal' and/or 'irregular' border-crossers and were assumed to be primarily 'economic migrants' (Frontex, 2016: 5); and their movement was framed as a direct threat not only to European economies, but also to public safety and security at large, with an explicit association made between migration and terrorism (Frontex, 2016: 8).

Many of these assumed characteristics of the 'migration crisis' – and the overarching claim that citizens, nations and Europe as a whole are threatened by external migration – were also to be found, albeit with varying emphases and degrees of intensity, in the narratives of anti-immigrant political movements, and indeed some governments across the continent. Right-wing and neo-Nazi groups – such as the *Alternative für Deutschland* (Alternative for Germany or 'AfD'), the *Nationaldemokratische Partei Deutschlands* (National Democratic Party of Germany or 'NPD') and the *Patriotische Europäer gegen die Islamisierung des Abendlandes* (Patriotic Europeans Against the Islamisation of the Occident or 'PEGIDA') in Germany, Golden Dawn in Greece, Jobbik in Hungary, the Five Star Movement in Italy and the English Defence League (EDL) in the UK, to name only a few – all sought to capitalise on the 'migration crisis' narrative in order to stoke anti-immigrant and pro-border sentiments among citizens who are typically deprived of clear and authoritative sources of information. These groups' highly gendered and racialised mediations of the 'crisis' invariably presented new arrivals as terrorists, sexual predators and uncivilised barbarians in order to call for tougher immigration controls and deterrent border security measures on land and at sea. Such mediations pre-date 2015, of course, but population displacements that year offered unprecedented opportunities to bring them to the fore (Krzyzanowski et al., 2018). These securitising representations were not limited to the extreme fringes of the political spectrum, however, as governments, notably in Austria, Denmark, Hungary and the UK, adopted increasingly populist slogans to justify physical fence-building along land borders and/or more restrictive national immigration policies. Thus, in defending the construction of the 523 km long and 4 m high fence along Hungary's land borders with Serbia and Croatia, for example, Prime Minister Victor Orbán asserted in a 2015 interview that 'the factual point is that all the terrorists are basically migrants' and that the 'number one job' facing the EU, EU member states and NATO is 'to defend the borders and to control who is coming in' (Kaminski, 2015). There was an overtly religious dimension to Orbán's border rhetoric, in that he sought to position Hungary as a 'civilisational border guard', which had defended Europe's Christian borders for over a thousand years (Scott, 2020: 11). Taken as a whole, Bauman (2016: 1) sums up the securitising narrative of the 'crisis' as one whereby migration is presented as 'ostensibly overwhelming Europe and portending the collapse and demise of the way of life we know, practice, and cherish'.

Humanitarian narratives of crisis

The mobilisation of a crisis narrative was not limited to securitising discourses in support of tougher deterrent border controls, however;

it also framed interventions in public policy debates made by prominent humanitarian non-governmental organisations. In a report entitled *The Mediterranean Migration Crisis: Why People Flee, What the EU Should Do*, Human Rights Watch (2015: 22) located the 'crisis situation in the Mediterranean' in the wider context of 'severe humanitarian crises around the world'. It argued that the response of the EU, in 'preventing departures and limiting arrivals', has 'contributed to the crisis' and urged EU governments to 'place a human rights perspective at the centre of efforts to respond to the crisis' (Human Rights Watch, 2015: 2). Similarly, a public statement released on 9 July 2015 by Amnesty International referred to the 'unfolding humanitarian crisis' in the central Mediterranean and the 'ever-growing refugee crisis' it was said to be a part of (Amnesty International, 2015: 1, 4). The statement used the language of crisis to draw attention to the inadequacy of the EU's search and rescue efforts, particularly after the closure of the Italian-led Operation Mare Nostrum, and to call on EU leaders to do more to 'rescue [...] people in distress' (Amnesty International, 2015: 4). While hailing the initial success of the EU's approach in reducing the death rate at sea, the document argued for EU countries to open 'more safe and legal routes for refugees to enter Europe' (Amnesty International, 2015: 4). Likewise, in a report published in November 2015, Médecins Sans Frontières (MSF) referred to the 'crisis' in Europe coming 'on top' of 'the global displacement crisis' (MSF, 2015: 3). The authors attributed the former to the efforts by the EU and member states to 'seal-off' the continent, to pursue 'an ever-increasing securitisation agenda' and to intensify 'numerous restrictive immigration policies and practices' (MSF, 2015: 4). They recognised that 'some limited action has been taken by the EU in 2015 to deal with the refugee crisis', but concluded by noting that 'in no way does the response match the scale of the crisis nor deal with the chronic lack of safe and legal routes' (MSF, 2015: 20).

Securitising and humanitarian narratives of Europe's 'migration crisis' in public policy debates clearly diverged in several key respects. The former took the sovereign state and its citizens as referent objects of security, which were presented as being threatened by transnational flows of 'migrants'; as such, the crisis was one seen as posed to the EU and its member states from an external source. A particularistic narrative designed to stoke a politics of fear was propagated in a bid to define 'the people' against an abstract notion of the 'migrant Other'; this legitimised otherwise exceptional measures in liberal democracies such as the construction of large-scale razor-wire fences. Humanitarian narratives, by contrast, took those on the move as referent objects of a non-statist understanding of security; from this perspective, the crisis was presented in humanitarian terms as demanding greater efforts by the international community to respond to the basic needs of those often framed as 'helpless victims'. A universalist narrative that appealed to notions of humanitarian compassion was mobilised in order to mount a cosmopolitan critique of states' (in)action and call for solidarity with those individuals caught up in a crisis that was not of their making. What made the European Commission's policy rhetoric – in the 2011 GAMM and renewed in the 2015 *Agenda* – so challenging to interpret was that it combined both securitising and humanitarian logics in one single governance narrative; mobile subjects were addressed by the Commission's policy framework as *both* threats to Europe *and* as lives that are threatened. This normative ambivalence meant that the policy-making environment, in which events were problematised by the European Commission as Europe's 'migration crisis', was confused and led to contradictory outcomes. Yet, despite some important differences – not least in terms of stated intentionality – both securitising and humanitarian narratives of Europe's 'migration crisis' were ultimately bound together by their common reference to – and reliance on – the concept of crisis to frame increased arrivals and deaths.

Academic narratives of crisis

The dominant narrative of crisis has been largely reproduced in extant interdisciplinary literature analysing the situation since 2015 in Europe. While any attempt to characterise and categorise such work is problematic, it is possible to identify at least three strands in this context. The first strand accepted the dominant policy narrative of the existence of a 'migration crisis' and did not address key questions about what and/or who is in crisis. Typically, the narrative of the 'migration crisis' was invoked as an explanatory factor in studies of the rise of Euroscepticism and populism (Pirro et al., 2018), the decline of liberal democratic values (Mounck, 2018), and other crises in the EU such as the 'economic crisis', 'terrorism' and 'Brexit' (Davis Cross, 2017; Krastev, 2017; Youngs, 2017). While this scholarship did not claim to offer a detailed analysis of the politics of the social construction of Europe's so-called migration crisis, it nevertheless reified that narrative – albeit unintentionally – which was assumed to be (and was reproduced as) a neutral and apolitical frame.

A second strand of work, more closely associated with critical migration studies, broadly understood, problematised the stock 'migration crisis' narrative as presented above. This narrative has been critiqued on the grounds of its Eurocentricity (Crawley et al., 2017), its empirically reductionist depiction of those on the move (McMahon and Sigona, 2018) and its ahistorical and geographically decontextualised understanding of global migratory dynamics (Crawley, 2016). More often than not, however, such work has challenged the dominant 'migration crisis' narrative only to then reframe the core issues at stake with reference to alternative crisis narratives, thereby retaining 'crisis' as the primary lens through which increased arrivals and deaths at sea since 2015 are viewed: a 'crisis of refugee protection' (Crawley et al., 2017); a 'geopolitical crisis' among EU member states (Crawley, 2016); and a 'crisis of the nation-state and of political representation in Europe' (Anderson, 2018), to name only a few. In these alternatives the referent object of crisis is shifted away from 'migrants' and/or 'refugees', but the use of crisis as an overarching metanarrative remains unchallenged. It may be that such reworkings seek to repurpose the language of crisis to a different effect, but the recycling of the crisis frame poses the question as to whether they constitute genuinely alternative narratives.

Narratives of 'crisis'

A third strand, connecting with the Foucauldian perspective of Roitman (2014), has sought to develop an explicitly 'anti-crisis' narrative frame. This position, as alluded to by Dines et al., involves rethinking 'migration' and 'crisis' as relational – that is to say, as separate phenomena brought together by different actors and for various reasons – rather than seeing their relationship as in any sense already given (Dines et al. 2018: 446). It is ultimately to this third – albeit least developed – strand of research that our study seeks to contribute by reclaiming the critical study of migration from the metanarrative of crisis politics. To do so, it is first necessary to consider at greater length what is at stake politically in the deployment of crisis narratives, to examine the work that 'crisis' does as a supplement to logics of security and humanitarianism in the context of migration, and to investigate how using this concept wittingly or unwittingly opens up and closes off certain modes of interpretation and response against the backdrop of increased arrivals and deaths in Europe, particularly since 2015.

The politics of narrating Europe's 'migrant crisis'

The general literature on the politics of crisis, while fundamentally heterogeneous, highlights the central point that crisis narratives are always intimately bound up with questions of authority, power, knowledge and governance. Koselleck's (2006) etymological work on crisis shows that, while today the concept is used widely in a somewhat undiscriminating manner, its origins in the Greek verb *krino* meant specifically to make distinctions, to judge and to decide at a critical juncture or key moment. He shows that in the ancient Greek medical context 'crisis' referred to the point that is reached when a decisive intervention is called for in response to deterioration in the condition of a patient. From the seventeenth century 'crisis' was transposed into political contexts such as the French and American revolutions to describe the emergence of secular transition points in history. This established 'crisis' as a historical-philosophical concept that was key to Europe's self-understanding of its own role in history – and the possibility of changing the course of the future – which arguably defines a specifically 'modern' approach to politics (Roitman, 2014). In the nineteenth century, 'crisis' became central in theories of political economy, notably Marx's identification of recurring crises endemic to capitalism and both the miserable and revolutionary potential of these dynamics. Today political analysis is concerned less with identifying a stable meaning of the term than to better understand, against the backdrop of the proliferation of crisis discourses associated with late modernity, how that concept is used, by whom and with what consequences (Milstein, 2015). Hay (1999) argues that *narratives* of crisis are fundamental to their performance; that is to say, the perceived symptoms of failure always require mediation. On this view, social and political crises cannot be viewed as an objectively existing 'property of a system', as implied by Marx, but rather as a 'lived experience'; for this reason, according to Hay, crisis narratives ultimately depend on widespread public appeal to gain traction and legitimacy (Hay, 1999: 333).

The political stakes of the securitising narrative of Europe's so-called migration crisis can be readily understood via the logic of sovereign exceptionalism, as paradigmatically outlined by Schmitt (2005 [1922]). In his influential theory, Schmitt argues that sovereignty is defined by the twinned ability to decide on *both* the existence of emergency conditions *and* the necessity of an exceptional mode of response. According to this formulation, which pre-empts Hay's insistence on the non-objective grounds for crisis narratives, it is precisely the designation of a given situation as constituting an emergency that enables non-routine measures to be invoked. As a subjective interpretation of events, the invocation of the concept of 'crisis' to refer to a given situation must be understood as a highly politicised intervention and ultimately as a sovereign move. On this view, governmental actors purport merely to respond to externally derived crisis conditions, but crisis is always internal to governmentality and creates new opportunities for intervention. In invoking the narrative and logic of crisis, the European Commission and other governmental actors interpreted the increase in arrivals and deaths at sea in simplifying ways. All people on the move, all migratory routes and all border sites were reduced as part of a single crisis narrative that focused on the notion that Europe was under threat. In turn, this homogenising depiction of a continent besieged from the outside was conducive to the introduction of a range of exceptional measures that would otherwise be unpalatable to liberal democratic societies in 'non-crisis' times: the militarisation of the Mediterranean and 'offensive interventions against migration flows' (Garelli and Tazzioli, 2018a: 182); the introduction of 'hotspots' as initial reception and identification hubs that function as 'pseudo protection zones, whereby legal protection becomes a de facto tool for advancing separation between citizens and non-citizens' (Papoutsi et al., 2018: 5); the acceleration of the process of externalising border controls to North African and sub-Saharan African states (McMahon and Sigona, 2018); the criminalisation of NGOs working at sea and those colluding with smugglers (Sigona, 2018); and the frenzied construction of border walls and the suspension of Schengen (Benedicto and Brunet, 2018). Further still, that the 2015 *Agenda* referred to the need for the EU 'to be prepared to act in anticipation of a crisis' suggested that, rather than a temporary phase, the future management of the EU's external borders would be permanently on a 'crisis' setting, with 'the reinforcement of Frontex [...] here to stay' (European Commission, 2015b: 11). In its embrace of the dramatising narrative of the 'migration crisis', as Scott (2020: 4) has argued, the European Commission was complicit in propagating an 'emotional geopolitics of fear' and the cultivation of a 'political context that favours populism' – and, we might add, the intensification of deterrent security measures and the resultant unprecedented loss of life at sea.

It might be argued that the European Commission's simultaneous embrace of the narrative of humanitarian crisis tempered the excesses of the securitising dynamics pursued by some populist politicians and far-right movements referred to above. Yet, as a number of authors have sought to highlight, some narratives of humanitarian crises – particularly those that position people on the move as 'helpless victims'

– are not free from the politics of exceptionalism either (e.g. Pallister-Wilkins, 2017). Fassin has demonstrated that the logic of humanitarian reason – 'the vocabulary of suffering, compassion, assistance, and responsibility to protect' – is an intensely political mode of governance (Fassin 2012: 2). In his genealogy of humanitarianism, Fassin (2012: 2) locates the emergence of the moral economy of 'us' helping 'them' in the context of Christian traditions of empathy and the eighteenth-century abolitionist movements in France, the UK and the US. Its outward emphasis on compassion makes humanitarianism appear apolitical and normatively desirable, but in managing, regulating and intervening in the bodies of some human beings – and not others – it is a governmental technology that inescapably 'qualifies and measures the value and worth of lives' (Fassin, 2012: 242). With reference to the opening of the Sangatte refugee centre in France during the 1990s, Fassin (2012: 226) argues that the removal of undesirable bodies from public life and their management in invisible spaces means that logics of securitisation and some forms of victimising humanitarianism are not incompatible or essentially contradictory, but conjoined as part of a single 'biopolitical' apparatus of government. As such, the referent object of humanitarianism is the 'biological life of the destitute and unfortunate' rather than the 'biographical life' of those on the move, understood as 'the life through which they could, independently, give a meaning to their own existence' (Fassin, 2012: 254). In the words of Anderson and colleagues, humanitarian interventions construct mobile subjects as 'objects of control, rescue, and redemption' instead of politically qualified 'full human beings' (Anderson et al., 2012: 78).

Ticktin (2016) draws out the wider implications of the politics of humanitarian exceptionalism in respect of the deployment of the 'migrant crisis' narrative in the European context: it does not recognise or allow for the mourning of particular lives lost; it sets up a sharp distinction between innocent ('real refugees') and guilty ('economic migrants') subjects with no scope for grey areas; the former are seen as passive victims and worthy of humanitarian succour, while the latter are cast as hyper-agentic criminals who are not; the focus on saving lives in the 'here and now' means that the temporal context of crisis humanitarianism does not allow for historical contextualisation; and in prioritising feelings rather than rights it does not allow for political change. Narratives of 'humanitarian crisis' were used strategically by NGOs in 2015–16 to raise the profile of deaths at sea, to critique the (in)action of states and to garner public support financially and politically. Yet while clearly not all humanitarian actors and motives are the same (Fassin and Pandolfi, 2013: 15; Squire, 2015a), the work of Fassin and Ticktin highlights why there are reasons to be cautious about seeing such crisis narratives as less analytically and politically problematic than their securitising equivalents. Ultimately, both securitising and victimising humanitarian narratives of Europe's 'migration crisis' ran the risk of taking the experiences of those on the move – including their deaths – outside of politics. Both crisis narratives were depoliticising not only in the sense that they abstracted increased arrivals and deaths from broader structural inequalities; they also worked to 'silence' the 'voice' of mobile populations and 'empty their subjectivity of agency' (Nyers and Rygiel, 2012: 8) (see Chapter 2).

'Europe's migrant crisis': a postcolonial critique

A further problem with diverse narratives of Europe's so-called migration crisis concerns the use of the prefix 'Europe'. At one level, as the work of Crawley et al. (2017) has already shown, there was a prevalent Eurocentricity to the dominant narratives of crisis used to frame increased arrivals and deaths in 2015–16. The staging of the 'crisis' in terms of 'uncontrolled and unregulated movement into Europe' – as depicted by large arrows pointing towards the European continent on Frontex risk assessment maps – constituted a highly problematic and innately political 'view from Europe' (Crawley et al., 2017: 2). If placed within a broader geographical context, then what was presented by Frontex as a situation of 'immense' proportions exaggerated the scale of the situation in Europe when compared to other regions implicated in population displacements globally during the same time frame (Frontex, 2016: 6); of 4.2 million Syrian refugees displaced between 2011 and 2016, for example, a total of 1.5 million fled to Lebanon, a country half the size of Wales (Crawley, 2016). Despite the moral panic over the arrival of approximately a million people in the EU during 2015, this constitutes a small percentage of the 65 million people classified as displaced that year globally as a result of violence and conflict (Crawley et al., 2017: 15). While these arrivals were deemed by the European Commission to be of sufficient magnitude to warrant the invocation of the crisis narrative, the total number was equivalent to 0.5 per cent of the EU's total population (Anderson, 2018: 1529). One explanation that has been put forward as to why 2015 was a turning point in the invocation of the crisis narrative is that, while large numbers of Syrian refugees had already been displaced to Lebanon, Turkey and Egypt since the onset of conflict in 2011, it was only when migratory routes shifted to Europe that this frame was pushed by EU policy-makers and further propagated by Western-centric global media interests (Leurs and Ponzanesi, 2018).

At another level, we argue that the dominant narrative of 'Europe's migrant crisis' – in both securitising and certain humanitarian forms – reflects a geopolitical imaginary that is more than simply 'Eurocentric', one that must be located in the deeper historical context of colonialism and its ongoing legacies. De Genova (2018) makes the stark observation that the 'racialised' dimension of the dominant crisis narrative is rarely acknowledged as such across policy, media and academic domains of knowledge and commentary. On his view, euphemistic and highly racialised terms such as 'migrant' and 'refugee' obscure the basic reality that the majority of those on the move are 'black bodies' whose entry to Europe from former colonies is systematically blocked by ever more violent means, thereby constituting a 'European colour line' (De Genova, 2018: 5; see also Samaddar, 2016: 89). A consequence of the failure to understand 'Europe's migration crisis' via the lens of race renders invisible the 'distinctly *European* colonial legacies that literally *produced* race as a socio-political category of distinction and discrimination in the first place' (De Genova, 2018: 6). In this way, De Genova highlights not only the dependency of Europe's external border regime on continued widespread assumptions about the 'utter disposability of black and brown lives', but also the reproduction of 'the entire fabric of the European social order' according to a perpetuation of colonial logics and fantasies of domination (De Genova, 2018: 15; see also Danewid, 2017).

These themes are explored further by Hage (2016) in his critique of the so-called European migration crisis *as* a crisis that is internal to colonial world order. On his view, notions of 'besiegement' and the loss of control of borders are central to the narrative that the 'crisis' was primarily a 'crisis' *facing* 'Europe' (Hage, 2016: 38). The idea of Europe being 'under siege' by 'migrants' – as expressed by the language of crisis, and readily apparent in the statements made by the European Commission and Frontex above – has a long colonial history and derives from attempts by colonisers to use the imagery of warfare to simultaneously 'delegitimise the resistance of the colonised' and 'legitimise [the] excessive use of violence against the colonised' (Hage, 2016: 39). Hage's argument draws on Levi-Strauss's definition of colonialism as 'a historical process which has made the larger part of mankind subservient to the other, and during which millions of innocent human beings have had their resources plundered and their institutions and beliefs destroyed, whilst they themselves were ruthlessly killed, thrown into bondage, and contaminated by diseases they were unable to resist' (quoted in Hage, 2016: 42). For Hage (2016: 43), colonial relations are not historically confined to what he calls 'the "classic" era of colonialism', however, and continue to structure global politics. Today, colonial relations are manifested spatially via the intersection of two types of border regimes that, taken together, form what he calls a 'global apartheid' (Hage, 2016: 44).

The first type of border Hage highlights – 'national borders' – are relics of the era in which arbitrary lines were drawn by European colonisers across what were once continuous lands in order to limit the mobility of the colonised, divide up exploited resources among the colonisers and regulate flows between the colonies and Europe (Hage, 2016: 44). The second type of border – the 'racialised class border' – supports the first type and operates by separating out the mobility of 'largely white upper classes' from the 'transnational working class'; the former move in frictionless ways across national borders whereas the latter face a series of checks and interventions at those borders, which in turn performatively reproduces them (Hage, 2016: 44). Crucially, for Hage, national borders are coming under increasing strain as a result of the transnational flows that they can no longer contain such that, 'like the badly maintained barbed wire of an aging and neglected farm, they are becoming less and less able to function' (Hage, 2016: 43). On his view, mobile populations challenge not only the system of containment created by 'national borders', but also the broader colonial logic of 'global apartheid' of which they are an intrinsic part. While Hage notes that the fear of a loss of control of borders has been 'exaggerated' and 'instrumentalised' by those seeking a politics of exceptionalism, in the final analysis he draws on Fanon (1967) to argue that 'if Western societies are feeling besieged, it is because they are' (Hage, 2016: 45).

One of the key elements of a postcolonial critique of the narrative of '*Europe's* migration crisis' is to examine how those on the move have been produced as governable subjects by apparatuses of European border security, and to locate these dynamics within the perpetuation of broader structures of colonialism. Jabri (2013: 4) develops the concept of the 'postcolonial subject' in order to refer to mobile populations across shifting global landscapes who are 'shaped and regulated into governable, manageable entities' by such technologies of government. On her view, postcolonial subjectivities are (re)inscribed via the 'colonial encounter' and their bodies are targeted by the disciplining apparatuses of a 'global military machine' that seeks to manage otherwise 'errant movements' by rendering them knowable and therefore governable (Jabri, 2013: 5). Jabri is careful to emphasise that postcolonial subjects are not '*determined* by the colonial legacy', however, and are always only partly constituted in 'a space of hybridity, negotiation, and articulation', which itself shapes the contours of global politics and is thus a form of resistance (Jabri, 2013: 12, emphasis added). Securitising narratives of the 'crisis' are most readily reflective of these dynamics, but Jabri recognises that it is also necessary to be attentive to the reproduction of colonial logics via humanitarian crisis narratives when the structural position of those who are doing the 'saving' is shored up and legitimised at the expense of the political agency of those being 'saved' (Jabri, 2013: 121).

Another key element of a postcolonial critique of the narrative of 'Europe's migration crisis' is to appreciate the role that colonial relations have played and continue to play in the constitution of Europe and its identity. Bhambra (2016: 188) argues that it would be a 'mistake' to limit the insights of a postcolonial approach only to 'those "others" who migrate to Europe'; rather, this needs to be situated within a broader understanding of how postcolonial subjects are historically connected with Europe *and* how Europe continues to be dependent on colonial relations for its own 'self-understanding' in the world. Such a move is important unless the emphasis of the postcolonial critique is to reprioritise the coloniser position in constituting the colonised rather than to appreciate the co-constitutive nature of colonial relations (Bhambra, 2016: 188). For Bhambra (2016: 194), the attempt to exteriorise the conditions of possibility for the 'migration crisis' can be understood as a strategic move by European politicians to deny the historical role that Europe's imperial projects have played in forcing people to flee from conflict, violence and poverty in former colonies today. On her view, the logic of exteriorisation in respect of the 'crisis' was not new, but rather a continuation of the self-enclosing European narrative of integration as being a peaceful distancing from the past rather than acknowledging that it is founded on the forced exploitation of land, labour and markets overseas, particularly in the African continent, as its constitutive outside (Bhambra, 2016; 197–198; see also Samaddar, 2016: 89). A significant problem with the prevalent Euro-centricity, then, is not only that it renders key postcolonial geographies and histories invisible, but that it also reproduces what Samaddar

(2016: 102) refers to as Europe's 'logic of innocence', which is of course profoundly violent.

Drawing on these theoretical critiques, we show throughout the course of this book that colonial relations continue to structure the lived experiences of people on the move as well as understandings of their own positionality vis-à-vis 'Europe' – key dynamics that are otherwise glossed over in Eurocentric and colonial narratives of crisis. As we shall go on to discuss in subsequent chapters, the continued impacts of the colonial legacy are a recurring theme that emerges in the narratives of people on the move about their experiences in the years before, during and in some cases after their arrival in Europe. One man from Ethiopia, for example, who had been granted refugee status in 2011 in Malta, draws explicitly on the language and logics of colonialism to narrate his understanding and interpretation of the situation he found himself in. Instead of abstract and decontextualising narratives of crisis, he speaks of the disjuncture between the '*pride*' he takes in who he is and the '*colour*' of his skin on the one hand, and his experience of being called '*ejja ebet*' or '*slave*' during his time in Libya on the other: '*I was not certain about tomorrow because nothing was certain*' (MAL1.26, man from Ethiopia, Skype interview).[1] Such narratives, which bring the postcolonial dynamics of the present into sharper focus, were systematically silenced in the social construction of 'Europe's migration crisis'. Instead, the dominant ahistorical and Eurocentric crisis narrative worked to re-secure a 'logic of innocence' via the continued exclusion of postcolonial voices from public debate.

For Hage, this form of exclusion is part of a more long-term dynamic whereby 'the more a colonising nation can shield its citizens from realities, carving out spaces where they are not exposed to the colonial conditions of their good life, the more civilised it appears' (Hage, 2016: 42). Maintaining the pretence of the 'logic of innocence' not only enables a historical distancing between coloniser and colonised – 'colonialism was something that happened to *them*; it had nothing to do with *us*' (Bhambra, 2016: 199). It also facilitates selective denial of the physically violent impacts of contemporary foreign and security policies – not least some EU member states' roles in supporting US military interventions in Syria, Afghanistan and Iraq, and hostile policies towards Iran and Lebanon (Samaddar, 2016: 102; see also Chapter 6). This silencing is of course ironic because, as Samaddar (2016: 119–120) points out, the very 'possibility of EU citizenship' and its attendant 'rights of life, labour, social security, and dignity' continue to be predicated on the reproduction of borders that deny such rights to those seeking to flee former colonies. By contrast, we argue that foregrounding and listening carefully to the testimonies of those on the move – whose experiences have been shaped by the legacies of colonialism – shatters the benign self-image of Europe as a civilised and civilising project. To do so reinstates the historical and contemporary linkages between increased arrivals and deaths on the shores of the continent and Europe's own policies and practices. Prioritising such testimonies prises open elite self-generating and self-enclosing narratives of crisis in both their securitising and humanitarian guises, and exposes new grounds for analysis, critique and contestation. For this reason, we argue that it is necessary not to modify but rather to move beyond a 'crisis' narrative.

Testimonies beyond 'crisis'

How might it be possible to think beyond the dominant narrative of Europe's so-called migrant crisis, and why might that be analytically and politically desirable? Roitman argues from a Foucauldian perspective that because the invocation of the term 'crisis' is ultimately nothing other than 'an observation that produces meaning' (Roitman, 2014: 41), its usage must always be problematised as a 'self-authorising ground for accounts of the emergent' (2014: 70). On her view, it is insufficient for critical analysis to simply map, problematise the usage of crisis narratives in diverse contexts, and re-problematise with alternative crisis frames. All crisis narratives impute a philosophy of history predicated on notions of success and failure in one way or another, which constitutes a particular normative starting point about how things ought to be. In turn, this has the effect of shutting down alternative knowledge and histories, which may hold the key to more effective thought, judgement and action than allowed for by crisis frames. Because every crisis narrative 'generates meaning in a self-referential system', Roitman (2014: 10, 90) claims that any invocation of the concept serves to deny 'alternative narratives' and 'other histories' and thus foreclose critique. Irrespective of how it is intended to be mobilised, Roitman suggests that analysis should dispense with crisis frames altogether and instead adopt a position that she calls 'anti-crisis'. That is to say, for Roitman, the key task facing critical scholars is to be open to the possibility of identifying and working with 'non-crisis narratives' (Roitman, 2014: 13): in other words, to suspend crisis as the basis for analysis and critique. While we acknowledge that not all crisis narratives are the same and that there may be strategic grounds to invoke notions of crisis in order to make particular interventions, in this book we take Roitman's 'anti-crisis' position as a starting point to develop alternative narratives for engaging critically with increased arrivals and deaths in the Mediterranean since 2015.

In their work on the mediation of borders in the contemporary European context, Chouliaraki and Musaro (2017: 545) draw a distinction between the 'narrated border' as officially presented in policy documentation and the 'enacted border' as experienced by those who encounter security apparatuses on the ground. With regard to the former, they argue that the European Commission's mediation of events in 2015 constituted 'an institutionally-sanctioned story of humanitarian security that constructs "us" as heroic benefactors and "them" as either passive victims or potential evil-doers' (Chouliaraki and Musaro, 2017: 545). The latter, by contrast, is always experienced by those on the move in highly nuanced ways involving a 'conflicted range of emotions' caught between securitised and humanitarian logics in ways that 'both confirm and undermine the official discourse' (Chouliaraki and Musaro, 2017: 545). Clearly, by starting with the exceptional politics of crisis, analysts run the risk of merely recycling the 'narrated border' rather than juxtaposing and assessing this idealised narrative in the light of the 'enacted border'. While there are several ways in which the 'enacted border' might be explored ethnographically, we take the first-person narratives of those on the move as a way of moving beyond the 'narrated border' and its attendant crisis politics. This is enabled by a research design that takes care to avoid securitising, humanitarian and/or crisis frames of analysis (see Introduction and Chapter 2). Instead, by privileging the detailed, complex and sometimes contradictory testimonies of people on the move, we seek to initiate a methodological and political shift from a catch-all interest in the 'biological life' of mobile populations to the 'biographical lives' of our participants (Fassin, 2012). Such a shift – from securitising and humanitarian narratives of crisis to testimonies of the contested politics of migration – allows for a repurposed emphasis on context and non-elite situated knowledge and experience at 'enacted border' sites. It contributes to wider efforts in critical migration and border studies to put mobility rather than control at the centre of the analysis (Mezzadra and Neilson, 2013; Nail, 2016a; Squire, 2011), to recover voices 'from below' (Nyers and Rygiel, 2012: 2; Johnson, 2012), and to develop new vocabularies beyond the language of Euro- and state-centricity (King, 2016: 16).

It must be emphasised that our adoption of an 'anti-crisis' perspective is not an arbitrary theoretical choice, but one that is an outcome of the findings of the body of research on which this book is based. That is to say, the argument that we should seek to abandon the dominant crisis frame is drawn from a close engagement with the content of the narratives of those we spoke with in producing our counter-archive. Tellingly, and as reflected in the opening quotation of this chapter, people on the move rarely describe themselves as being caught up in a 'migration crisis' facing Europe in ways that straightforwardly echo the dominant narrative. Certainly, no one identifies themselves as posing a security threat to Europe; yet, importantly, neither do our research participants express themselves merely as helpless victims in need of 'saving' or humanitarian succour. The array of alternative starting points that are invoked – of the need to escape what we call the 'complex intersecting drivers and conditions of flight' – are explored in subsequent chapters. For now, it is worth highlighting three key recurring themes that underpin and signal the need for the 'anti-crisis' position, informed by a postcolonial perspective, that is adopted here.

First, rather than posing a security threat to Europe – as depicted by securitising narratives of crisis – the testimonies from our counter-archive point to the violent and threatening circumstances people on the move found themselves in. This is powerfully summed up by a woman from Cameroon, interviewed in Rome, who turns the dominant and highly gendered securitising narrative of crisis on its head in saying that '*total insecurity is pushing us to migrate*' (ROM2.16, woman from Cameroon, Rome). When security is read exclusively through the dominant lens of crisis it is the security of the state and/or EU citizens that is privileged as the referent object, rather than the lives of those who are exposed to violent conditions in Europe's former colonies. However, this does not mean that testimonies straightforwardly justify humanitarian narratives of crisis associated with universalist notions of human security.

Second, and as we shall go on to investigate, there are many political claims made in the name of a common humanity and demands to be treated with dignity and respect (see Chapter 6), yet we also hear powerful testimonies. For example, a 41-year-old surgeon from Syria who was interviewed in Malta provides a harrowing account of his journey in a rubber motor boat from Libya across the Mediterranean Sea towards Malta. In a chase lasting four hours, his boat was shot at by men with Kalashnikov rifles on another vessel who had followed them from Tripoli. They managed to escape, but the damaged rubber boat started to take on water. At that point, approximately one hundred kilometres from Lampedusa, the surgeon called the Italian authorities for assistance, but was told that they were in Maltese territorial waters. He had not heard of Malta before, but after a request for assistance a small aeroplane appeared. At that moment, the boat stopped, the captain lost balance, and the vessel capsized. The Maltese authorities rescued thirty-four people and thirty bodies. For ten days while in detention the surgeon did not know the whereabouts of his family who had been with him on board. He was offered food, but went on hunger strike in protest – not at being detained; all he wanted was information about his family, who remained missing. He says: '*Everybody was very kind, but nobody gave us what we needed at the time, which was information, that's all, we don't need food, we don't need protection, they start teaching us about our rights, but nobody care*' (MALI.MGI, man from Syria, Malta). By listening to such testimonies we can better appreciate why 'kindness' and humanitarian succour in the form of food and shelter is not necessarily what those fleeing war, poverty and 'total insecurity' are seeking; in the case of the Syrian surgeon, it was information about lost family members, above all else. The needs and demands vary depending on the biographical details of individuals' experiences and circumstances, and may evolve dramatically during the course of journeys that are commonly years or decades in duration (see Chapter 4).

Third, while crisis politics in both securitising and humanitarian modes has a distinctive temporality – that of urgency, emergency and rupture – one of the most striking themes throughout the testimonies presented here was that of continuity rather than change in the context of individuals' lives. Whereas the narrative of Europe's so-called migration crisis typically drew a sharp temporal border around the 2015–16 period as one of exception and excessive movement, this temporality is challenged by those whose lives have been marked by violence. The exposure to sustained violence and exceptional conditions was narrated not only with reference to conditions in 'countries of origin' prompting flight in the first place, but also by those we met who had been stranded in Europe as a result of the Dublin Regulation, which normally expects people to apply for asylum in the first state they arrive to in order to claim asylum. Rejected asylum seekers in Malta, for example, were effectively in a permanent state of limbo, with return to their country of departure not being an option for many, and with limited access to rights. One man from Ivory Coast had been granted temporary protection status ten years prior to the interview taking place. He expressed frustration because, despite contributing to the Maltese economy for a decade, he was treated as if he had just arrived on the island. He says: '*They need to change the policy for those who are living long time in Malta. Ten years is not the same as one day. But you spend ten years here, you treated like you are here only for one day*' (MAL1.23, man from Ivory Coast, Malta). These insights, in keeping with postcolonial perspectives on the philosophy of history, challenge dominant Western temporal imaginaries based around logics of crisis, collapse and discontinuity (Whyte, 2018). Testimonies such as those offered by the man from Ivory Coast living for ten years in Malta highlight that constant change and exposure to violence is not an aberration for many, but a function of ongoing colonial relations and dynamics 'as a late consequence of Europe's violent encounter with the Global South' (Danewid, 2017). In the final analysis, testimonies of this kind not only assist in the task of repoliticising and recontextualising events narrated in the crisis frame; they also powerfully illustrate that to talk glibly in terms of Europe's 'migrant crisis' is politically naive.

Conclusion

In this chapter we have identified and sought to problematise the dominant narrative of Europe's so-called migrant crisis as a starting point for understanding and responding to increased arrivals and deaths since 2015. While variants of this narrative exist – notably in securitising and humanitarian guises – the literature on the politics of crisis highlights the limitations and implications of adopting the metanarrative of crisis. Applying these insights more specifically to the recent EU context, we have sought to emphasise three critical points. First, securitising narratives of crisis silence the experiences of violence of those on the move, reducing them to security threats that need to be better deterred and/or 'known' and therefore governed (see Chapter 3). Second, humanitarian narratives of crisis, though

Narratives of 'crisis'

varied in terms of content and motive, fail to engage with the hetero-geneous range of political claims and demands of those in flight (see Chapter 4). Third, in focusing on Europe, crisis narratives invariably reproduce colonial power relations and, with a temporal emphasis on the 'here and now', distract critical attention away from enduring exposure to violence (see Chapter 5). In developing an 'anti-crisis' position, we have argued for an abandonment of these crisis narratives and have set out an alternative approach that acknowledges the politics of crisis while explicitly seeking to go beyond this. By prioritising detailed empirical analysis of specific migratory routes, particular sites of mobility and attempted control, and the multiplicity of grounded experiences of those on the move, we discover that dominant postco-lonial narratives of Europe's 'migration crisis' are limited in both their analytical purchase and potential to respond in practical policy terms. Drawing out the complexities, contradictions and demands found in the rich narratives of our counter-archive, we problematise and disag-gregate what has become retroactively constructed as Europe's 'migrant crisis' in search of alternative frameworks and counter-narratives. In shifting the analytical frame from the politics of crisis to that of the contested politics of testimony, we are better able to address more fundamental questions about the implications of increased sea arrivals and deaths, which is the task of the rest of this book.

Notes

1 This Skype interview was conducted from Malta with a man from Ethiopia who was located in Norway. A limited number of Skype interviews were carried out with contacts that had passed through Malta previously. Please see Chapter 2 for fuller details of the research methodology.

2

Reclaiming voice

… what we want is our voice to be heard in the world … We just want our voice to be heard in the world.

(KOS1.02A, woman from Syria, Kos)

Am I not human? Anything that is useless, gets thrown out. When I see that I'm useless in my country, useless in Europe, useless in other countries, then who am I? A hidden pronoun? In the Arabic language we call it a hidden pronoun. An invisible subject.

(IST2.28, man from Iraq, Istanbul)

Introduction

As we saw in Chapter 1, people travelling by boat across the Mediterranean Sea were at the centre of intensified political debates during 2015 and 2016, with increased attention focused on what was predominantly viewed as a refugee or 'migrant crisis'. Humanitarian and security-oriented narratives not only converged in policy circles, but also in wider political debates at the time. For example, media and communications scholars have shown how humanitarian articulations of global suffering circulated in the global media, particularly during the early stages of the so-called crisis (Zhang and Hellmueller, 2017; see also Georgiou and Zaborowski, 2017: 3). Researchers have also highlighted how media coverage played into fears about the arrival of dangerous 'undeserving migrants' (Holmes and Castaneda, 2016), with some suggesting that a security frame became increasingly evident over time (Greussing and Boomgaarden, 2017). While this book does not undertake a detailed analysis of media representations, what it does suggest is that the convergence of security and humanitarian narratives of crisis in broader political and public debates contributed to the closure of opportunities for people on the move to advance concrete and nuanced testimonies about the journey across the Mediterranean to the EU. Indeed, scholars have suggested that even where people on the move were given an opportunity to have a voice on media platforms, this was usually framed in terms of an assumed victimhood whereby people were presented as spokespeople for a broader collective without any contextualisation of their distinct migratory experiences (Chouliaraki and Zaborowski, 2017).[1] It is precisely this absence of the situated voices of people migrating that this book takes issue with. We argue that such a silencing involves a form of epistemic violence against those most directly affected by the preventative policy agenda: people on the move themselves.

As the opening quotes from the Syrian woman in Kos and from the Iraqi man in Istanbul suggest, the silencing of people on the move was not lost on those making precarious journeys to Europe in 2015 and 2016. Emphasising the need to be '*heard in the world*' and speaking of the trauma of being '*an invisible subject*', these testimonies point to the 'pernicious ignorance' that consistently leads to 'harmful practice[s] of silencing' (Dotson, 2011: 239). In the attempt to challenge this ignorance, *Reclaiming Migration* engages what we call a counter-archive of migratory testimonies – testimonies that we collated directly with people on the move across the Mediterranean in 2015–16. This chapter suggests that this counter-archive contrasts with official forms of knowledge production, enabling an appreciation of the diverse narratives, practices and projects of migration that are otherwise rendered invisible (see Chapter 1). Our analysis does not aim to 'give voice' to people on the move, but rather seeks to speak *with* those making precarious journeys whose calls so often go unheard. Yet, as we will see, the production of a counter-archive is by no means a straightforward process. The risk of silencing involved in practices of 'giving voice' are continually present, as is the risk of exposing voices in terms that undermine silence as a personal choice and political tactic in and of itself. Indeed, questions of positionality – in particular the uneven power dynamics between researchers and research participants – continue to haunt this book, and remain irresolvable despite the commitment of the research team to embedding the principles of participation, respect and equality in the project design. It is in this sense that we emphasise the importance of those moments in the research process in which people on the move 'take voice' in terms that undermine the very grounds on which the study is based. We argue that these moments are critical dimensions of a counter-archive that seeks to unsettle the predominance of a singular account of Europe's 'migrant crisis', along with the power dynamics through which knowledge of the situation in 2015 and 2016 was produced.

Epistemic violence

Those who are doing the research, what they can be help to us? Or what they can think that we can do together to change our situation to better?
(MAL1.22, man from Ivory Coast, Malta)

Epistemic violence refers to a form of harm or injustice that results from the silencing of particular groups of people. It does not stand in isolation from physical violence, as we will see in this book, but it is a distinctive form of violence in its own right. The term is often traced to the work of Spivak, a postcolonial scholar who provocatively asked the question: 'Can the subaltern speak?' (Spivak, 1988). Although Spivak's description of colonised or previously colonised communities as 'subaltern' might be seen as problematic, what her work importantly brings to the fore is how some groups of persons are prevented from speaking about their interests because others claim to know those interests better. In other words, she draws attention to the ways in which the knowledgeable or knowing subject is constituted on the basis of the delegitimisation of other subjects and forms of knowledge. This is understood by Fricker (2007) as a form of 'epistemic injustice' that involves disbelief or oversight of the knowledge produced by members of a particular group (testimonial injustice), as well as a more basic failure to understand experiences that are alien to the conceptual framework of dominant groups (hermeneutic injustice). Going further, Dotson conceives these harmful practices as involving a form of 'pernicious ignorance', which is based on a 'failure to meet the vulnerabilities of speakers in linguistic exchanges' (Dotson, 2011: 238). Indeed, such processes of delegitimisation, ignorance and non-reciprocity are not only evident in the widespread silencing of people on the move across the Mediterranean during 2015 and 2016. They also reflect more long-standing trajectories that involve hierarchical relations of colonial power and racialised violence (see Danewid, 2017; Mayblin, 2017).

So how can academic practices of knowledge production challenge these hierarchical dynamics and processes of silencing? It is worth noting that the production of a counter-archive based on migratory testimonies is a relatively novel intervention in the field of critical migration and border studies, despite some important works along these lines over recent years (e.g. Heller and Pezzani, 2015). Many critical scholars have rightly exercised caution in undertaking research directly with people on the move, not least due to the risks of producing knowledge that re-inscribes the power dynamics associated with epistemic violence. Rather than carrying out research *on* people who migrate, such scholars have often focused instead on critically inter-rogating security and humanitarian regimes of governing migration that drive and consolidate epistemic violence (e.g. Albahari, 2016; Jones, 2016). These works are important in exposing the ways in which people on the move are subjected to a range of different forms of violence, including the material violence of bordering practices (e.g. Davies et al., 2017) as well as violence resulting from discriminatory attitudes and stereotypes about people who migrate (e.g. Mavelli, 2017). Indeed, caution regarding the use of migratory testimonies is often underpinned by a concern that research does not fall into the trap of narrating stories in terms that reiterate assumptions about the victimhood of and/or threat posed by people on the move (Johnson, 2012). Such caution is understandable, because assumptions about 'risky' forms of migration involve well-established discourses and practices that both disempower and discipline those deemed as threatening and/or threatened (see Aradau, 2004). In this context, the presentation of migratory stories out of the context is a particular concern, because such an approach both risks dehistoricising migratory struggles and depoliticising the struggles of people on the move (Malkki, 1996). Indeed, an analysis of migratory stories in these terms also risks feeding into a 'control bias', which involves a drive to understand migration in order to manage it better (see Scheel, 2019).

A question nevertheless remains for scholars of critical migration and border studies as to how research can respond to the demand to *'change our situation for the better'*, as expressed by the man from Ivory Coast cited at the start of this section. In what ways might we respond to the call for support, while avoiding a replication of the disempowerment or victimhood of people on the move and while remaining respectful to the demand to do something 'together' in order to contribute to a transformation of migratory politics? This is a question to which we seek to respond through engaging our counter-archive of Europe's 'migrant crisis'. Basing our intervention on a solidaristic ethics of respect rather than on a philanthropic ethics of compassion (see Ticktin, 2016), we analyse the counter-archive based on an appreciation of our ongoing responsibility as witnesses to the violence and harms that people on the move faced during 2015 and 2016, and that many people still experience in various ways and contexts today. This might be understood in terms of a form of alliance building, whereby we draw on our academic knowledge and resources to support people on the move to make their voices heard in the face of trauma, harm and violence. Such an approach is not one that seeks to present the 'authentic' voices of people migrating. Rather, it seeks to make a distinct intervention in a given context on the basis of an engagement with such voices. Specifically, we reject the silencing of people on the move in policy debates and seek to involve broader publics in bearing

Reclaiming voice

witness and taking action to reject the violence and harms that people on the move continue to face. As such, this book can be understood as contributing to a wider body of critical research that has in different ways challenged the situation that people face when making precarious journeys to the EU (see Garelli et al., 2018). It does so based on an appreciation of the demands for change that emerge in multiple forms through our counter-archive, and that directly challenge a preventative policy agenda.

Engaging a counter-archive

Open the doors. Help them reach a place where they can study, complete their studies. A place where there are doors open in front of them.
(IST2.20, woman from Syria, Istanbul)

What does it mean to engage a counter-archive of Europe's so-called migrant crisis of 2015–16? Before answering this question, it is first instructive to consider what it means to engage an archive. An archive can be understood in infrastructural terms as holding a privileged place in practices of knowledge production. Conceived as a material entity which is comprised both of a general structure (often a building) and material content (usually written documents), an archive is conventionally understood as the property of society at large, with anybody being able to claim access to its contents (Mbembe, 2002: 20). Nevertheless, this is not to say that the archive is an open repository that embodies the principle of equality. Mbembe (2002: 20) points to the colonial violence of the archive, arguing that it embodies within it processes of despoilment and dispossession, since the documents it holds no longer belong to their authors. Indeed, a range of scholars have shown how the production of an archive precisely represents the power of law or command over the production of truth. For example, Derrida suggests that the archive can be understood in relation to the Greek concept of *arkheion*, the house of the superior magistrates,[2] with the *arkhons* (magistrates) not only playing a commanding role in housing the archives but also in interpreting them (Derrida, 1995: 9–10). He argues that the archive 'shelters in itself the memory of the name *arkhe*, the principle of commandment' while also sheltering this memory from itself (Derrida, 1995: 9). As a pledge, or a 'token of the future' (Derrida, 1995: 18), the archive in this regard is bound up with the power and violence of the law to define the truth of a given situation. It is, Derrida implies, the forgetting of this violence or power of command that renders the archive so problematic.

How might we understand the 'truth of the situation' in 2015 and 2016, as this was produced through the 'official archive'? The answer to this question is relatively complicated, because a range of states and agencies were implicated in the production of knowledge about migration across the Mediterranean to the EU during this time. For example, the deaths of those en route were documented in different ways by local coroners across various states, while those arriving to the EU alive were identified and documented by local police authorities as well as by EU agencies such as Frontex, Europol, Eurojust and the European Asylum Support Office (EASO). States as well as intergovernmental organisations such as the International Organization for Migration (IOM) and the United Nations High Commissioner for Refugees (UNHCR) collated data about migratory journeys, while digital records of travellers were transferred between states through databases such as the Schengen Information System (SIS) and Visa Information System (VIS). What this represents is a large and complex system of documentation which is not housed as a distinct archive in a given building, but that circulates and is subject to continuous use and reuse by a range of border security, migration management, humanitarian and law enforcement agencies. As we have already seen in Chapter 1, a key effect of this circulation of knowledge has been the production of an official truth regarding the situation in 2015 and 2016 as one of 'crisis'. While concerns surrounding deaths at sea and increased arrivals proliferated, state and interstate agencies also produced a 'truth' regarding the correlation of the humanitarian 'crisis' with the 'crisis' of state borders. For example, it was argued that search and rescue operations effectively perpetuate rather than resolve the

Reclaiming voice

situation of deaths at sea (see Steinhilper and Gruijters, 2017). This led to a situation whereby an assumption regarding the need to increase preventative border security operations predominated over one about the need to provide support to people on their journeys (see Forensic Oceanography, 2016). That doors could be 'open' as suggested by the Syrian woman in Istanbul cited at the start of this section thus became unsayable in this context, with calls for the intensification of search and rescue operations and the opening of legal pathways increasingly delegitimised over time.

It is precisely this power of the official archive to shape meaning – to constitute knowledge –that Foucault points to in his archaeological work. More than simply an institution, he argues, the archive 'stands as a system of statements, or rules of practice, that give shape to what can and cannot be said' (cited in Hamilton et al., 2002: 9). Foucault's insights have been important for anthropologists of colonialism, who challenge the order of truth that the colonial archive gives rise to. Archives, from this perspective, function as sites of 'knowledge production' rather than of 'knowledge retrieval', and can be engaged both as 'monuments of states' and as 'sites of state ethnography' (Stoler, 2002: 85). Stoler argues that the ordering of 'criteria of evidence, proof, testimony, and witnessing' effectively constructs 'moral narrations', which critical scholars unpack through writing 'un-stated histories' that 'demonstrate the warped reality of official knowledge and the enduring consequences of such political distortions' (Stoler, 2002: 90–91; see also Stoler 2009). One way in which such 'un-stated' histories might be developed is through the engagement of 'counter-archives' such as that produced here, which work in tension with the official production of meaning. Carolyn Steedman (2001) suggests that the archive 'will not go away', but that the counter-archive represents an interruption of stories 'half way through' (cited in Motha and van Rijswijk, 2016: 2). In other words, a counter-archive can expose the partialities of a commanding system of knowledge production, while disrupting the smooth functioning of such knowledge through its multiplication and contestation. This might be understood in terms of what Shapiro (2013: 83) calls the 'non-juridical justice of the archives', which lends itself to an opening of the archive to an uncertain future. As Derrida (1995: 26) argues, more than a thing of the past, the archive should '*call into question* the coming of the future'.

Multiplying the sources of documentation and bringing to bear voices that are silenced by the 'official archive' is particularly important in providing openings for the 'un-stated histories' of people crossing the Mediterranean during 2015 and 2016. Such work has already been started by projects such as Forensic Architecture and activist groups such as Alarm Phone, which have documented the impact of military vessels and other search and rescue authorities on people making distress calls at sea (Heller and Pezzani, 2015; Stierl, 2016). The testimonies of people on the move have been crucial to these forms of knowledge production, and remain so in order that migratory struggles are not precluded by the growing concern to document border deaths (e.g. M'charek and Black, 2019; Missing Migrants, 2019). Indeed, a consideration of migratory testimonies is critical both in producing knowledge that challenges state representations of crisis, and in advancing legal and political challenges against the abuse of rights on the part of states (see also Sossi, 2013). The contribution of *Reclaiming Migration* to this body of work lies in its detailed engagement with first-person narrative accounts of the situation in the Mediterranean during 2015 and 2016, as these are advanced by people on the move themselves. Working with and through the testimonies of those making the dangerous journey across the Mediterranean to highlight the claims and demands that are directed to EU policy-makers, the book emphasises the contested nature of knowledge production and draws attention to the ways in which people on the move directly question the legitimacy of governing authorities and the forms of knowledge that these produce. As we will see in the next section, this involves addressing people travelling across the Mediterranean as 'experts' in the field of migration, and engaging a counter-archive that 'function[s] as [a] critical intervention … [which] challenge[s] established forms of representing and responding to violence' (Motha and van Rijswijk, 2016: 2).

Reclaiming voice

Migratory 'expertise'

Consider us as humans, humans who can contribute not only to the economy but also in policy-making. We can contribute, and that would be a better solution. I think.

(MAL1.26, man from Ethiopia, Malta)

Reclaiming Migration engages a counter-archive based on in-depth qualitative research across multiple sites during 2015 and 2016. This research was carried out by a team that included the authors of this book, as well as two further investigators, seven research assistants and various site-based interpreters. The team conducted research in two phases across seven locations, focusing on the island sites of Kos (Greece), Malta and Sicily (Italy) during 2015, and the urban sites of Athens (Greece), Berlin (Germany), Istanbul (Turkey) and Rome (Italy) during 2016. Overall 257 interviews were conducted with a total of 271 people who had made – or who had contemplated making – the dangerous journey across the Mediterranean Sea by boat.[3] The study also involved site-based observational research, where possible. The majority of the interviews were recorded and transcribed in full, and where necessary translators were employed to interpret directly during the interview. Research participants were recruited using a targeted snowball sampling method, which was designed to reflect the diversity of migratory experiences at each site. Interviews followed a semi-structured format, which gave thematic structure to the questioning based on the project's overarching research questions, but without fixing the interview too rigidly. Open-ended questions provided a guide for each individual interviewer, yet also enabled flexibility dependent on the research participant's responses to different thematic areas of questioning. Emphasis was focused on providing support to research participants to share their migratory stories; to address the ways they made decisions and gained information throughout the migratory journey; and – critically – to draw out their experiences of and responses to policy interventions at different phases along the way. The semi-structured interview format facilitated a responsive approach, allowing participants to 'speak back' to the research and to share their experiences in a participatory way. This renders the project findings unique in the sense that the qualitative data produced is not replicable or standardised, but instead represents a reflexive engagement between the research team and research participants (see also Squire et al. 2017).[4]

Our work is influenced by participatory traditions of qualitative research, which seek to involve participants in the research process based on relations of equality and respect. While all marginalised groups face significant barriers to their meaningful engagement in research (see Pain and Francis, 2003; Bergold and Thomas, 2012: 197), there were of course additional barriers for people on the move across the Mediterranean in 2015 and 2016. Research is not a priority for those in precarious situations and, given our focus on new arrivals to the EU, it was not possible to involve participants in the early stages of the research design. Neither did those we interviewed usually take up our offer of remaining in contact with the project and team. Indeed, undertaking in-depth semi-structured interviews with people in precarious social and legal situations is complex, and the difficulties of creating a 'safe space' for research is a significant barrier to a more engaged, participative approach (see Bergold and Thomas, 2012). Some people we approached for interviews did not take up our invitation, and we had to persevere with interview requests at a given site over a period of time, often with the support of 'fixers' or local support workers at the formal and informal accommodation sites where we conducted our research. Despite these various barriers to participation, the research team remained committed to providing a supportive and engaged experience for the people we interviewed, in order that the process of knowledge production remained a sensitive and negotiable experience. Interviews usually lasted at least an hour and a half, and sometimes included limited follow-up support. It was not always appropriate to ask all the questions on the interview schedule, since emotional issues and research fatigue was often a concern, or sometimes people simply did not want to share everything with us or had specific issues to air. Hence, a flexible approach grounded in respect for research participants remained paramount throughout the research process (see also Squire, 2018).

Relations of privilege and disadvantage, along with the unequal positionalities of researcher and researched, are particularly stark for research such as that on which *Reclaiming Migration* is based. Indeed, the unequal benefits of participation continue to haunt this book, particularly given that the testimonies are ultimately 'owned' by a university in the Global North while the financial and reputational benefits of this book benefit the publishers and authors rather than the research participants. While limited in these important ways, the approach we have developed nevertheless attempts to expose and subvert sedimented relations of inequality by engaging people on the move in precarious conditions as those with a form of 'expertise' often overlooked by researchers and wider publics. Specifically, our work adopts an approach in which we seek to combine our academic expertise in policy and legal developments with the concrete experiential expertise of people on the move. As we will see in Chapter 6, this facilitates appreciation of people on the move as *theorists* of migration rather than simply experiential 'experts'. On the basis of this, what we seek to do '*together*' to change the situation '*for the better*' (MAL1.22), to echo the question posed by the man from Ivory Coast cited earlier in this chapter, is to assess the impact of the European policy agenda. Specifically, we do so from the perspective of those that the agenda affects most directly: people on the move themselves.

The value of the approach that we seek to develop is evident in Johnson's discussion of the role of narrative research in migration studies. She argues that it is important to engage people on the move not as research informants, but as 'autonomous and creative subjects' who are authors in their own right (Johnson, 2016: 383). The significance of this move, Johnson claims, is that it moves away from 'the division between elite and marginalised, the powerful who frame and sustain the dominant narrative, and the subaltern, who are silenced within it' (Johnson, 2016: 384). As the Ethiopian man we interviewed in Malta cited at the start of this section indicates, people on the move can *'contribute'* to a *'better solution'* precisely *'because we are experts in our life'* (MALI.26). He continues:

> *Nobody is more expert than us. I lived it* [my life on the move] *for nine years, and somebody come in Europe and sit in Norwegian parliament and says that he knows better than me about migration … I don't think so. I don't think so.*
> (MALI.26, man from Ethiopia, Skype interview)[5]

It is precisely by amplifying the voices of people on the move, in the way that this Ethiopian man suggests is critical, that we seek to 'authorise' the voices of people on the move (Johnson, 2016: 389). Indeed, rather than *extracting* knowledge from research participants, we seek to assess policy developments *with* research participants through the collaborative production of knowledge (see Tilley, 2018). In so doing, this book seeks to challenge the conventions that silence people on the move by rendering them as 'unauthorised speakers' in political debates (Johnson, 2016: 389). By engaging our research participants as people with the authority to speak, we highlight claims that are otherwise discounted as unauthorised or illegitimate. As such, this book can be understood as an invitation to bear witness to the violence and harms experienced by people on the move, through the engagement of a counter-archive that is co-produced with those who are best placed to narrate the situation that emerged across the Mediterranean during 2015 and 2016.

Taking voice

> *Now, every person here has their story. Every person who left Syria has a story and suffering and we're still suffering. European countries must look at this situation from the perspective of human rights.*
> (ATH2.27, woman from Syria, Athens)

> *The most important thing for politicians is to follow a humane policy. If they follow this in Turkey, they won't lose anything. But unfortunately everyone is playing a game, cat and mouse.*
> (ATH2.29, man from Syria, Athens)

Reclaiming voice

Rather than simply documenting the journeys and telling the stories of people on the move in 2015 and 2016, *Reclaiming Migration* seeks to produce knowledge *with* those migrating, by approaching research participants as 'experts' who can make an important contribution to the assessment of migration policies and their impact. This is important because it does not represent an attempt to 'give' people voice, but rather to listen to and learn from the testimonies of our research participants directly – often with considerable discomfort. While such a focus can be understood as an attempt to foster openness to 'the vulnerabilities of speakers in linguistic exchanges' (Dotson, 2011: 238), it also involves a rejection of the tendency to reproduce such vulnerabilities through the research process. Indeed, our research specifically seeks to find ways to challenge assumptions about the vulnerability of people on the move. It does so by acknowledging the difficult situations that people face and by considering the claims and demands advanced by people on the move to European politicians and policy-makers in the light of such experiences. As is evident in the opening quotes of this section, this manifests in a series of demands directed towards policy-makers such as those about the need for human rights to be respected and about the need for policy-making to be humane. Yet, rather than simply 'giving voice' to such demands, our research seeks to create situations whereby people on the move can 'take voice' in their own terms. Instead of enabling voice only for the purposes of our research, this opens opportunities for more disruptive narratives to emerge in terms that undermine the very grounds on which the research rests.

Scholars in the field of refugee studies have long paid attention to the question of voice. For example, Liisa Malkki's pioneering work focuses on the criticality of voice in terms of the ability to establish 'narrative authority over one's own circumstance and future, and, also, the ability to claim an audience' (Malkki, 1996: 393). Malkki (1996: 393) argues that 'this is not to make a simple, romantic argument about "giving the people a voice", for one would find underneath the surface not a voice waiting to be liberated but even deeper historical layers of silencing'. Rather, she emphasises the importance of voice in providing insight into refugees as historically embedded political actors, whose claims extend beyond their perceived vulnerabilities and involve distinctive political struggles. Indeed, many of our research participants made claims or demands for support, including with administrative procedures (ATH2.32), accessing services (ATH2.36; IST2.25), family reunification (ATH2.30; BER2.12A; IST2.19) and information provision (ROM2.02B). At the same time, however, people also spoke directly to the ways in which vulnerabilities were being produced by policy-makers, and made broader appeals to freedom in this context. For example, one woman from Syria we spoke with in Athens describes how policy risks '*kill[ing] people of frustration and exhaustion – they're killing them psychologically*' (ATH2.33, woman from Syria, Athens). Going further, she explains:

> *I want our message to reach the whole world. We are not coming here to beg! We are coming to work hard and raise our children. We are not coming to be humiliated. I want us to reach a better level. You see us waiting in line for food, but it's not in our control. What happened to us was not our doing. What more can I say?*
> (ATH2.33, woman from Syria, Athens)

This quote is indicative of the way people we spoke with 'take voice' through the research process, and, in so doing, contest the vulnerabilities that are imposed on them.

Yusef Qasmiyeh (2019: np) argues that voice is 'something which cannot be given (to anyone) since it must firmly belong to everyone from the beginning'. He suggests that voice can be understood as a way in which people create their 'own meaning in this narrow-vast world', and he refers to this in poetic terms as a process of 'embroider[ing] the voice with its own needle'. For many of our research participants, the interview process can precisely be understood in such terms. For example, people explained to us how this was an opportunity to '*tell you what is inside my heart*' (ATH2.41, man from Afghanistan, Athens), and '*to meet someone to talk of these problems* [that I face]' (IST2.10, man from Afghanistan, Istanbul). The act of listening, in this regard, appears to

Reclaiming voice

be a powerful intervention in its own terms (see Johnson, 2012). Yet people we spoke with also wanted us to do more. '*Is it possible for you to go to Ankara to speak to the employees and to convey our complaints to them?*' (IST2.29, man from Iraq, Istanbul). '*I think* [it would be good] *if* [you can] *tell me* [whether] *it will be good if we go another place to find the life or to stay here?*' (MAL1.27, man from Comoros, Malta). These requests, so important to those we interviewed, highlight our limitations as researchers. While we did suggest places to access support, we did not provide any resources or services for those we interviewed beyond basic refreshments, and we did not have a position of authority that could directly impact in any immediate sense on the situation of research participants. Explaining this in the interview process was often an uncomfortable process, which exposed the ways in which the research is ultimately grounded in relations of privilege and inequality. Differences of positionality in this regard render acts of speaking and listening a distinctly 'fraught' process (Pedwell, 2014, 2016), exposing 'troubled identifications' that require continuous navigation (Ratcliffe, 2005).

Despite these fraught engagements, the privileges of the research team were directly engaged as a resource by the people we interviewed in many cases. People emphasised the importance of the research team sharing findings '*to tell people the truth*' (ATH2.39, man from Afghanistan, Athens), to '*tell our problems*' (ROM2.26, man from Eritrea, Rome), and to '*spread the message*' (BER2.14, man from Iraq, Berlin) by '*conveying our message and stories and our voice to the outside world*' (BER2.11, man from Syria, Berlin). We were told that those who '*lack humanity*' need to hear '*this story*', because '*one nice word will heal your wounds*' (BER2.26, man from Syria, Berlin). Moreover, many people we spoke to asked us to share their problems with '*people who are responsible*' (ATH2.37, man from Afghanistan, Athens), with '*those in positions of responsibility*' (IST2.26, man from Syria, Istanbul), the '*responsible ones*' (IST2.27, man from Syria, Istanbul), '*the decision-makers*' (BER2.20, man from Iraq, Berlin; BER2.21, man from Syria, Berlin; IST2.14, man from Afghanistan, Istanbul), '*policy-makers*' (BER2.13, woman from Syria, Berlin; IST2.14, man from Afghanistan, Istanbul), '*big* [powerful]

Reclaiming migration

leaders' (IST2.16, woman from Syria, Istanbul), *'the media and politicians'* (IST2.05, man from Syria, Istanbul), and *'the committees of the European Union and the United Nations'* (IST2.21, man from Syria, Istanbul). This facilitated more critical demands on the part of those we interviewed, which were directed towards various governing authorities. For example, one woman from Syria says:

> *They say that there is relocation, let them prove it. There is protection, let them prove it. There is such and such from the state, let them prove it. We don't want money. We just want them to make it easier to leave and to offer services for this. These offices should help us. Put employees in them. We have our proof of identity, our papers, translations from Arabic to Turkish. They said that this space would be open for us, but they didn't open it.* [Interviewee's mother interjects –] *'They refused us a visit visa'.*
>
> (IST2.17, woman from Syria, Istanbul)

Posing a direct challenge to those responsible – in this case the embassy officials working for an EU state in Turkey – the demands of the women in this interview highlight how research participants made use of our team in 'claim[ing] an audience' (Malkki, 1996: 393). By asking us to advance demands to those deemed as responsible for the difficulties that they were facing, this exchange forms an important moment of contestation enacted by the women in a wider context of silencing. As a research team we sought to honour such requests by developing a range of outputs and activities designed to reach policy and wider public audiences.[6] Beyond simply reflecting relations of privilege and vulnerability, the interview situation can in this sense be understood as a site of contestation over situations of precarity and inequality.

While many people we spoke to engaged with our research team as allies in the struggle against broader processes of silencing, others challenged us more directly during the research process. At the end of the interview, we usually raised a question asking what should be the purpose of the research, but in one case our research participant challenged the interviewer before she got that far. The man from Syria says:

Reclaiming voice

You sit with us and ask us. All of you ask about our past, what happened to us. Nobody asks, nobody says, 'can I help you?' Sorry. You, you, as people, like your government. You are sympathising with me now ... Maybe if you see me in the street, in the U-Bahn, in the bus, your approach will be different. So the question to be asked [by you must be], *'what can we do for you?'*

(BER2.09, man from Syria, Berlin)

Others echoed this concern, suggesting that to ask people what they need is to show respect and value for people. For example, a man from Iraq stresses:

The best thing is to ask about the conditions of refugees and to respect them as humans. 'What are your problems? What do you need?' Ask. This is good. I mean, we thank you for your respect and value for human beings.

(IST2.30, man from Iraq, Istanbul)

Although some saw the interview process as a potentially positive experience offering opportunities for support, others were more sceptical. This is evident where a man from Syria comments:

You are not the first and you will be not the last to interview us. You – it's a good thing that you convey our message and voices to the outside world, but believe me we don't expect anything in return, a lot of people came, we had so many interviews done, even high-ranking employees came to this site, we spoke to them but nothing has changed.

(BER2.22, man from Syria, Berlin)

Interview fatigue is a serious issue here, in particular for those who have faced media interviews and who have had numerous interviews for their asylum application. Moreover, the last statement draws attention to some of the problematic limits of an attempt to counter the silencing of people on the move – our failure to make a difference directly to the lives of those we interviewed. As we will see in the next section, this is a key issue that our team has grappled with throughout the research process. While producing a counter-archive of 'Europe's migrant crisis' with people on the move is an important critical intervention that was largely appreciated by many of those we interviewed, it is by no means without its limitations.

Retaining silence

So when we got visits from journalists, media sources, I didn't want to speak with them. I told my further refugees, my friends, not to speak with anybody. Don't misunderstand me, but they are also businessmen, dealers, they take what they want from you, they don't offer anything in return. Some time, I spoke with some … to the journalists like yourself because I felt that they have, they come, they do that with good heart, good intention, which made me some time speak to them, but I felt sorry, they didn't give us anything in return, any help in return. Not even stay contact with us. Like ourselves, we sit with, asked for answers, and that would be it. They don't care about us. They don't visit us again … They come to take the information they need. Once they are done, you are done.

(BER2.30, man from Syria, Berlin)

The decision not to speak, not to 'take voice' in situations of vulnerability, violence and harm is one that cannot be underestimated. The quote above points to the decision '*not to speak with anybody*' as a means to maintain personal integrity in a situation where people '*don't care*'. Indeed, this remains a particularly fraught concern for our research team, the members of which certainly do care, but who were often not able to provide the support required by our research participants, as indicated above. The decision *not* to talk is completely understandable in this context, and one that our research team has been committed to respecting at all times. It is thus worth paying attention to both how and when people take voice, as well as to when they do not. We found that it is relatively common for people to ask for advice after the interview was finished, once the tape recorder has been stopped. This is significant, because it is indicative of the ways in which people on the move often *don't* want to speak if there is a chance that it may be exposed to those in positions of authority or power. Expressions such as '*I have no idea*' (IST2.08, man from Afghanistan, Istanbul; ROM2.30, man from Sierra Leone, Rome) or '*I don't know*' (IST2.15, man from Afghanistan, Istanbul) may be genuine expressions of a lack of knowledge, but they may also represent something more far-reaching. For example, if someone gives a large sigh when asked if they have any final comments about European policies (ATH2.30, woman from Syria, Athens), might this perhaps be symptomatic of a desire to hold back information that risks compromising their personal situation? That some people didn't want to speak to us at all may also be significant in this regard.

It is important in the light of cases where people do not take voice to reflect on what Papadopoulos, Stephenson and Tsianos refer to as the 'imperceptible politics' of migration, whereby people on the move challenge 'historical configurations of social and political control' through the *subversive* act of escape (Papadopoulos et al., 2008: 203). This suggests that our engagement of a counter-archive has important limits that must be respected, in order that any hidden tactics of people on the move in precarious conditions are not exposed in terms that perpetuate violence and harm.[7] The way we have dealt with this is to focus on the explicit claims and demands of people on the move, rather than on people's tactics of migrating. Nevertheless, this is always a messy and difficult process, and the risks of contributing to a 'control bias' (Scheel, 2019) remain even where many of our research participants ask us to publish our findings. It is worth noting that differences of positionality on the part of people on the move can be significant in relation to this question of how far people on the move engage in hidden tactics or present more open demands in the attempt to challenge the violence and harms that they experience. For example, many Syrians along the eastern route to Greece prompted us to share our findings and the demands that they advanced to policy-makers. By contrast, many Afghans on the eastern route and sub-Saharan Africans travelling via the central route to Italy were generally less inclined to engage with the question of how we should use the research, and were often more reticent to advance claims aimed at policy-makers directly. In other words, some people have (or perceive themselves as having) a greater capacity to 'claim an audience' than others, thus directing demands to policy-makers with greater confidence. Neverthe-less, the picture is by no means clear-cut and a complex range of silences and demands are evident for different groups in our research. As such, an approach which recognises the importance of – and does not betray – silence is important, just as an approach that shares the demands of those on whom silence is often imposed is also important. One of the troubling silences in our research relates to the power imbalances structuring the research process, which remain integral to the interview situation despite the commitment of the team to embedding the principles of participation, respect and equality in the project design at all stages. One point that emerged as important in this regard was that we, as researchers, did not fall into the trap of personal or collective self-congratulation when faced with positive responses to the project:

> *It's a great idea. All people from Europe all good people. They always care and they love the human. They don't behave like animals. It's a good idea, this research.*
> (ATH2.34, man from Afghanistan, Athens)

> *I don't know what the benefit is of this or where this voice will reach. I don't know. But I really relaxed talking to someone! (laughter) Really. Thank you so much for giving me the opportunity.*
> (IST2.03, woman from Syria, Istanbul)

> *I consider your coming to us, as they say, a revolution. It didn't cross my mind that a journalist, a doctor, would come to us. This means that there is good, that they are using the likes of you to do the work. As long as there is a person like you, it means there is good in this society and it came into my house.*
> (IST2.22, man from Syria, Istanbul)

While the power dynamics between different interviewers and interviewees are variable based on differing positionalities and their complex intersectionalities, the praise for our research by some people on the move remains a difficult dimension of the project in many regards. This is particularly the case given that it was relatively rare for research participants to speak about their concerns or criticisms of the project. Important in this regard is one research participant's suggestion that: '*You benefit from this information and this evidence*' (ATH2.31, woman from Syria, Athens). Countering Europe's 'crisis' with that of the Syrian people, he goes on: '*If it wasn't for our crisis, we wouldn't have left*' (ATH2.31). This represents an important caution to researchers who, as indicated above, do indeed benefit in various ways from researching the violence and harms that people on the move face – regardless of intention. Our research participant in this case takes voice in terms that does more than simply challenge singular accounts of 'Europe's migrant crisis'; he also questions the power dynamics within which the research process is itself grounded. Such claims remain critical in exposing the limits of a counter-archive, along with the power dynamics through which such a form of knowledge production is grounded.

While retaining silence is in many ways an important dimension of our counter-archive, it is also vital that the risk of re-silencing is challenged as this emerges throughout the process of analysis. As indicated above, our project was participatory in a limited sense, meaning that we sought a collaborative approach with people on the move through the interview process, rather than in the broader sense by involving research participants in the design and analytical dimensions of the research. This is of course not surprising given the precarious situations of those we spoke with, along with the practicalities of undertaking research in relatively unstable conditions. Yet it also means that our analysis might be charged as involving the 'despoilment and dispossession' of the testimonies of those who collaborated with us in producing the counter-archive (Mbembe, 2002: 20). Critically, our research is not based on the assumption that we are better placed to assess the interests of people on the move than they are themselves (see Spivak, 1988). Indeed, our analysis explicitly and openly focuses on developing *through* migratory testimonies a critical assessment of the 2015 *Agenda* (please see Introduction and Chapters 3–6). This is not necessarily an endeavour that all our research participants wanted to be involved in, or agreed on in the terms that our project envisaged. For some, this did not appear to pose a problem: '*You know better*' (ATH2.40), '*You academics know your milieus better than me or anyone else*' (IST2.26). Nevertheless, others had much more specific demands that we were not able to convey through our analysis: '*I can suggest the people living in the camp – this campsite – give them apartments, assign them jobs or something to do, keep them busy*' (BER2.20); '*Communicate that there is difficulty in smuggling, that people are dying, that people are stuck in Greece for four or five months, no one is moving*' (IST2.27). Drawing together collectively the expertise of people on the move with the academic expertise of our research team through the counter-archive in this regard remains an imperfect as well as a fraught process, but nevertheless involves a sustained commitment to countering the silencing of people on the move.

Conclusion

This chapter has provided an overview of some of the key conceptual and methodological dimensions of the project on which *Reclaiming Migration* draws, while situating the research in relation to a broader body of scholarship in the cross-cutting fields of critical border and migration studies. Specifically, it has made the case for an approach that contributes a counter-archive of migratory testimonies, in order to 'challenge established forms of representing and responding to violence' (Motha and van Rijswijk, 2016: 2). Our efforts to produce a counter-archive of Europe's so-called migrant crisis of 2015–16 reflect a concern to address people on the move as 'experts' in assessing the impact of the EU policy agenda. We seek to foster appreciation of the diverse narratives, practices and projects of migration that have been rendered invisible in the midst of 'crisis', while at the same time challenging the control bias that emerges where governing authorities and rationalities hold command over the production of knowledge. The chapter has suggested that such an endeavour involves the forging of an alliance between researchers and research participants, in terms that reject the 'pernicious ignorance' that consistently leads to 'harmful practice[s] of silencing' people on the move (Dotson, 2011). Nevertheless, this is not to suggest that the production of a counter-archive is without problems or limitations. The uneven power dynamics within the research process remain a key concern, as do the dangers of 'giving voice' and exposing the hidden tactics of people on the move. As several of our research participants importantly highlight, the research process is

Reclaiming voice

one in which people on the move rarely benefit in any sustained way, while as researchers we do in various ways – whether we want to or not. Advancing a critique of the preventative policy agenda in terms that remain committed to challenging the dynamics of power and racialised violence through which people on the move have been silenced is thus critical. It is to this task that we will now turn.

Notes

1 As Lilie Chouliaraki and Rafal Zaborowski argue, this misrecognition of refugees as apolitical, asocial and ahistorical actors in effect maintained a 'strict hierarchy' that ensured that people on the move remained 'firmly outside the remit of "our" communities of belonging' (Chouliaraki and Zaborowski, 2017: 613).

2 In Latin, this is translated as *archivuum*, 'residence of the magistrate' (Stoler, 2002: 90).

3 The first phase was completed during September to November 2015 and involved 136 interviews with a total of 139 participants at three island arrival sites: Kos, Malta and Sicily. Difficulties in recruiting research participants in Malta due to reduced arrivals resulting from an 'agreement' with Italy during the time period of our research led to some of the interviews being carried out at this site between December 2015 and March 2016, and also led to some Skype interviews being carried out with those who had moved on from Malta to other EU states. The second phase was completed during May to July 2016 and involved 121 interviews with a total of 132 participants at four urban sites: Athens, Berlin, Istanbul and Rome.

4 For full information on the project sample and methodology, please see the final project report, Squire et al. (2017), at www.warwick.ac.uk/ crossingthemed.

5 This Skype interview was conducted from Malta with a man from Ethiopia who was located in Norway.

6 For example, we produced a detailed report on the basis of the research and shared this with various policy audiences (see www.warwick.ac.uk/ crossingthemed). We also created an openly accessible online map which we used to share the research with various public audiences (see www. warwick.ac.uk/crossing-the-med-map).

7 This is a continuous concern for a project that does not simply produce a counter-archive for critical analysis by the research team, but also produces a database that might be used by future researchers in a multitude of ways.

3

Rejecting deterrence

But what I wanted to tell is what I was hearing when I was in Sudan, about Libya, about the Sahara, that it was very, very bad. And when I was in Libya what I was hearing about the sea that it was very, very bad. And that is what I was telling, when people were asking me about Sudan to give them information when I was in Libya. I was telling them that it was very bad, but nobody was listening. I never listened to them when they say, 'people are dying', 'the Sahara is hot' because I was already in fear, and then what am I going to fear?
(MAL1.26, man from Ethiopia, Skype interview)[1]

There is no solution. Either smuggling or stay here for a year. They closed the border but they opened the door to the smugglers. You opened the door to illegal migration. You're saying that you want legal migration but it's the opposite. I don't mean you personally, I'm talking about the European countries. You opened the door to human trafficking.
(ATH2.15, woman from Syria, Athens)

Introduction

The 2015 *European Agenda on Migration* marked the intensification of a preventative or *deterrent* approach to migration management and border security, broadly understood as a range of policies and practices designed to discourage unauthorised migration to the EU (see Introduction). Such an approach assumes the effectiveness of deterrence in stymieing 'undesirable' forms of migration at source, and in changing the behaviour of people on the move in precarious conditions. This chapter draws on our migratory testimonies in order to problematise these core assumptions and highlight the ineffectiveness of the deterrence paradigm. In so doing, it emphasises the ways in which deterrence involves practices of racialised violence that reflect long-standing colonial dynamics. By contrasting the stated aims of the 2015 *Agenda* with the lived experiences of people on the move, the analysis opens up space for critical reflection on recent policy developments. We challenge the suggestion that intensified border policing, the limitation of rights and increased deportations form effective deterrents to migration. By drawing on our counter-archive, we contribute to conceptual debates about the limits of the deterrence paradigm through arguing that deterrent measures are ineffective on two primary grounds. First, in order to be effective, deterrence presupposes *knowledge* of deterrent measures by those the authorities seek to deter. Yet a common refrain among the people we spoke with was that they were largely unaware of key policy instruments such as detention and deportation. To improve 'knowledge' and increase awareness of these measures among people on the move as part of a deterrent approach would be to miss the point, however. We see a glimpse of the limitations of this logic in the extract above from the man from Ethiopia interviewed in Malta, who explains that, despite warning others of the situation in Libya, '*nobody was listening*' (MAL1.26). Second, in reflecting the elite assumptions of a crisis frame that invokes long-standing colonial dynamics, a deterrent approach fails to understand *why* people migrate in the first place. As such, it represents an approach that fundamentally underestimates the drivers of migration and conditions of flight (see Chapter 4).

Anti-smuggling is central to deterrence, yet our counter-archive challenges the dominant policy framing of smugglers as the 'problem' at hand, highlighting the drivers that necessitate movement as well as the wider conditions that make smuggling the only viable option for escape. Migratory testimonies, such as that above of the woman from Syria interviewed in Athens, contest the dominant framing by noting the complicity of authorities in the conditions that allow smuggling networks to thrive – '*You opened the door to illegal migration*' (ATH2.15)

– while also highlighting common instances of corruption and collusion among border police and smugglers. Foregrounding the very sources of knowledge and expertise among people on the move that were excluded from the 2015 *Agenda* demands a reassessment of the deterrence paradigm as well as of anti-smuggling. We argue that efforts to externalise border controls increase the risk of racialised violence and abuse that individuals face on their journeys, at times far beyond the EU's territorial borders and independent of whether the intended destination is Europe. Testimonies show that people on the move face a continuum of border-related violence when travelling towards and across the EU, in their encounters with border guards, police, smugglers and the material environment. Presenting nuanced accounts of the relationships and encounters of people on the move with smugglers, our counter-archive thus highlights the dangers of anti-smuggling, to present a damning critique of the preventative policy agenda as an extension of Europe's colonial history. Although deterrent border security measures are highly ineffective on their own terms, the experiences of people on the move are paramount – though often neglected – in any assessment of the preventative approach. For this reason, as well as acknowledging the predominance of drivers of flight, we also suggest that it is important to emphasise the *lived experiences* of deterrent bordering practices, through which migratory journeys become more perilous.

The deterrence paradigm

With its emphasis on both 'working in partnership with third countries to tackle migration upstream' and putting in place 'concrete measures to prevent hazardous journeys' *before* they take place (European Commission, 2015b: 5), the European Commission's 2015 *Agenda* represented a complex deterrent approach to the management of the EU's external borders. As we have already outlined in the Introduction to this book, two of the four 'pillars' of the 2015 *Agenda* reflected the logic of deterrence, namely: 'Reducing the incentives for irregular migration' and

'Border management – saving lives and securing external borders'. In emphasising the 'danger' of journeys at sea, the need to 'address root causes in third countries', the effort to 'fight against smugglers and traffickers' and an increased focus on returns, the first of these two pillars aimed to reduce the incentives for the initiation of journeys (European Commission, 2015b: 8–9). The other pillar, with its efforts to 'support third countries developing their own solutions to better manage their borders' and 'to strengthen the capacity for countries in North Africa to intervene and save the lives of migrants in distress', focused on increasing the externalisation of border controls such that mobility is effectively stymied at the point of departure from 'key African and neighbourhood countries' (European Commission, 2015b: 11–12). In this way, the *Agenda* brought together both securitising and humanitarian narratives of crisis to justify and further entrench a deterrent approach. Before we go on to assess the effectiveness of the EU's preventative policy agenda, it is first instructive to locate the deterrent approach within the general trajectory of the criminalisation of migration.

In their authoritative analysis of the relationship between deterrence and the criminalisation of migration, Hastie and Crépeau (2014: 213) argue that the opening decades of the twenty-first century have witnessed the 'slow and steady progression towards restrictive immigration policies' in the Global North. On their reading, it is in response to the globalising dynamics in which new forms of transnational mobility are made possible that states have sought new forms of border control based on the political distinction between 'legal' and 'illegal' forms of movement (Hastie and Crépeau, 2014: 213; see also Dauvergne, 2012). The rise of a 'crime-control' response to migration has in turn constructed people on the move as potentially 'dangerous' subjects and, in feeding populist xenophobic narratives of mistrust and scapegoating, justified the use of 'increasingly punitive measures' against those deemed to be 'irregular' (Hastie and Crépeau, 2014: 213; see also de Haas, 2008). Such measures – including fingerprinting and the collection of biometric data, the use of administrative detention, and surveillance at sites of arrival and places of work – have proliferated especially since the attacks of 11 September 2001 (Hastie and Crépeau, 2014: 217; see also Huysmans, 2006; van Munster, 2009). What these narratives, policies and practices amount to is the de facto 'illegalisation' of migration, albeit outside of the parameters and processes of criminal law, which means that there is greater exposure to 'criminalisation' and yet fewer opportunities to access rights and protection (Hastie and Crépeau, 2014: 220). Underpinning these dynamics is the logic of deterrence, which Hastie and Crépeau (2014: 223) conceptualise as deriving from criminal law and as forming 'an important goal of penal sanctions and measures'. They suggest, however, that this logic is not only about 'raising the cost of crime'; it is more fundamentally about 'influencing and conditioning social behaviour' (Hastie and Crépeau, 2014: 223). As such, deterrence can be understood as an attempt to establish a direct causal link between the introduction of ever more punitive measures, on the one hand, and 'the future conduct of the targeted group', on the other (Hastie and Crépeau, 2014: 223).

Rather than marking a break with previous policy in the EU context, the 2015 *Agenda* continued the existing deterrent approach to migration management and border security (see Introduction). Woods and Saucier describe death and suffering in the Mediterranean as an '*ongoing*' process, which has impacted the lived experiences of 'black people' in the region 'for the better part of the past and present millenniums' (Woods and Saucier, 2015: np, original emphasis). It is on this basis that the 'migrant crisis' is best understood 'as part of Europe's ongoing encounter with the world that it created through more than 500 years of empire, colonial conquest, and slavery' (Danewid, 2017: 1680; see also Sharpe, 2016). The policing of migration across the Mediterranean reflects the ongoing significance of this encounter, which Saucier and Woods (2014: 57) suggest to be the manifestation of a historically informed social order that is premised on anti-black violence. Indeed, the measures taken to impede 'undesirable' migration towards the EU have intensified markedly since the early 1990s, not only in the Mediterranean but also more widely. As is by now well documented, the past three decades have witnessed the technologisation of internal mobility checks within the Schengen area (Dijstelbloem and Meijer, 2011; Walters, 2002), the increased reliance on detention and deportation across EU member states (De Genova and Peutz, 2010; UNGA, 2013), the externalisation of the common refugee protection framework to undemocratically elected regimes in North Africa (Gammeltoft-Hansen, 2011b), the offshoring of bordering practices to third countries via mobility partnerships and juxtaposed controls (Bialasiewicz, 2012), and the neoliberal outsourcing of controls to private security companies and local militias (Andersson, 2014). These measures reflect what Anievas et al. (2015: 4) call the 'global colour line', and can be understood as representing a 'continuation of the organising logics of the "colonial matrix of power"' (Lemberg-Pedersen, 2019: 248). Indeed, since the onset of the so-called 'Arab Spring' in 2011 the gradual proliferation of deterrent measures designed to criminalise migration from Africa to the EU has only intensified (Hastie and Crépeau, 2014).

The 2015 *Agenda* is significant, because it further deepened, extended and justified the remit of the deterrence paradigm by conjoining it with the narrative of crisis and politics of exceptionalism (see Chapter 1). While this was to some extent already evident over preceding decades in the increased securitisation of migration, the prominence of a narrative of humanitarian crisis in the 2015 *Agenda* marked a further development in the genealogy of deterrence. People on the move were not only seen as potential criminals, but also as subjects in need of 'saving' through the humanitarianisation of the deterrence paradigm (Little and Vaughan-Williams, 2017). Importantly, this double appeal to humanitarianism and security – as well as concomitant attempts to externalise black mobilities – is by no means unprecedented, with similar dynamics evident in eighteenth-century anti-slavery politics (Lemberg-Pedersen, 2019: 253). More recently, responsibility for the risk of making the journey has been placed on the individual subject, who is warned not to endanger their life by seeking unauthorised entry to the EU in the first place. In this regard, people remaining undeterred can only be 'saved' by authorities acting on behalf of the

EU, which creates further opportunities for the management of mobile populations while effectively criminalising the activities of non-governmental organisations seeking to support people on the move (see also Squire, 2020a: 159–161). For these reasons, it is increasingly important to acknowledge the complementary ways in which strategies of deterrence – as reflected in the 2015 *Agenda* – work in both securitising and humanitarian directions as part of a single apparatus of control. Questions arise, however, as to how far this approach has been 'effective' on its own terms in responding to the European 'migrant crisis'. What happens to an understanding of the politics of deterrence when we shift the standpoint away from elite crisis narratives to the perspectives of the very people that are supposed to be deterred? It is to these questions that the analysis will now turn.

The ineffectiveness of deterrence

Interviewer: *At that time, did you know whether you might be taken to the detention centre or not?*

MAL1.02: *We didn't know at that time. We thought that they are going to give us something and let us go free. We had no idea about being taken to the detention centre.*

(MAL1.02, man from Ethiopia, Malta)

While a key operating assumption of the 2015 *Agenda* was that a deterrent approach to migration management and external border control is both *possible* and *effective* as a paradigm for responding to 'crisis' conditions, the effectiveness of deterrence in the context of criminal law and its application to the management of migration more generally has been subject to a sustained critique. Hastie and Crépeau (2014: 223) argue that the application of deterrent measures to migration is ineffective due to a failure to engage with 'the underlying meaning and behaviour of individual migrants', and a resultant 'lack of a correlative effect' between the range of 'deterrent measures', on the one hand, and the 'future conduct of the targeted group', on the other. Our analysis supports this problematisation. We draw attention to the widespread ineffectiveness of more punitive deterrence mechanisms mobilised in response to the 'migration crisis', including detention and deportation as contemporary manifestations of colonial attempts to striate space and produce governable subjects (Jabri, 2013). Our counter-archive suggests that these measures are largely ineffective because knowledge of such measures among people on the move was very limited – if to some extent variable according to route – as illustrated by the lack of awareness of mandatory detention referred to by the man from Ethopia cited at the start of this section. In addition, our counter-archive indicates that insofar as deterrent measures are known in advance and/or encountered en route, these have less significance in the decision to migrate than the various drivers of migration. For this reason, it is also important to underscore the ineffectiveness of 'information campaigns' in disseminating knowledge of deterrent measures, which fail to hit their target (Nieuwenhuys and Pécoud, 2007).[2] Our engagement of people on the move as 'experts' rather than as objects of deterrence thus highlights the ineffectiveness of the 2015 *Agenda* empirically, as well as methodologically and politically.

A lack of knowledge about deterrent measures

As stated, the logic of deterrence underpinning the 2015 *Agenda* presupposed widespread knowledge and awareness of deterrent measures among people on the move. It is important to note that there is significant variation in terms of levels of knowledge and awareness across the different routes, as well as in the context of different national and regional networks. Some of those travelling along the eastern route, for example, indicated that they had received prior information about onward border closures in central Europe and major policy developments such as the EU–Turkey Joint Actions. One area in which people provided testimonies of knowledge-sharing across all routes relates to the implications of fingerprinting in the context of the Dublin Regulation, which expects people to have asylum applications processed in the first country of arrival in the EU. Yet, people often expressed a demonstrable *lack* of awareness, both of long-standing deterrent measures and those introduced under the auspices of the 2015 *Agenda*. This was particularly, though not exclusively, the case among those travelling along the central Mediterranean route. We focus here on knowledge about three specific deterrence measures with a history in the EU context prior to 2015, in turn: detention, deportation and military-led search and rescue missions.

One of the central governmental strategies in the attempt to deter unwanted entrants to EU member states in recent decades has been the threat of detention on arrival (UNGA, 2013). Article 15(2) of the 2008 EU Return Directive (2008/115/EC) states that the use of detention under a repatriation order must be as short in duration as possible – it 'may not exceed six months' unless 'the third-country national does not cooperate, or where there are delays in obtaining the necessary travel documentation from the migrant's home country', in which case it can be extended for up to eighteen months. The 2008 Directive also specifies that detention must only be used if there is a prospect of removal, that specialist detention facilities should be used, that detention decisions should be reviewed regularly, and that detainees must be allowed contact with legal representatives, families and consular authorities, and be informed of their right to challenge the decision. Despite these legal provisions, however, the widespread use of detention across the EU has been subject to long-standing criticism on account of failure to adhere to these standards and to protect the legal and human rights of detainees (Pro Asyl, 2012; Amnesty International, 2013; UNGA, 2013). Indeed, Article 18 of the 2008 Directive permits states to relax certain standards under 'emergency conditions', which, according to a 2013 report commissioned by the EU Education, Audiovisual and Culture Executive Agency, 'exposes migrants to inconsistent treatment and the abuse of power' (EACEA, 2013: 11).

If we consider the case of Malta, for example, successive governments have sought to capitalise on the narrative of crisis and the politics of exceptionalism to enforce a mandatory detention policy of up to twelve months for asylum seekers and eighteen months for rejected asylum seekers (Mainwaring, 2016).[3] This policy has largely been justified on the basis that detention acts as a deterrent for unauthorised arrivals, conceived in humanitarian terms (Vaughan-Williams and Pisani, 2020). Nevertheless, the majority of those we spoke with in Malta had no prior knowledge of the policy, and this came as a complete surprise to many on arrival, as the excerpt opening this section indicates. Indeed, a lack of awareness of detention was not limited to the Maltese context. When this was raised during a discussion in Kos, for example, a man from Afghanistan expressed disbelief that '*such a thing*' could '*happen in Europe*' because he had been told by smugglers that '*after Turkey the rest of the journey is better*' (KOS1.05, man from Afghanistan, Kos). Some describe how they had heard that '*Hungary and Bulgaria are placing people in camps*', indicating that they do '*not know why*' (KOS1.40, man from Syria, Kos). Others express faith in notions of natural justice that they associated with the political and legal systems in Europe: '*I do not know if there is detention or not ... but I know that if you are in a country and you are not doing anything illegal then you will not be detained*' (KOS1.28, man from Syria, Kos).

In contrast to detention, the extent of knowledge and awareness about the threat of deportation from EU member states was far more varied. Under the 2008 Return Directive, 'illegally-staying third country nationals' can be removed to their country of 'origin', 'transit' country or a 'third country' (Article 3). Despite removal being another key instrument of deterrence, several people we spoke with claimed that they were unaware of this risk prior to arrival (ATH2.25; SIC1.20; ROM2.16). Some only realised that they could be deported once they had arrived in the EU and were able to access information via social media and/or internet searches (BER2.19). Many more were aware of deportation as compared to detention, however, even if the quality and accuracy of the information they had received was inconsistent. For example, an Iraqi man in Istanbul explained that deportation was possible '*from Greece*', but not '*from Europe ... Greece isn't Europe. I have good information about this. Greece is a poor country. It's not like European countries ... The important thing is that the refugee who goes to Europe is not deported unless he requests it'* (IST2.24, man from Iraq, Istanbul). A number of people said they had heard that all Syrian and Iraqi nationals are exempt from being returned and that they had decided to proceed with their journey on that basis (BER2.20; ATH2.18; ATH2.21). In Berlin, Istanbul, Kos, Malta and Rome, several expressed having a general knowledge of the widespread existence of returns as a policy instrument, but said that this was nevertheless insufficient to deter them from making the journey (BER2.16B; BER2.17; KOS1.31; KOS1.37; IST2.09; IST2.16; MAL1.24; ROM2.03). This general sentiment is summed up by an Afghan woman in Istanbul, when she says: *'Yes, I heard about these cases, but I think that even if it will be the last day of my life I will try to get there because of the problems that I had in Iran'* (IST2.09, woman from Afghanistan, Istanbul).

A third key area in which knowledge of EU deterrence measures was limited among people on the move relates to awareness of military-led search and rescue missions across the Mediterranean region. In November 2014, Frontex launched Joint Operation Triton with the dual aim of 'managing borders and saving lives at sea' (European Commission, 2016b). This superseded Operation Mare Nostrum, the Italian government-led naval and air search and rescue operation, which had begun in October 2013 in the aftermath of several major shipwrecks. From 22 June 2015, Operation Sophia, led by the EUNAV-FOR MED task force, aimed to 'identify, capture, and dispose of vessels' that were 'used or suspected of being used by migrant smugglers or traffickers' under the auspices of the 2015 *Agenda* (European Commission, 2016b). In 2016, a NATO-led intervention was subsequently launched in the Aegean Sea to prevent migration to Greece as the 'hotspot' approach to reception and identification was being set up (see Introduction). Garelli and Tazzioli suggest that these successive search and rescue missions can be understood as constituting the Mediterranean and Aegean Seas as complex 'military-humanitarian' spaces of 'contested geographies of escape, control, and rescue' (Garelli and Tazzioli, 2018a: 686).

Rejecting deterrence

Securitising and humanitarian narratives of crisis thus come together through what are described as contradictory and highly ambivalent 'overlapping configurations' of power, in which the outcome of encounters between EU authorities and mobile populations from the Global South is often unclear (Garelli et al., 2018: 666; see also Vaughan-Williams, 2015). On this basis, Garelli and Tazzioli suggest that the missions subsequent to Operation Mare Nostrum – with their dual focus on saving lives *and* disrupting the business model of smugglers – are more akin to a form of 'hybrid warfare' (Garelli and Tazzioli, 2018b: 184). They suggest that militarised search and rescue operations have in recent years become 'vessels of dissuasion', whose missions need to be addressed as part of the wider 'strategy of deterrence against migrant departures from Libya ... and as an attack on the logistics of migrant crossing' (Garelli and Tazzioli, 2018b: 191–192). Nevertheless, we contend that an exclusively top-down focus on the governmentality of military-humanitarianism risks reproducing the dramatic scenes of rescue and control on which dominant narratives of crisis and policies of deterrence are predicated. By contrast, analysing the contested politics of search and rescue from the multiple and diverse standpoints of those populations targeted by military-humanitarian missions adds nuance and complexity to this picture, and recovers the experience and agency of those constituted as 'postcolonial subjects' (Jabri, 2013). In this regard, our findings highlight very different experiences according to the routes taken by people on the move.

Many of those travelling on the central Mediterranean route were unaware of the military-humanitarian operations referred to by Garelli and Tazzioli (2018a, 2018b). For this reason, none of the people we spoke with discussed being deterred from leaving the shores of Libya in fear of encountering and being contained by military-led operations at sea. Their testimonies cast doubt on the veracity of claims that widespread awareness of search and rescue missions across the central Mediterranean act as a 'pull' factor in stimulating 'irregular' movement. Rather, many people interviewed in Malta and Rome were either largely (MAL2.09; MAL1.25) or entirely (MAL1.10; MAL1.15; ROM2.01;

ROM2.08) unaware of the possibility of being rescued by the Italian coastguard or other agency. As a man from Sudan explains: '*We didn't have any idea, [it] just happened in front of us – like a miracle*' (MALI.10, man from Sudan, Malta). Some suggested that they had been led to believe their boats would be chaperoned all the way to the Italian coastline and thus it had come as a surprise when they found that they had been abandoned. For example, a woman from Eritrea says: '*We didn't wait to be saved, because the traffickers said they'd take us all the way to Italy, not that they would abandon us in the middle of the sea. That's why we didn't think about being rescued*' (ROM2.09, woman from Eritrea, Rome). Only one man from Eritrea indicated that he had prior knowledge of the possibility of search and rescue in the context of the central route prior to embarkation. He explains: '*Yes I know that … They have rescue numbers. And they give you GPS. If you suffer, just phone one of these numbers they say to you. All the smugglers they say this idea, if you suffer you phone this number, they will rescue you*' (ROM2.14, man from Eritrea, Rome).[4]

By contrast, the situation as narrated by those travelling along the eastern Mediterranean route differed considerably. Here, with few exceptions (KOS1.46A; KOS1.46B; KOS1.22A), testimonies repeatedly emerged in which people expressed prior awareness of – and dependence on – the existence of search and rescue missions. Many in Athens, for example, emphasised their '*hope*' that the '*Greek coastguard*' would come and '*save*' them (ATH2.20H, man from Syria, Athens). They report being informed by '*Turkish smugglers*' that they should place their faith in European surveillance systems and that ultimately the Greek authorities would not let them die: '*As we were leaving, he said "whatever happens to you, you're being watched by Europe … They know that you've left Turkey. They're watching your boat. If you're drowning, they'll come get you. Don't be scared"*' (ATH2.24, man from Syria, Athens). Others say that they had acquired information about search and rescue prior to arriving in Europe via dedicated Facebook pages '*where you can talk with the people who went before*' (BER2.21, man from Syria, Berlin). Not all accepted at face value information provided by smugglers or through social media networks, however. A number of people we spoke with had heard of stories about those who had encountered difficulties, had not been rescued, and had drowned at sea (IST2.27). Several also expressed their scepticism about the probability of being 'saved' by European authorities. For example, one man from Afghanistan explains: '*No matter what they said, I didn't believe them because I knew people had died. And although I knew that, I had to come here … I was forced to … because of my needs. I surrendered myself to God and I said I am going. I had no other choice*' (KOS1.05, man from Afghanistan, Kos). It is precisely this notion, that people on the move often feel compelled to escape situations of extreme precarity whatever the consequences, that we now explore in greater detail.

The predominance of migration drivers

Since governmental models of deterrence largely ignore the diverse perspectives and the experiences of people on the move, they are severely limited in their understanding of why people are motivated to undertake migratory journeys in the first place, and largely reflect assumptions made by governmental actors about the drivers for migration (Hastie and Crépeau, 2014: 223). One of these assumptions is that those migrating are 'rational actors', as understood in the context of social science models of human behaviour. As Hastie and Crépeau (2014: 226) emphasise, however, this fails to consider the possibility that the risk of not migrating may outweigh the risk of not being deterred. Our research supports the argument that deterrence-based approaches to migration are ineffective 'because of their inability to connect with the true reality of the situation' (Hastie and Crépeau, 2014: 226). However, we also go further to ground this conceptual and methodological critique in an analysis of the *lived experiences* of people on the move. By drawing on migratory testimonies from our counter-archive, we thus seek to advance understanding of the ways in which the ineffectiveness of deterrence is related to ongoing dynamics of racialised violence against people crossing the Mediterranean in 2015–16, an area that remains under-analysed in the literature to date.

The testimonies from our counter-archive repeatedly indicate that the *drivers* of migration have an indomitable potency that far exceeds the so-called 'pull factor' of Europe (the latter being a key dimension in a crisis-based framing of the situation in the Mediterranean in 2015–16, as well as in a logic of deterrence). While explanations for seeking entry to the EU diverged particularly in relation to different national groups, people we spoke with often described similar circumstances that rendered their migration necessary. A group of Somalis, for example, recount personal stories related to violence and insecurity, and, particularly in the case of younger men, the need to avoid recruitment into militant groups: '*The situation was fucking bad … They* [Al Shabaab] *told us "come and unite with us to kill with enemy in the country, and be like bomb". After they beat us, they cut, they put in the inside of the room and they closed it*' (MAL2.04, man from Somalia, Malta). Indeed, we heard a recurring set of narratives about exposure to violence whereby, even in countries generally regarded as 'safe', the threat of persecution and harm became so severe that people felt compelled to leave. As one man explains: '*I left Gambia because of corruption and dictatorship … People missing for no reason and no one knows where they are, some lost their uncles because of the dictatorship*' (MAL2.05, man from Gambia, Malta). Regardless of people's origins, the search for personal safety and peace was consistently listed as the primary motivating factor for fleeing. Thus, a man from Somalia says: '*Actually I didn't have any destination, I evacuate Somalia … for lack of security and I didn't want to fight Al-Shabaab … Kenya was the nearest country and so I went there*' (MAL2.06, man from Somalia, Malta).

Since the concept of deterrence implies a pre-emptive attempt to change people's behaviour or actions, it also presupposes that those who are targeted by deterrent measures are free to choose to behave or act differently. However, the high incidence of exposure to violence and the need to flee from sustained threats to personal safety – coupled with the absence of adequate protection and access to rights – means that many people on the move do not speak straightforwardly of 'choosing' to leave, or indeed 'choosing' to seek entry into Europe as a specific destination (see also Chapter 5). Many on the eastern route – especially Syrian nationals – described Europe as a last resort in the face of bad treatment or difficulties in accessing Arab countries. For example, a man in Kos explains: '*I was aware of what I would face here ... I knew that when you come illegally, it is difficult, I knew this was a deadly route ... but I have no other choice. I knew I would have to suffer all this*' (KOS1.26, man from Syria, Kos). Others in Turkey discussed exploitative work conditions and a form of life reduced to basic survival (see Mbembe, 2003). On the central route, many who had travelled via Libya told us that they had never planned to come to Europe. Conditions in Libya – including the difficulties of migrating back through a country where they had already suffered torture, abuse, forced labour and imprisonment in dire conditions – rendered onward travel to Europe their only option. Far from a choice that might be changed due to an appreciation of the risk of detention, deportation and militarised 'rescue', the dominant theme in our counter-archive is the necessity of escape.

Shockingly, several people we spoke with along the central route described a process of being forced onto boats to Europe, either against their will or without them knowing what was happening; this often occurred after requesting money from employers. For example, a man from Ghana, explains:

> *I told him that I need only 3,000 Euros to send it for my kids, he told me ok no problem ... he told me to sit inside his car ... I trust this man so much that I never think any bad intention about this man, I know he cannot do any bad against me ... I don't know, we just entered like a bush ... Before I realise they just ... tied me down, took me, there is nothing I can do: only me, four, five people or six people ... Then they just throw me ... I can hear some sound of sea, the breeze of the sea.*
>
> (ROM2.08, man from Ghana, Rome)

Another man who had been imprisoned in Libya describes how he was subsequently forced to embark on a boat bound for Italy:

> *I was working there for one month, police arrived ... they caught a lot of people, I did fifteen days in prison once again. They sent me directly to the beach ... there is a big yard there, always police is going to send [us] there till one hundred or*

two hundred people … when they worked a lot, they push them to get into some boats that are over there – they sent there one hundred and twenty people.

(SIC1.40, man from Mali, Sicily).

Indeed, none of the people we spoke to in Malta claimed that the country was their intended destination, with many revealing that they had never heard of the island. This is encapsulated by a man from Ethiopia, who explains: '*To be honest, I didn't know anything about Malta. We just came here by chance and we didn't intend to come here – we never imagined coming to Malta*' (MAL1.04A, man from Ethiopia, Malta). Our counter-archive thus suggests that a choice of final destination is rare, and that plans often change along the way based on preconceived expectations and a generalised hope of something better. As a woman from Ethiopia explains: '*Your country is your country, but you expect something different. Sudan was a little bit better than my country. And then the situation was changed in Sudan; you try to go to another country when you find something better – you expect better*' (MAL1.15, woman from Ethiopia, Malta). Taken together, these testimonies shatter the reductionist image of hyper-agentic 'economic migrants' who 'choose' freely to leave their countries of origin and head directly for the EU in a linear and frictionless manner. Rather, journeys are often stimulated by fear of violence or even death and are frequently made as a last resort, with people on the move exposed to yet further forms of violence as they pursue an uncertain destination and future.

Anti-smuggling

The smugglers are not bad … they are helping people and they are more afraid about the people than they are afraid for themselves … If this is true about the fight against the smugglers, they can go there and bring people in Europe legally so that the smuggler doesn't have to work. Find a way for people to come legally so they don't have to pay the smugglers.

(KOS1.48, man from Syria, Kos)

I have heard about smugglers who are unjust. For example, someone I met in the camp told me that the smuggler put the gun to his head and forced him to get in the inflatable rubber boat even though there was water leaking in. Someone like

Rejecting deterrence

this they should definitely prosecute. But to prosecute them just for the job they do, no. I'm working, let's say for example that I am a smuggler and you want to travel. I didn't force you to travel with me. Do you see?
(ATH2.27, woman from Syria, Athens)

We have shown that the deterrent approach rests on two flawed assumptions: that people considering a migratory journey are aware of deterrent policies, and that such knowledge might actually impact on the decision-making process. Anti-smuggling, as a key dimension of a deterrent agenda, is also based on misplaced assumptions. Though by no means new in 2015,[5] anti-smuggling efforts intensified markedly from April 2015, when then European Commissioner Dimitris Avramopoulos announced in Malta: 'Europe is declaring war on smugglers' (European Commission, 2015f). Beyond the military-humanitarian developments at sea discussed above,[6] additional measures aimed at combatting smuggling were advanced, including the strengthening of cooperation between Europol and Frontex, a greater focus on anti-smuggling in existing Common Security and Defence Policy missions in Niger and Mali, and additional funding designated for this purpose as part of the EU Emergency Trust Fund for Africa. In May 2015, the Commission put forward a new EU Action Plan Against Migrant Smuggling (2015–2020). The 2015 *Agenda* thus acted as a catalyst for escalating the 'war against smugglers' by the EU to new levels.

We suggest that this declared 'war' is highly problematic for several reasons. First, it absolves the EU and its member states of responsibility for the suffering and deaths at their borders, simultaneously positioning them as 'modern-day abolitionists' aiming to 'save black lives' (Saucier and Woods, 2014: 69). Yet as Saucier and Woods (2014: 69) suggest, 'stepping up patrols of the Mediterranean in order to limit the loss of life does not recalibrate the station of blackness within the Western imaginary; on the contrary, it facilitates greater surveillance and control over black bodies'. Second, the so-called 'war on smugglers' is based on flawed assumptions regarding people's relations with smugglers on the one hand, and smugglers' relations with law enforcement on the

87

other. The testimonies in our counter-archive suggest that relationships between smugglers and smuggled are considerably more complex than indicated by simplistic policy narratives about saving helpless migrants from ruthless smugglers. Moreover, testimonies also suggest that smuggling and law enforcement are not straightforwardly opposed to one another as assumed by anti-smuggling measures: patterns of corruption and collusion exist between police forces and smugglers across different countries and migration routes. In addition, we found that anti-smuggling measures increase the reliance of people on the move on smuggling networks and heighten the risks en route, effectively exposing those who are seeking a place of peace and safety to perilous journeys and further harms.

Complicity, corruption and collusion

... the police themselves participate in smuggling people, but when they do this, they don't wear police uniform – they put on civilian clothes.

(MALI.15, woman from Ethiopia, Malta)

It's them [the policemen] who work as traffickers ... it's them the Mafiosi, the traffickers.

(ROM2.10, man from Palestine, Rome)

Since anti-smuggling focuses on strengthening enforcement in order to reduce smuggling, policing and smuggling activities are understood to be diametrically opposed to one another. This assumption is problematised by our counter-archive, highlighting patterns of cooperation, complicity and collusion between law enforcement and smugglers across both the central and eastern routes (see Andersson, 2014). For example, people we spoke with questioned the role of governments in the countries they had travelled through, suggesting the likelihood of cooperation between smugglers and border authorities. For example, one man from Syria asks: '*You're the central authority, you can't control your beaches? From which people are being smuggled? The smuggler takes $700 from each person, the government takes $200 and he keeps $500*' (ATH2.29, man from Syria, Athens). Similarly, a woman from Eritrea explains: '*I know*

Rejecting deterrence

very well that also the government in Egypt, in Syria, Libya, Sudan, they earn behind those traffickers, I am very aware of that' (ROM2.09, woman from Eritrea, Rome). This knowledge of corruption is echoed by a man from Iraq, who says: '*I think this is an agreement with the Turkish government to smuggle people … So dealing with, done with smugglers, on the open road on the street, and the police don't see them? No, they see it. But they don't interfere with them*' (BER2.10, man from Iraq, Berlin). People on the move here suggest that governments stand to gain in various ways from tacitly tolerating or even supporting unauthorised migration. Our counter-archive thus indicates that to address smuggling as a criminal activity universally condemned by state authorities is too simplistic, with testimonies highlighting likely entanglements of various government authorities in the smuggling industry.

Beyond reporting complicity with smugglers on a governmental level, people on the move also described concrete experiences of cooperation between police and border guards. In particular, people told us that smugglers would 'buy roads' for them, allowing them, in effect, to bypass border controls. Following the statement by a Kurdish man from Syria that '*they* [the smugglers] *cheat us, with what we call in Syria: we bought the road*' (BER2.02, man from Syria, Berlin), a translator in Berlin offered his own explanation:

> *The smugglers in Syria, they are saying "I buy the road," which means I bribe the army or the police to clear the road for me. So this is my road for, let's say, half an hour or one hour, and then there comes the next one. That's what we mean by buying a road. I pay money to have the road clear for one hour maybe.*
>
> (BER2.02, translator for a man from Syria, Berlin)

While the phrase 'buying the road' was used most often in relation to the Turkish–Syrian border, testimonies include accounts of bribery of the police by smugglers in Iran, Libya and at the Turkish–Greek sea border: '*The smuggler was Iranian and I believe that they had paid off the Iranian police. So with the Iranian guards we didn't really have any issues*' (ATH2.07, man from Afghanistan, Athens); '*They* [Turkish border guards] *sell the border for about 2 hours, $50,000, they have a deal between* *them. This is why you can be sure that nothing is going to happen'* (ATH2.13, man from Syria, Athens). These testimonies indicate that border police can be involved in cooperative behaviour with smugglers, undermining the assumption that strengthening policing will weaken the business of smugglers. For people on the move in precarious situations, enlisting smugglers who have connections to the police can make the difference between escaping unsustainable situations or being 'pushed back' or 'pulled back', as this man from Ghana explains: '[The smugglers] *say these* [members of the coastguard], *the duty of these peoples, they are not my duty, so these peoples, this week or the next week people is my duty, so the time that it his duty* [I] *can push you … Because when they push you, you can reach Italy. But when it's not his duty and they push you, they can catch you back'* (ROM2.07, man from Ghana, Rome).

Departing without ensuring the tacit support of the relevant border guards can thwart migratory projects or expose those travelling to racialised violence and abuse. Indeed, our testimonies indicate that encounters with border police who have not been paid to look the other way are often fraught with physical harm: '*Smugglers in Turkey are partners of the government. Because some people tried to buy their own boat and go on their own without using through the smuggler and they drowned them'* (BER2.26, man from Syria, Berlin). Along both the central and the eastern Mediterranean routes people on the move experienced violence from different authorities, including at border crossings. Testimonies included accounts of beatings, shootings or attempts to sink boats while crossing from Iran to Turkey, Syria to Turkey, Turkey to Greece, Sudan to Ethiopia, Eritrea to Sudan, Morocco to Spain, Greece to Macedonia, and inside Libya and Burkina Faso. Such incidents were not limited to authorities outside of Europe. People on the move also spoke of physical violence and dehumanisation experienced at the hands of the Greek coastguard, in Maltese detention centres, Italian hotspots and along the Balkan route. As one man from Afghanistan explains: '*The only police that he was really aggressive with us, it was a Macedonian police. That they, the only police that they beat us'* (BER2.19, man from Afghanistan, Berlin). In addition, a man from Syria says: '*while we were trying to get on the ship they* [the Greek Coastguard] *hit me … They slapped me twice. They hit me! This was the rescue'* (KOS1.26, man from Syria, Kos).

Beyond individual instances of bribery ensuring that border crossers could continue travelling while avoiding police violence, those passing through Libya spoke of a complete blurring of police and smugglers. Facing violence, abuse and extortion by smugglers, police, criminal groups, employers and people on the street, the people we spoke with struggled at times to tell the difference between law enforcement and smugglers. A woman from Ethiopia says: *'You know, when I was in Libya, I always wondered to know who the police officers are and who the ordinary civilians are. I left Libya before I grasped this. They always say "we are police officers"'* (MAL1.13, woman from Ethiopia, Malta). Experiencing situations of general lawlessness and extreme violence, people travelling through Libya also told us that police forces were directly involved in the smuggling of people there, as the quotes at the beginning of this section illustrate. The case of Libya is extreme in regard to this complete blurring of police and smugglers, with people being 'sold' between groups that were not clearly identifiable:

> Interviewer: *Is this both the police and the smugglers?*
> MAL1.31: *Yeah. We don't know. They wear soldier clothes, they have guns, even they shot in your head.*
> Interviewer: *Did it look like the smugglers and the police were working together?*
> MAL1.31: *Yeah! Exactly. Yeah. Even when we reach in Libya, the police take us to another place to Tripoli. It is like they have connection. They take money. They buy us. Like things. Maybe the police man he take two peoples and he take 200 or 300* [dinar] *or something.*
> (MAL1.31, man from Eritrea, Malta)

In a situation where law enforcement officials and smugglers seem to merge, and both are involved in the detention and smuggling of people on the move, the strengthening of law enforcement cannot be expected to decrease smuggling in a straightforward sense. In the light of these findings, a focus on strengthening police forces, regardless of their human rights record, is likely to be ineffective; not only will bribery and collusion persist, but there is also a risk that the racialised violence faced by people on the move during precarious journeys will be further exacerbated, as discussed below.

Complex smuggled–smuggler relations

If the smuggler is good he won't force people to leave. If he's not good, or mean, sometimes people are scared to get on the balam [inflatable rubber boat] *and he starts shooting in the air and screaming at them ... Our smuggler was half and half. He wasn't very bad but he wasn't very good. There are others that are worse.*

(ATH2.23, man from Syria, Athens)

They [the smugglers] *are not the same. Some of them they are very brutal, some they are good people.*

(ROM2.03, man from Chad, Rome)

Anti-smuggling efforts frame smuggling as an 'evil' that needs to be addressed. When migration policies aim at combatting 'ruthless smugglers', the emphasis is placed on 'saving' or 'protecting' migrants, as the 2015 *Agenda* stressed: 'Action to fight criminal networks of smugglers and traffickers is first and foremost a way to prevent the exploitation of migrants by criminal networks' (European Commission, 2015b: 8). In rationalising anti-smuggling in such terms, the Commission not only fails to address the issue that many of those to be 'saved' actively seek out smuggling networks to escape insecurity, as they have no alternative options to reach safety. It also presents an overly simplified understanding of smuggler–smuggled relationships as exploitative and violent. At times, smugglers are likened to modern-day slave traders (e.g. Frontex, 2014; see also Graham-Harrison, 2017), which Saucier and Woods (2014: 69) argue positions border guards and police forces involved in anti-smuggling measures as modern-day abolitionists. Testimonies from our counter-archive challenge this depiction of anti-smuggling as seeking to protect vulnerable migrants from cruel smugglers, with relationships between those who are smuggled and those who smuggle described as considerably more varied and complex (see also Perkowski and Squire, 2019). Nevertheless, this is not to say that stories of exploitation and

Rejecting deterrence

violence by smugglers are absent in our counter-archive. Indeed, many of those we spoke with shared horrific details of their encounters with smugglers, in particular in Libya:

> *The day we were supposed to take the boat ... we were kidnapped ... We endured five days of kidnapping: beatings, traumas, and even rape by old people ... They mistreated us every day. We had to pay to free ourselves. So we paid the ransom and after five days we were liberated. We were stripped off, forced to undress in front of the men, and then body-searched, even in the buttocks; we were searched everywhere, as they were looking for money ... I wake up at night and relive the trauma, I endured five days of kidnapping, five days of violence, each night a man would abuse me.*
>
> (ROM2.11, woman from Cameroon, Rome)

Accounts of extortion and violence along the central Mediterranean route were common, with many sub-Saharan Africans travelling through Libya being held against their will and forced to call relatives to send money at some point: '*Their language is money, if you pay you move, if you don't pay you die. They don't care*' (ROM2.14, man from Eritrea, Rome). As the quote from the woman from Cameroon above illustrates, women face the added risk of sexualised violence in a climate of generalised aggression.

Although stories of violence and abuse along the eastern Mediterranean route were not as pervasive as they were among those travelling through Libya, they nevertheless were an integral part of the journey for many who arrived in Europe along this route. Thus, some of those moving along the eastern Mediterranean route also experienced or witnessed gendered forms of violence at the hands of smugglers, though rape and abuse were not as ubiquitous as in Libya. A man in Kos explains:

> *What I saw during this route ... what I saw with my own eyes ... Even now that I am talking to you about it, it makes me cry.* [The smugglers] *put their hands into the underwear of the women to look for money, to take money, dollars, euros ... from men and women ... What happened in Iran ... that they did not give us food ... They stole our money, they took our money ... And the rapes ... They rape women ...*
>
> (KOS1.31, man from Afghanistan, Kos)

Reclaiming migration

In addition to accounts of sexualised violence, beatings and extortion, some individuals were forced at gunpoint to board boats, unable to turn back when they realised how risky the crossing would be. As a man from Syria describes: '*Actually it was one smuggler in the boat. And he had to point a gun at me, to get on the boat, because I was trying to get back. It was very, very crowded in the boat. I thought it was going to drown. But I was forced to get on boat. Either I get killed or … Yeah*' (BER2.29, man from Syria, Berlin).

At first sight, accounts of violence and abuse seem to confirm the understandings invoked by anti-smuggling measures, of smugglers as ruthless and exploitative. While this is one of the realities people on the move face, the quotes at the beginning of this section also indicate that there are vast differences between different smugglers and the ways they treat their 'customers'. As a trans woman from Somalia explains: '*some [smugglers] were more human and understanding and some were very inhuman looking at human beings like goods and services*' (MAL2.09, trans woman from Somalia, Malta). Whereas anti-smuggling measures focus almost exclusively on the brutality of smuggling networks, the people we spoke with had more varied experiences of smugglers. At times, they were acquaintances, friends or family members, or members of migrant communities: '*The smuggler we used, as I told you, was a relative, so there wasn't any difficulty*' (ATH2.32, male from Syria, Athens). Some told stories of being offered a place on a boat to Europe for free in order to escape a difficult situation; others told of smugglers freeing them from detention; while a third group described smugglers simply as providers of an urgently needed service. In sum, presenting smugglers as ruthless criminals fails to capture the complexity of relationships between people on the move and smugglers. Indeed, our migratory testimonies provide nuanced accounts of smuggling as both exploitative and liberating, and contest one-dimensional, vilifying depictions of smugglers. This is suggestive of the ambivalent role smugglers often play in the lived experiences of people on the move: on the one hand, facilitating movement in a situation where legal routes are scarce, while on the other hand enacting violence, extortion or theft.

Rejecting deterrence

Increasing the risks en route: a continuum of violence

Our counter-archive not only supports existing critiques that point to the ineffectiveness of deterrent measures such as anti-smuggling, but also offers grounded insights into the adverse consequences that these have on the lived experiences of people on the move. In the following passage, a Syrian man demonstrates the complexity of the decision-making process as it relates to diverse obstacles to mobility. Plans to return are put on hold as the context at 'home' deteriorates, basic survival demands that routes shift and expectations change about destinations at each point, while employment and income security becomes the priority. Friends and networks are an important resource, but efforts to travel in a legal manner can be hijacked by unforeseen circumstances, including visa restrictions, racism and violence. The extract illustrates precisely the dynamic nature of encountering and negotiating barriers to movement of various kinds, as plans and obstacles are negotiated, avoided, conceded and overcome to varying degrees:

> *The main problem for me was no job in Turkey ... so I started searching for another place to work ... I start calling my friends, in all the Arab countries, it was closed completely, because of Syrians, I tried my friends in Europe, the United States, very, very difficult, to travel ... For me the first opportunity was to get a job in Libya, because one of my friends was in Libya ... So I fled to Libya, from Syria to Libya, from Syria to Turkey by car, and I crossed legally, and I got a visa and a contract, because I got a job, in this moment there was no thinking of going to another place ... People there they act with foreigners as slaves ... even your car, there is a plate on your car that identifies your nationality, so you are a target, a moving target, everywhere, and we heard stories everyday about ... an Egyptian driver who was stolen and killed and beaten and they are laughing ... We are safe in the short term but in the future no one knows what's happening, anybody can kill you.*
>
> (MAL1.MG1, man from Syria, Malta)

This narrative reflects the experiences of several people we spoke with and their multiple efforts to negotiate state borders as well as a range of racialised social, economic and political bordering practices – with varying degrees of success.

Reclaiming migration

To suggest that this experience was common to all, however, provides only a partial understanding, since bordering practices represent different things to different people, and the historical and – ever-shifting – spatial and temporal dynamics cannot be ignored. Defying barriers to mobility erected along migratory routes, one man from Afghanistan explains: '*I didn't care about borders. All I cared about was to save my life, seriously*' (ATH2.39, man from Afghanistan, Athens). Others we spoke with describe their experience of the volatile nature of visa granting practices, highlighting how it became difficult to get visas as conditions of flight multiplied in the context of the Syrian war: '*it wasn't possible for Syrians to get visas because of the war*' (BER2.29, man from Syria, Berlin). Working off a map to explain his journey, a man from Ivory Coast in the following passage provides some important insights into how people on the move can negotiate state borders as colonial 'relics' (Hage, 2016: 44), by employing different tactics, relationships and vernacular knowledge:

> So, here is Ivory Coast, this one is Cote D'Ivoire. Here is Burkina Faso, we have border with Burkina … But there are barriers you know to control … So it is like something you are hiding already, we start hiding just to cross or to pass because you can't come from here, you have to go from here, from there, you know? There already is a system in place that is guiding these things … It is like a network yes.
>
> (MAL1.22, man from Ivory Coast, Malta)

Indeed, many narratives demonstrate the complex mobilisation of networks to negotiate and overcome borders as manifestations of a governmental regime of global apartheid, while also pointing to the range of different actors involved – including relatives, friends and formal contacts within and across national groups – in making travel arrangements. The following excerpt, for example, provides some illuminating insights as to how the journey can be experienced. This man, from Ivory Coast, describes how he started the journey alone. As the journey panned out, he became part of a network of people that he discovered were making the same journey. Despite the dangers encountered during the journey, the group appears

Rejecting deterrence

to provide a source of support and sense of personal security and safety:

> *In these places it was really incredible because when I left my country I realised that there is a lot of people like me who are trying the same like I am trying because before I didn't know that I will meet that amount of people with different languages and different culture, yeah but then you feel more comfortable, you have people you know even if it is something that is risky or since you are certain of group it is not like you taking a risk alone, and it is not only of you.*
>
> (MAL1.22, man from Ivory Coast, Malta)

Given the continued absence of legal routes and increased enforcement of deterrent policies, the people we spoke with had very little choice but to travel in unauthorised ways; deterrence thus generates rather than stymies the very forms of unauthorised migration that it claims to forestall.[7] Rather than giving up on their plans to move – which the logic of deterrence implies might be expected – many we spoke with considered taking even more dangerous and costly routes when faced with tightening border controls. Invariably, those who had heard about the risks of travelling before starting their journeys were not deterred by such measures, as illustrated by the testimony of the man from Ethiopia interviewed in Malta, with which we opened this chapter. As his story illustrates, pursuing a deterrent approach to migration management fails to consider the importance of the drivers of migration. Crucially, deterrence renders those on the move even more vulnerable to exploitation and violence en route: *'I never listened to them when they say, "people are dying", "the Sahara is hot" because I was already in fear, and then what am I going to fear?'* (MAL1.26, man from Ethiopia, Skype interview).[8] As we go on to argue, deterrence thus stimulates rather than prevents increased reliance on smuggling networks.

Increasing the reliance on smugglers

> *We know that the smuggler is committing a murder ... it's criminal* [what he is doing] *... and when he arranges an appointment, you know you are putting yourself in danger. But of course, we will get involved in the smuggling because there is no other way ...*
>
> (KOS1.12, man from Syria, Kos)

Reclaiming migration

Three decades of migration policies shaped by deterrence have rendered unauthorised travel to the EU increasingly difficult, as people on the move must navigate a complex web of controls, checkpoints and patrols that are no longer limited to official border crossings alone. Through externalisation and partnership agreements with third states to manage migration, barriers to movement proliferate not only around the EU, but along migratory routes far beyond EU borders. As migration drivers continue to compel people to migrate, the criminalisation of migration and the absence of legal routes have increased demand for smuggling services, as a man we spoke with in Rome indicates: '*Me as a Sudanese for example, it's not easy from Sudan to go legally to Europe or everywhere. Even if the money is there, corruptions, it's not easy. This if there are no smugglers that means* [I] *cannot arrive here …*' (ROM2.13, man from Sudan, Rome). Measures aimed at dismantling smuggling networks without providing legal alternatives to people on the move thus demonstrate a simplistic understanding of the wider context in which unauthorised migration takes place, and fail to engage with the predominance of migration drivers. The Syrian woman quoted at the beginning of this chapter highlights the cynicism of closing legal routes on the one hand, and declaring a 'war on smugglers' on the other. She notes that a thriving smuggling business is the direct result of an absence of alternative options to access protection in Europe, most importantly safe and legal routes: '*They closed the border but they opened the door to the smugglers*' (ATH2.15, woman from Syria, Athens). For another Syrian woman, smuggling constitutes the only viable path to safety. She explains: '*Why did people have to resort to smugglers? Isn't it because of the politicians themselves? If I could leave Lebanon legally, wouldn't I have done so?*' (ATH2.33, woman from Syria, Athens).

As well as increasing the reliance of people on the move on smugglers, deterrent anti-smuggling policies also render the smuggling process as a whole much riskier. The quality of boats over recent years have notoriously deteriorated, with inflatable rubber boats (the *balam*) rather than wooden boats common across both the central and eastern routes during 2015 and 2016. Increasing dangers do not deter, however,

Rejecting deterrence

as a man from Syria indicates: '*When you are in danger every day and you do not have another option you just say "I will do it, I will try it".* *When you are living in Syria, you are not afraid of these things. When you see your brothers dying in front of your own eyes, when your house is being bombed then you do not care. You are not afraid of the sea*' (KOS1.06, man from Syria, Kos). Beyond this, however, our testimonies also indicate that the dangers of engaging with smuggling networks worsen in a context marked by intensified anti-smuggling measures:

> *Yes, I was aware of* [the EU's fight against smuggling], *because all these smugglers were saying that if something happens, they would go to jail, they would lose their lives in jail for twenty or thirty years. Because I asked one of the smugglers why they were treating us like that, why they were hitting us, why we should not speak at all. And he said 'Do you know that if we get caught our lives will be in danger? We will get locked in jail for thirty years.'*
> (KOS1.09, man from Afghanistan, Kos)

What this man from Afghanistan highlights is the ways anti-smuggling measures perpetuate the harms people are exposed to when they have no choice *but* to engage with the smuggling industry. Feeding into a wider continuum of violence that implicates various governmental authorities and that makes the relations between smugglers and the smuggled increasingly tense, a deterrent anti-smuggling approach in this regard forms part of a postcolonial present in which the EU exposes people on the move to increasing harm.

Conclusion

This chapter has mobilised insights from testimonies of people on the move across the Mediterranean in 2015 and 2016 in order to challenge assumptions about the effectiveness of the deterrence paradigm underpinning the 2015 *Agenda*. Deterrence assumes that unauthorised movement *can* be stopped by changing the behaviour of those on the move, specifically through discouraging them from attempting the journey towards Europe in the first place. Yet, our counter-archive shows that this preventative approach is based on a range of flawed assumptions surrounding the knowledge and decision-making of people migrating, rendering it ineffective on its own terms. That is not to say, however, that the paradigm of deterrence does not *do* things in a performative sense. Indeed, the very failure of deterrence serves as a condition of possibility for the framing of migration as a crisis, which in turn facilitates an extension of EU migration policies in terms that perpetuate racialised hierarchies and long-standing colonial dynamics of control. Our testimonies thus reveal that, whereas deterrence does not work in the way it is claimed, its ineffectiveness enables the persistence and reinforcement of both securitising and humanitarianising narratives that variably position people on the move as potential 'criminals' or as subjects in need of 'saving'. In so doing, deterrence ultimately produces and perpetuates the precarity of people on the move as postcolonial subjects. The proliferation of border controls and the criminalisation of unauthorised migration far beyond the geographical outer edges of the EU render it more difficult for those seeking a place of peace and safety to escape from unsustainable or harmful situations. When attempting such journeys, people face a continuum of border-related violence, including by border guards, police and smugglers. Deterrence thus renders people on the move more vulnerable to exploitation and racialised forms of physical violence en route, including by increasing their dependency on smuggling networks and by leading to longer and riskier journeys. As such, it forms part of a long-standing history of colonial violence within (and beyond) the 'Black Mediterranean', potentially alienating and even breeding contempt among those who are compelled to flee – in particular those who come to Europe with an expectation of finding freedom and a rights-based approach (see Chapter 5).

Notes

1 This Skype interview was conducted from Malta with a man from Ethiopia who was located in Norway.
2 Our findings challenge the prevalent 'control bias' underpinning widespread notions in both policy and some academic literature that deterrent border

security is an effective paradigm for the management of migration (Scheel, 2019). At the same time, however, we also depart from scholarly accounts that seek to simply overturn the hierarchy and reprioritise the ontological primacy of migratory movement over control (Mezzadra and Neilson, 2013; Papadopoulos et al., 2008); this would be to pay insufficient attention to the detailed testimonies of border-based violence and human rights abuse that many told us they encountered in seeking entry to the EU. Rather, we argue that foregrounding the voices of those on the move calls into question simplistic dichotomies between control and autonomy and emphasises the need for a more nuanced account (McNevin, 2013; Squire, 2011).

3 Malta applied a form of mandatory detention of up to eighteen months if international protection was rejected. In December 2015 the Maltese government published a new migration strategy reducing mandatory detention to nine months.

4 Since the research was undertaken we are aware of evidence that there is increasing contact between those seeking to leave Libya and groups such as Alarm Phone (see Stierl, 2016).

5 Human smuggling was first defined and penal sanctions reinforced on the EU level with the 'Facilitators Package' in 2002 (Directive 2002/90/EC and Framework Decision 2002/946/JHA). The EU became a signatory of the UN Protocol against the Smuggling of Migrants by Land, Sea and Air in 2006 (Council Decisions 2006/616/EC and 2006/617/EC).

6 It was shortly after Avramopoulos's statement that the EU naval operation EUNAVFOR MED was launched 'to transform smuggling networks from "low risk, high return" operations for criminals into "high risk, low return" ones' (European Commission, 2015b: 8), followed by the NATO mission in the Aegean Sea as discussed above (Withnall, 2016). In June 2016, EUNAV-FOR MED was extended and two new tasks were added to its mandate: training the Libyan coastguard and navy and the enforcement of the UN arms embargo on the high seas (European Council, 2016b).

7 Restrictive rules on family reunification were particularly significant here, as the following quote illustrates: '*We registered with the UN in Turkey. The guy there told my dad your wife and daughter might not be covered by reunification. He told us we can have a lawyer in Germany but it would cost us a lot. "See what you decide." That's why my sister and I went into the balam* [inflatable rubber boat]' (ATH2.32, man from Syria, Athens) (see also Chapter 5).

8 This Skype interview was conducted from Malta with a man from Ethiopia who was located in Norway.

4

Contesting protection

I moved from Afghanistan's capital to Nimruz, from Nimruz to Pakistan, and from Pakistan to Iran … From Iran, we moved to Turkey. We were fifteen days in Iran before that. When we moved to Turkey we spent fifteen days more there … Then we decided with my friend that we should go to European country because the Turkish people were not preparing anything.

(ATH2.37, man from Afghanistan, Athens)

I don't have a problem to live in any European country as far as they provide me protection. I would go to any country that can provide me with protection in order to live … Any European country.

(KOS1.50, man from Pakistan, Kos)

Introduction

Chapter 3 examined the intensification of a preventative approach to migration as this was embedded in the 2015 *European Agenda on Migration*, and revealed deterrent measures to be ineffective due to flawed assumptions about the knowledge and decision-making of people on the move. The chapter also emphasised deterrence as playing a performative role in advancing a form of crisis politics that relies on securitising and humanitarian framings of people on the move as 'criminals' and 'victims', and in exposing those migrating to increased risks of violence. This chapter extends the analysis of the harmful effects of a preventative policy agenda, specifically by challenging assumptions concerning the qualification of people on the move across the Mediterranean in 2015 and 2016 for humanitarian protection (or as more usually described, asylum and protection). As outlined in Chapter 1, the 2015 *Agenda* employed the language of crisis in both its humanitarian and its securitising form. Much of the *Agenda*, and EU migration policy more broadly, rests on embedded assumptions about people who are moving to find safety or protection and about how EU member states should respond to such situations. For example, the 2015 *Agenda* spoke of 'the immediate imperative' being 'the duty to protect those in need' (European Commission, 2015b: 2). It also claimed that 'the EU [had] a duty ... in helping displaced persons in clear need of international protection' – a duty to 'save lives' (European Commission, 2015b: 4). Such references to the 'displaced', to 'beneficiaries' and to 'saving lives' reflect the EU's adoption of the humanitarian narrative of crisis, its rendering of people on the move as victims, and its approach towards humanitarianism, asylum and protection. This remains reliant on an EU legislative framework (the Common European Asylum System) that is acknowledged by the European Commission to have weaknesses and failures of interstate mutual trust (European Commission, 2015b: 12), yet that nevertheless remains central to its interpretation and implementation of protection.

This chapter addresses the EU's humanitarian narrative of crisis and its approach to asylum and protection by exploring the journey and arrival of people on the move as a continued search for peace and safety. It draws on our counter-archive of migratory testimonies, to contest the many limitations of European asylum and protection policies. The chapter explores the notion of journeying to safety and reveals how many of those we spoke with were forced into seemingly 'unending' journeys, often experiencing increasing and cumulative precarity. Our analysis challenges the very notion of a 'migration crisis' by revealing the longevity of many journeys outside EU territory, their fragmented nature and what we call varied and 'intersecting drivers and conditions of flight'. The significance of colonial histories that bind states, and which are ignored – even silenced – in the *Agenda* and in asylum and refugee law, is also brought to the fore through

Reclaiming migration

the testimonies, along with the racialised exclusion inherent in the EU protection regime. Furthermore, we show how the idea of a 'duty to protect' was not extended to providing assistance to people traversing these complicated land routes in 2015–16, instead remaining largely territorially bounded to those who succeeded in reaching Europe and who met stringent legal requirements. Indeed, our counter-archive reveals the violence of an asylum system that requires cross-border travel irrespective of the difficulties and risks that this imposes. It suggests that while many people were actively seeking asylum or protection on arrival in an EU state (as exemplified by the quotation from the Pakistani man we spoke with in Kos, cited above), others were simply seeking peace and safety. Few understood the significance of asylum or protection as framed by EU law and policy, with many having no alternative other than to apply for asylum, with the potential for further injustice and violence (see Chapter 5). By contesting the cumulative experiences of precarity faced both before and after arrival to the EU, people on the move advanced a multiplicity of claims and demands, importantly drawing attention to the limits of assumptions about the need for the EU to provide humanitarian succour.

Journeying to safety?

IST2.06: *My plan first when I left Iran, I left by myself. I did not let my parents know about it because I am sure they would not let me go. I didn't tell anybody that I had a plan to go to Europe ... There is nothing in Iran, they do not support Afghans and there are many millions of Afghans living there. It's a very hard situation, they are refugees, they have to pay the government once a year for living permit. I wanted to travel to see other places. That is the reason I decided to get out of Iran and come to Turkey. When I got to Turkey, I didn't have much money to come to Europe, so I didn't try it.*
Interviewer: *So you didn't have a specific place in mind in Europe?*
IST2.06: *No, only wanted to get to Europe. Of course I had in my mind that if I get to Greece, where I would try to go. The first step would be Italy, so after Italy I would probably go to Switzerland or Finland, I like some countries with nature, the silence.*
(IST2.06, Afghan man born in Iran, Istanbul)

Contesting protection

This exchange highlights the complexity inherent in many migratory journeys. Chapter 3 suggested that policy-making generally relies on a limited understanding of migratory decision-making, yet it also relies on a limited understanding of when the journey starts and ends, the nature of – or reason for – the journey, the differences between journeys, what can transpire during the journey, the impact of colonial legacies on the journey and the transformative effect of the journey on the individual. For a considerable time, EU laws, policies, reports and statements have focused on jeopardy, often describing journeys undertaken by migrants as 'perilous', 'dangerous', 'hazardous'.[1] Yet use of such a broad and arguably reductive term as 'journey' is ubiquitous in the migration field and in-depth study of the journeys of those on the move has, until recently, been relatively rare. Zetter and Benezer (2014: 301) note that '[t]he journey, as lived experience, metaphor, concept or construct has not been the object of systematic study', particularly in relation to refugee journeys. However, the journeys of 2015 and 2016 provided important opportunities for scholars to address this lacuna in the research literature. It also enabled such works to provide a counterweight to the lack of nuance and the simplification by the EU, by individual member states and by the UN or non-governmental organisations when describing the migration into Europe (see Crawley et al., 2017). One such example is a special issue of *Geopolitics*, in which Mainwaring and Brigden bring together a range of scholars from different disciplines to compare clandestine migration journeys in North America and Europe, with many utilising ethnographic data. In the introduction, they seek to conceptualise 'the journey' broadly 'as an experience with indeterminate beginnings and ends', which 'encompasses imagined journeys before migration, journeys from countries of origin through countries of transit to destination, as well as deportation journeys' (Mainwaring and Brigden, 2016: 244). They argue that it 'is not simply a space between arrival and departure, a temporary moment of mobility between more "normal" static existences, but a social process that shapes migrants and societies alike' (Mainwaring and Brigden, 2016: 247). For them, the analysis of the (clandestine) journey affords greater appreciation of the linkages between the lived experience and the politics of migration (Mainwaring and Brigden, 2016: 245).

This important emphasis on the migratory journey has coincided with increasing recognition of the fragmented nature of migration. As Collyer wrote in 2010, '[l]engthy and dangerous overland journeys are now a significant component of global migration systems' and '[t]he development of fragmented migration and the resulting situation of stranded migrants calls for greater attention to the significance of the journey in academic and policy work on migration' (Collyer, 2010: 290, 291). Zetter and Benezer, too, have pointed to the illusion of fixity in migration, which is increasingly acknowledged by 'the significant and influential post-modernist mobilities paradigm' (Zetter and Benezer, 2014: 298), while Mainwaring and Brigden (2016: 247) agree that the single journey is rarely linear or premeditated. This chapter supports Collyer's description of fragmented migration as 'broken into a number of separate stages, involving varied motivations, legal statuses and living and employment conditions' (Collyer, 2010: 275). It supplements the call for greater analysis of the journey to safety and the relatively recent recognition of the importance of providing a conduit for the perspectives of people on the move (for example, Schwarz, 2018; Mainwaring and Brigden, 2016; Triulzi and McKenzie, 2013, Schapendonk, 2012; Khosravi, 2011; Collyer, 2010, 2007). Specifically, we focus on the narratives of people on the move – such as the Afghan man we spoke with in Istanbul, cited above (IST2.06) – as the source of critical insights on how the journey is experienced, with the aim of fostering appreciation of the claims and demands that such experiences give rise to. In so doing, we emphasise the importance of migratory testimonies in lifting the silence surrounding the ongoing legacies of colonialism and racialised measures of migration control. Building on existing analyses of fragmentation, the chapter points to what we call the diverse and cross-cutting 'drivers and conditions of flight'. These, we argue, lead to cumulative experiences of precarity and reflect the 'fluidity' of

Contesting protection

many journeys – that is, a lack of pre-planning and an ongoing negotiation of the migratory experience. It is to these lived experiences that we will now turn.

Fluid and fragmented journeys

In the period of intense migration to Europe in 2015 and 2016 that was characterised by rising numbers of deaths at sea, there was increasing focus on the two routes taken by people to the EU: those arriving from the east either by land or sea; and those coming from Africa via the central Mediterranean (see Introduction). Many of the images in circulation at the time were striking – pictures of small vessels filled to capacity with men, women and children; long lines of people slowly winding their way through fields, over fences and alongside roads; maps of dotted lines ostensibly revealing the routes travelled. Some images were graphic and distressing, exposing immense suffering, ill-treatment and death. While such reporting can provoke feelings of pathos and compassion or fear and hostility from its European (and global) audience (Chouliaraki and Zaborowski, 2017), it fails to provide a comprehensive or nuanced perspective on the many journeys of those involved or on the various individual and personal experiences of flight. Rather, with a focus on the movement of people across EU states and the Mediterranean Sea, the imagery was largely bounded, both temporally to 2015–16 and geographically within the EU territorial space, thereby feeding the EU's narrative of crisis in both its securitised and humanitarian forms (see Chapter 1).

In focusing attention on the personal biographical contexts of those migrating, we draw attention to the many limitations of the preventative policy agenda along with the discursive and visual imaginations on which this relies. The people we spoke with are diverse, and their journeys varied depending on whether they were travelling across the eastern or central Mediterranean route. People of different nationalities and backgrounds often had different objectives, faced different challenges, travelled by different routes and were subject to different migration policies. On the eastern route, journeys lasted anywhere between two days and twelve years, with the majority taking less than six months; on the central route from Libya to Sicily or Malta, however, journeys took between three months and twenty-six years, with many lasting more than one year (see Squire et al., 2017: 58). Some had left their own countries many years previously, and had lived for considerable periods in countries such as Libya, Sudan, Dubai, Lebanon, Jordan or Turkey before being driven to embark on the next stage of their migratory journey. Furthermore, those who had been in the EU for a considerable period – for example in Malta – had different experiences; some saw themselves as relatively settled, while others still perceived their journey as incomplete and hoped to move on to another EU state.

Many Syrians travelling from Turkey to Kos and onward to mainland Europe were moving relatively quickly when we spoke to them in 2015, having spent limited time in Turkey or Greece. For most, their main objective was to move on before borders closed. A young man from Idlib in Syria is typical in this regard. He crossed from Syria into Turkey, remained ten days in Turkey, mainly on the streets in Bodrum, before reaching Kos by boat, where, at the time of the interview, he had been waiting for seven days for permission to take the ferry to Athens (KOS1.01, man from Syria, Kos). At this stage his journey had been fairly direct, with only minor interruption, and he expected this to continue to be the case: '*even if there is* [detention in other European countries], *it will only be for some hours, like twenty-four hours*'. Equally, however, we spoke to Syrians whose journeys were much more fragmented and had lasted much longer. For example, a Syrian woman and her husband described a complicated situation of movement between – and through – countries, with various periods of residence. They first left Syria for Lebanon, where they remained for six months, but felt forced back to Syria due to extreme conditions in Lebanon. She explains:

> *We stayed there* [Lebanon], *the owner of the work took our money, and the owner of the house ... changed the keys in the middle of the month and we stayed*

Contesting protection

in the streets for maybe 20 days…we were hungry, we were really hungry … we were really cold … So, we were really cold, hungry and our back was really hurting because we could not lie down to sleep. It was really shit. It was really shit that time. After that, we went back to Syria, we tried to work and there was nothing in Syria. We worked as bartenders.

(KOS1.23A/KOS1.23B, woman and man from Syria, Kos)

Due to rising costs in Syria, this couple tried to re-enter Lebanon, eventually succeeding. After staying a further year in Lebanon, they decided to leave again: '*We cannot do anything … my life had stopped literally … waiting, just waiting … we do not rent a house, we rent a room in a shared apartment and the room was at least like $500 or $600 and my salary was $500.*' Taking a flight from Beirut to Turkey, they travelled to Izmir, Bodrum and finally, by an inflatable rubber boat [*balam*], to Kos. The precarity faced by this couple in Lebanon and the lack of opportunity was a major contributing factor in prompting them to join the Syrian migration to the EU. The drivers of their migration were therefore complex, including flight from war as well as from poverty, and a loss of both dignity and hope.

Kos provides an interesting site of study in this regard; not only did it reveal different journey routes and journey times for the same nationality – as with the Syrians described above – but people also voiced their concerns that non-Syrians were being held on the island for much longer periods, possibly indefinitely. For example, a man from Iran had been stuck in Kos for more than two months; his documentation permitting him to remain in Greece for thirty days had expired and he was hoping that his sister, based in the UK, would somehow arrange a flight from Kos to the UK (KOS1.39, man from Iran, Kos). While most in Kos who were waiting for their paperwork from the police considered that this interruption to their journey was a temporary delay (including Afghans, Pakistanis, Bangladeshis, Iranians and Nigerians), those we spoke with in other sites felt a sense of abandonment, 'strandedness' or 'stuckedness' in the sense of an experience of existential immobility (Hage, 2015). For example, many in Malta had been there for several years and, without refugee status

109

or documentation, faced extremely difficult conditions: '*Five years in Malta … till now my life is bad. Till now. OK I don't have documents, ok … I don't have nothing*' (MAL1.29B, woman from Ethiopia, Malta). Moreover, the situation for many Syrians in Turkey changed following the EU–Turkey Statement of March 2016.[2] Those interviewed in Istanbul in the summer of 2016, for example, were frustrated – either because they felt that their plans for onward travel had been interrupted or they were resigned to remaining in Turkey for the foreseeable future, on account of the Statement.

> IST2.23: *I swear, for me, the future has stopped. It has stopped definitively. I just want to secure the life of my children and we are waiting for the decisions. Honestly, we are waiting.*
> Interviewer: *You are waiting.*
> IST2.23: *We are waiting for the decisions that they will arrange for us. We don't know. Even now we are living in suspense. A decision might destroy us. A decision might return us to Syria. A decision might enslave us.*
> (IST2.23, Kurdish man from Syria, Istanbul)

The central route across the Mediterranean was more clearly characterised by fluid decision-making and fragmented journeys. Unlike the Syrians, Afghans and Iraqis crossing the Aegean in 2015, who were often certain about their country of destination by the time they reached Kos, many of those arriving from sub-Saharan Africa who we spoke with in Malta, Sicily and Rome did not plan to reach a specific European destination in advance of their departure from their home. Indeed, some had never intended to travel to the EU (see Chapter 3). A man from Gambia provides a very succinct description of the way decision-making en route alters in the face of conditions on the ground and increasing precarity:

> When I arrived in Libya, I thought I would have found life easier there, that I could work to make some money. I start helping people back home, mothers and brothers back home. As soon as I arrived in Libya, I found that that place was not so peaceful … as soon as we reach the country … wow … what we thought [and] what we found there is going different. So, to come back and cross the Sahara desert, to come back … you could still lose your life. Now, the only thing is at least to work in Libya, to accumulate some money and finance your journey

Contesting protection

to the Mediterranean, to cross ... still, you could still lose your life. This is vice-versa: going back to the Sahara? You could still lose. Coming to Italy? You could still lose your life.

(SIC1.01, man from Gambia, Sicily)

Similarly, a young Eritrean interviewed in Rome in 2016 explained how he initially went to Sudan to work, with the intention of returning to Eritrea, but that life in Sudan proved very expensive and his wages as a mechanic were insufficient. His rationale for making the decision to migrate is presented in straightforward terms: '*I want to change my life*' (ROM2.14, man from Eritrea, Rome).

The narration of expectations of the journey was an extremely important part of the testimonies of the people on the move that we spoke with in 2015 and 2016, challenging widespread assumptions about motivations for seeking to enter the EU (see Chapter 5). As we saw in Chapter 3, one of the stated aims of the EU's preventative agenda and the anti-smuggling policies was 'to prevent hazardous journeys' (European Commission, 2015b, 5). Yet, it is worth noting that this has been a long-standing objective, and was not wholly new in the EU's response to increasing deaths and arrivals during 2015 and 2016 (Gammeltoft-Hansen, 2011a, 2014). Our conversations with people on the move show the limitations of such policies: while many were aware of potential dangers they might encounter, they were not familiar with the many EU and member state deterrent polices (see Chapter 3). Two men – an Afghan seeking to reach Europe along the eastern route and an Oromo travelling along the central route – describe the dilemma they faced in determining whether to undertake '*risky*' and '*very, very bad*' journeys:

> Interviewer: *When you were leaving Iran in 2012, what kind of information did you have about the journey to Europe? What did you know about the journey?*
>
> IST2.06: *I knew about the journey. It was very risky, there were people who got arrested and deported back to Afghanistan. And I knew that Iranian border control was very strict and if they see anything they try to fire. So I knew about that, but I didn't want to tell my mom and dad about that.*
>
> (IST2.06, man from Afghanistan, Istanbul)

Reclaiming migration

But what I wanted to tell is what I was hearing when I was in Sudan, about Libya, about the Sahara, that it was very, very bad. And when I was in Libya what I was hearing about the sea that it was very, very bad.
(MAL1.26, Oromo man from Ethiopia, Norway via Skype)[3]

These narratives of journeys – interrupted and uninterrupted, planned and unplanned, with and without knowledge – counter wider political and public debates surrounding migration across the Mediterranean during 2015 and 2016, which often presumed that the majority of people hoped to reach Europe as an ideal destination or a place where humanitarianism and protection were promised (see Chapter 5). The suffering over months and years in long and arduous journeys from sub-Saharan countries, such as Eritrea, Ethiopia, Gambia, Ivory Coast, Mali, Nigeria, Senegal, Somalia and Sudan, cumulates over time as people experience fragmented journeys based on fluid decision-making processes. Alongside such fluidity and fragmentation, personal narratives of migration disclose considerable complexity in the drivers and conditions of flight, to which we will now turn.

Intersecting drivers and conditions of flight

The claim that people migrate either because of war or human rights abuses – often described as 'genuine' reasons or 'push factors' – or for economic reasons – frequently seen as unacceptable or even bogus 'pull factors' – is not borne out by our counter-archive of testimonies from those making complex journeys across the Mediterranean in 2015 and 2016 (see also Crawley et al., 2017). Indeed, the testimonies challenge the refugee/migrant and forced/voluntary dichotomies that continue to dominate EU and state policies and politics (Sigona, 2018). The issues that prompted many of our research participants to move were multifaceted and cross-cutting, and often changed along the journey depending on circumstances faced by the individual concerned. We call these *intersecting drivers of flight* (Squire et al., 2017: 62–63). Intersecting drivers of flight refer to the many ways in which people experience danger or harm from which they need to escape. This can occur prior to the act of migration, as well as throughout the migratory journey. For those we spoke with, such drivers included: war and conflict, torture, kidnapping, extreme discrimination and exploitation, violence by authorities or by local populations, threats posed by terrorist or cult groups, being targeted by governments for conscription or for punishment, societal ostracism, family problems, the absence of employment, limited opportunities for integration, work or access to education, language difficulties and governmental policies of exclusion of non-nationals (Squire et al., 2017: 62). For some, particularly those travelling on the central Mediterranean route, colonial legacies played a key role in driving migration, whether due to past colonial ties or as a rejection of present-day European intervention in many African countries. As we shall see in Chapter 6, at times the colonial ties are clearly articulated in the testimonies; at other times the silenced legacy of colonialism is subtly revealed through the unfolding narrative.

Alongside the term intersecting drivers of flight, we also refer to *intersecting conditions of flight* that can affect an individual during the migratory journey, and which can also compound precarity for certain groups of people on the move (Squire et al., 2017: 63). Our counter-archive reveals how such conditions relate to social categories such as religion, nationality, sexual orientation, gender, age, illness or disability, educational background, linguistic ability and financial situation, and lead both to societal or cultural discrimination as well as institutionalised exclusion and racialised violence. These forms of violence and discrimination can prompt or inhibit ongoing movement, thereby fundamentally influencing the journey. Yet, rather than considering these drivers and conditions of flight or movement independently from one another, our counter-archive highlights a situation in which there are often connections between different drivers and conditions, which accumulate over time. Thus, it was not unusual, for example, for people to describe how an earlier driver of flight was compounded by a new set of conditions that either prompted further onward travel, or influenced the migratory decision-making process. This is evident in the testimony of a woman from Ivory Coast, who explains how a flight from persecution in her home country became a struggle for survival in the first country of potential asylum, Togo:

> *There was a political party in Ivory Coast called Laurent Gbagbo's FPI who actually is in prison. Well, my husband was part of the youth of the FPI and that's why he was threatened a lot until 2010, 2011 when we had elections … At the evening, when we came home, we found a letter under the door: 'If you don't stop, we will behead you', letters like this or they wrote us messages on the phone … One day when he left, he came back, he found the door open. They destroyed the door, they took everything, everything stolen from the house, the TV, the fridge, there was nothing left … he came looking for me and we left for Togo … But in the situation we have been in Togo, we didn't have any of that. Nothing. We only had a bit of money to eat. Often we eat one time a day, often we didn't eat. It wasn't easy at all in Togo, it wasn't easy.*
>
> (SIC1.34, woman from Ivory Coast, Sicily)

In this case, persecution in Ivory Coast as a driver of flight was compounded by a struggle to eat in Togo, which forced the woman and her family members to undertake additional and increasingly dangerous journeys, culminating in their arrival to Sicily.

In contrast to such basic challenges of survival, an unaccompanied minor from Gambia, who we also spoke with in Sicily in 2015, gives a harrowing account of the violence he faced in Africa in the statement below. He reports how he left Gambia because he '*was chased by somebody*' and '*decided to run away*'. Heading to Libya, and travelling with his brother, he passed through Senegal, Mali, Burkina Faso and Niger, before eventually reaching Libya. Having described how his brother died in an accident between Niger and Libya, he explains that, alone, he managed to survive racialised violence, including kidnap, beatings and ill-treatment in Libya:

> *First, they kidnapped me three months in Sabha, in a place called Sabha. My first arrival in Libya. Yeah because it is just like a business. When you come, when you arrive there and the driver who brought you there will show you to some people … so those people give him money so after then you go to those people. When you go there, they will kidnap you and call your people and ask for money. That is what they were doing but luckily, I don't have anybody to call back to give me money because I don't have anybody at my back. After they kept me there, maltreating me, especially food problem because we were facing real difficulties. Even there were giving us food once in a day and every time before they give you food they*

must beat you. And they beat you … after then they give you food to eat and it is just a small food. That is how we spend our lives those three months.

(SIC1.23, unaccompanied male minor from Gambia, Sicily)

The young man concludes ruefully that he had never wanted to leave home but felt compelled to do so:

I never imagine even to move from my country, due to certain things it was difficult on my side and I was so afraid so I decided to move … because there is no place like home. No place can satisfy me like my home. It is because I don't have peace in my home that I decided to run. If I was having peace in my country I will not go out. I will go with my education because that is what I have and my vocation too.

(SIC1.23, unaccompanied male minor from Gambia, Sicily)

Only in Libya did the idea of travelling to Italy arise, on the advice of others, because '*it is better* [to] *move to Italy because here too is dangerous!*' (SIC1.23). As an unaccompanied minor, the age of this young man, as well as his lowered status as a sub-Saharan African in Libya, elevated his vulnerability to harm and abuse. It was thus, on finding that his existence had become increasingly precarious on account of both original drivers and ongoing conditions of flight, that he decided to continue his journey to Europe.

Such descriptions of cumulative precarity during fluid and frag-mented journeys are copious in our counter-archive, particularly on the routes from sub-Saharan Africa via Libya, where we repeatedly heard accounts of extreme violence, overt racism and exploitation. The following testimony closely mirrors that provided by the young man from Gambia above, and is indicative of the systemic and pervasive brutality of the smuggling and kidnapping industry as well as of endemic racism in Libya:

The treatment is very bad. Even when they call you they say 'oi negro'. I cannot explain it. I'm walking in the street, 'oi negro', sit down they say. Sometimes 'stop oi negro, sit down', and then you move further and then they go after you … [they] take whatever you have, mobile, money. It's normal, they are armed. Normal they can take you from the road, they close you in a room and they say phone your family, ask for money. They open the microphone and they beat you. They pour water and they beat you and open the microphone to make your parents hear. They beat you to make your family hear you suffer.

(ROM2.14, man from Eritrea, Rome)

Reclaiming migration

Distressingly, there has been no end to the racialised violence and misery over recent years – as graphically illustrated by an Associated Press report, 'Migrants stranded in Libya endure sewage, maggots, disease' (Michael, 2019). In the face of growing collaboration between the EU and Libyan authorities, particularly surrounding search and rescue operations at sea, many people have been thwarted in their attempts to escape such circumstances, thus facing longer journeys and increased precarity over time.

Not all the people we spoke with refer to overt violence as the sole motivating factor for their escape or onward movement. An Eritrean woman in Rome, for example, relays a complicated story of rape by an Eritrean soldier which led to a child that she handed over to the father, her marriage to an Eritrean resulting in two children, cross-border movement from Eritrea to Sudan as a refugee, divorce due to infidelity of the husband and a second marriage in Sudan resulting in three further children. As a Christian whose husband's family are Muslim, she speaks of religious discrimination as driving her decision to move to Europe with her three children by her Sudanese husband:

> Interviewer: … *And then when did you decide to leave Sudan?*
> ROM2.09: *Three years ago. We wanted to leave because in Sudan we had no right, but at least in Europe we get food, clothing, a shelter where we can sleep, whereas there we had no right. You get in and you decide what to do, you live on your own, and for this reason I thought 'what am I waiting for?' There is racism in Sudan, between Muslims and Christians. If we sell, trade, they take part of our earnings. The soldiers or the policemen come and they take half of what I earned, and they say: 'that is for us'. But they don't behave like this with everyone, only with Christians from Eritrea. If you try to say no, they will either kill or jail you. So we decided to leave.*
> (ROM2.09, woman from Eritrea, Rome)

She concludes by pointing out that current legal routes to the EU are ineffective due to corruption and abuse of process and power in both Europe and Africa, thereby helping to create the precarious conditions that force people to choose unauthorised means of travel and access to EU countries:

Contesting protection

I wanted to tell you something else. The UN helps Sudan for Eritrean refugees, but nothing gets to us. Everything goes to Sudan, we get nothing. We are on the streets; we are treated poorly. Even if I manage to get a contract for a job from another European country, sent by my relatives who are in Europe to get the visa from Sudan, the Sudanese sell it to another Sudanese or Eritrean at a different price; they falsify everything and take the money and give me nothing. Because they tried to pursue this legitimate route, to send a job contract, get a visa to come to work. For this reason, people throw themselves in the sea to come here. There, in the European embassies, they use operators, or employees of the country, it's them who destroy and falsify everything.

(ROM2.09, woman from Eritrea, Rome)

Intersecting drivers and conditions of flight come together here in cumulative terms, with sexualised violence, the brutality of corrupt authorities, institutional racism and religious discrimination combining with EU deterrent policies in terms that produce and perpetuate the precarity of this woman from Eritrea and her three children.

The way precarity can arise, increase and become endemic, due to the actions of states and EU policies, is clearly apparent in many of the conversations we had in Istanbul in 2016. Most of those we spoke with there were Syrian, but we also met Afghans and Iraqis. They had all fled to Turkey, either with the aim of remaining there or further migrating to the EU. As discussed above, following the EU–Turkey Statement, people's ability to cross the eastern Mediterranean was severely limited, resulting in a sense of 'stuckedness' and serious dissatisfaction with life in Turkey. It was not unusual to find gender, age and financial constraints combining to influence decision-making as well as giving rise to increasing precarity. For example, a Kurdish woman from Syria with a husband and eight children explains how her family had arrived in Turkey in 2013 with the hope of going to Europe, but had not managed to raise sufficient funds to pay smugglers despite all of the children bar the youngest having to work to make ends meet rather than attend school (one daughter was already united with her husband in Germany at the time). She says:

I have the aspiration to go to Europe. I have two children who were university students. One of them registered for the university and we left. And one was in the last year of university. And I have my son fifteen years old, he didn't study.

Reclaiming migration

He was in the seventh grade and we left. And I have this young one too who we recently put in a Turkish school. I don't have the financial means. My husband has his years [is not young] *and my children are not accustomed to work. They were students. These conditions are hard for them. Turkey is harsh. I hope to go to Europe but I'm not able to.*

(IST2.16, Kurdish woman from Syria, Istanbul)

She nevertheless goes on to acknowledge that the conditions are also not faultless in Europe, as reported by her daughter in Germany: '*But she's also not happy. She's not finding a house, she's living in disgusting conditions. They are students, they graduated from universities, they are accustomed to cleanliness and order*'. Indeed, the quest for a '*normal life*' – an expression used by many – is often not realised in the countries to which people flee.

A second Syrian Kurdish family offers further insights into the intersecting conditions that affect decision-making and perpetuate precarity – in this case, gender, age, earning capacity and education. The family comprises two frail parents, two sons (one married with four children) and two daughters. The youngest son, daughter and grandson have already travelled to Germany. The conversation takes place with the remaining daughter and elder son (sister and brother). It becomes clear that the whole family wanted to go to Europe but did not have the financial means to do so: '*There was no money. If we had the money, we would have left with them*' (IST2.18S, woman and man from Syria, Istanbul). Conditions are difficult: the family all live together in one apartment; the brother earns a low wage and the children are receiving no education: '*Rent is 400 lira. Water and electricity about 250. It reaches 800. And that doesn't include food, clothes … The children don't go to school. They have no future.*' The sister is taking care of their parents, whose health is poor: '*My mother was sick. She had heart failure in addition to diabetes, high blood pressure, inflammation. Her legs were hurting her, she couldn't walk.*' The brother hopes for a way out, with recourse to the smugglers and borrowing money from friends: '*We will take care of ourselves and we will leave. This is the goal. Living here without schools, we can't bear it.*' The sister, by contrast, must remain to look after her parents,

Contesting protection

but considers the idea of 'asylum' in Turkey as anathema because of the 'humiliation' she feels due to the family's treatment:

> IST2.18S: *You mean to get asylum in Turkey? No! Never. Never in my life would I take refuge here.*
> Interviewer: *Why not?*
> IST2.18S: *I experienced humiliation here. If you experience humiliation, you won't return someplace. Wherever the place may be. Whatever it gives you of life. If you experience humiliation, especially financial humiliation, you can't return. They don't say 'you are coming from war, you fled your house in your clothes.' They say 'you are Syrian'.*
> (IST2.18S, woman and man from Syria, Istanbul)

One of the major grievances that people raised about the situation in Turkey related to working conditions and hours. The brother we spoke with above identified this as a key condition impacting his decision to find an opportunity to escape (IST2.18B). Similarly, a young Syrian man, who had succeeded in reaching Athens after living for over four years in Turkey, describes how his family had '*worked all the time*' in Turkey where '*the situation was bad*' (ATH2.32, man from Syria, Istanbul). The work undertaken by family members varied – '*house cleaning, cleaning hotels. I worked in a laundromat. My mother worked packaging, cleaning, these sorts of things.*' The family '*worked a lot … from 8.30a.m. to 7.00 at night*' and were required to work night shifts: '*If you didn't work the night shift, they'd fire you.*' Pay, however, '*was very little*'. In his view, '*Syrians, wherever you went, were getting exploited*' (ATH2.32).

Such concerns were widespread in the testimonies from our counter-archive, although, as we will see in the next section, the solution was not necessarily found in the EU. Language, too, proved an unassailable challenge for some and a significant factor in decision-making. Our discussion with a Syrian man in Berlin exemplifies this well. He explains how he had stayed in Turkey for seven months, with the intention of remaining there, but found learning Turkish too difficult. This, together with a feeling of failing care by the Turkish authorities, prompted onward movement to the EU:

> *I tried to learn the language, but I couldn't. I don't know why. But I couldn't learn the language. I couldn't communicate with people, and … and Turks are*

Reclaiming migration

very poor English speakers. So I had to use sign language. It was very, very difficult for me. And in Turkey, you don't ... you don't get support from the government. You need to spend all your money on rental and food, and ... and even water. You have to buy your own water. No, no support. Not even a dime. I didn't get any support.

(BER2.29, man from Syria, Berlin)

Intersecting drivers and conditions of flight play a central role in the decision-making processes of many people who decide to leave their country of birth or permanent residence and undertake a journey into the unknown. Even if a single factor prompts their initial departure, circumstances during the migratory journey often create additional reasons for continued movement. Few of those we spoke with had a single motivating factor and the majority provided accounts that revealed that once travel had commenced, further justification for migration often emerged, compounding the complexity of 'the journey' to safety. Moreover, as the next section will show, those who had expectations that 'the arrival' would provide a resolution to their challenges were frequently disappointed.

Reaching safety?

Asylum for me would make me feel safe because I know that you put yourself under international protection. This country is responsible for you in general, from a humanitarian perspective, on your health, your life, that you are not threatened by danger, that you do not sleep in the street, that you do not sleep hungry. These things are the most important for humans. Safety and being in a protective place.

(IST2.03, woman from Syria, Istanbul)

The idea that 'the arrival' forms a fixed end point of the migratory 'journey' is very much open to question, and this is clearly evident in testimonies from our counter-archive. Many people spoke of traumatic experiences during their journey to – and within – the EU, trauma that did not necessarily end on arrival to a given member state. Indeed, the hardships that people confronted across the EU often acted as new conditions driving onward movement. Some people adopted the pervasive 'crisis' terminology to describe the financial austerity

Contesting protection

confronting Greece and Italy as a reason for further migration. For example, a woman from Morocco explains that she left Greece without authorisation '*because of the economic crisis … there was no work*', but adds that '*when I arrived in Italy, I saw the crisis also here and I wanted to join my family in France, but now I'm Christian, all in my family are Muslims and they don't want to see me … I left in Denmark, I stayed there five months and after I came back in Italy*' (SIC1.44, woman from Morocco, Sicily).

In our exchanges with people who had reached Germany, Greece, Italy or Malta, it was apparent that a large number were intent on claiming asylum. Indeed, many described circumstances that prompted decisions to move which would meet the legal requirements for asylum and protection as provided under international and European Law – the UN 1951 Convention relating to the status of refugees/1967 Protocol ('Refugee Convention').[4] However, EU states, amongst many others, have long regarded the asylum system as a means by which people intentionally seek to circumvent immigration law – widely referred to as 'the abuse of the asylum system' (e.g. see Squire, 2009; Stevens, 2004). Indeed, the 2015 *Agenda* itself is illuminating on this point. It states openly that '[s]trengthening the Common European Asylum System also means a more effective approach to abuses'. 'Too many requests are unfounded', it claims, 'hampering the capacity of Member States to provide swift protection to those in need' (European Commission, 2015b: 12; see also Chapter 5). The implication here is that the 55 per cent of rejected asylum applicants have no protection needs and that the system is faultless. However, such an assessment is problematic because the 'unfoundedness' of a claim is often based on a very narrow interpretation of refugee law, which ignores the challenges and protection issues frequently experienced en route. In other words, the focus of refugee law on harms experienced in the 'country of nationality' or of 'habitual residence', as per Article 1A(2) of the Refugee Convention, means that neither the fragmented nature of many journeys, nor the intersecting drivers and conditions of flight outlined in the last section, play a significant part in formal refugee/ beneficiaries of international protection determination decisions or in the identification of individual protection needs. Consequently, this enables EU member states to limit substantially their acclaimed 'duty to protect'.

It is also important to recall that the 1951 Refugee Convention was originally drafted to address the post-Second World War refugee situation – that is, it was concerned with European refugees already in European states (Goodwin-Gill and McAdam, 2007: 36). While states signatory to the Convention could elect to extend its remit to include events 'in Europe or elsewhere' (Art 1B), and thereby people from outside Europe, this was interpreted by the UK, for example, to exclude colonial subjects, who comprised a significant part of the global population (Mayblin, 2017: 146). Their inclusion was hard won. Indeed, as Mayblin argues forcefully, 'the fact that non-Europeans can apply for asylum is a result of successful struggles for decolonisation, and then the subsequent struggle of non-Europeans to be included within the remit of the Refugee Convention' (Mayblin, 2017: 178). While some might consider the present day to have overcome these historical problems of international refugee law, our counter-archive confirms that the limitation of asylum and protection along long-standing colonial lines continues to be relevant, just as the silence surrounding the colonial connections along the migratory routes remains deafening. No less important is the fact that there is also a fundamental disconnect between the expectations and experiences of asylum/protection of those affected and the application of law and policy. Drawing on similar statements to those of the woman from Syria which open this section (IST2.03), the discussion below draws out alternative perspectives on the meaning and experience of protection from the viewpoint of those making claims to asylum – claims which stress the need for justice and practical solutions as opposed to humanitarian succour or aid (see also Chapter 6).

Contesting 'asylum' and 'protection'

Our counter-archive indicates that, while in 2015 and 2016 there was widespread awareness of concepts such as 'asylum' and 'protection'

Contesting protection

amongst Syrians, Afghans and Iraqis in particular, knowledge varied across different routes and sites, and by no means involved uniform understandings along the lines advanced by EU states (see also Stevens and Dimitriadi, 2019). In answer to our interview question, 'What does asylum mean to you?', there was a notable emphasis on safety, protection and rights. Many travelling on both the eastern and the central Mediterranean routes voice a desire to be granted safety: *'If he doesn't have safety in his country, safety is the most important issue, if he doesn't have safety that means he can't live in the country'* (IST2.14, man from Afghanistan, Istanbul). Often, the direct reason for leaving is expressed as a desire to realise safety: *'The first thing I say is that if my country were safe, I wouldn't have left'* (ATH2.17, Palestinian woman from Syria, Athens); *'I left Afghanistan to save my life'* (SIC1.12, man from Afghanistan, Sicily); *'I decide to leave in November just because of some kind of group that was after my life … I decided to run away so I was able to save my life'* (ROM2.18, man from Nigeria, Rome); *'then when the beginning of war we do not have another alternative, we save our life, and we try to cross the Mediterranean Sea. But it is difficult'* (MAL1.29a, Eritrean man from Ethiopia, Malta). A Nigerian woman we spoke with in Rome in the summer of 2016 says, in straightforward terms: *'Protection. Our protection. Low harm, better than Nigeria, we are safe'* (ROM2.03C, woman from Nigeria, Rome). A man from Eritrea volunteers a nuanced response: *'For me you feel free, you feel justice, economic justice, social justice, this means for me protection. Human dignity'* (ROM2.12, man from Eritrea, Rome).

In Istanbul, we spoke to a Kurdish woman from Syria who provides an expansive answer to the question of what asylum means to her, the core of which is a desire for protection, to *'live a normal life'* and not be too demanding on the state (*'I don't want anything more'*). She explains:

> When a refugee seeks refuge in any country they are fleeing something. Dangers, war … Syria was good. But as soon as the situation became bad, everyone started fleeing. Everyone is seeking asylum. Asylum in Europe. I want, for example, asylum in Germany. Why do I want asylum? They protect me, they give me a house. I live a normal life. I don't want anything more. I don't want more. I have asylum.

Reclaiming migration

A refugee is a human fleeing war, a bad situation, bombs. Asylum is living a normal life. Nothing more.

(IST2.20, woman from Syria, Istanbul)

By contrast, many travelling along the central route were less familiar with the notion of asylum and only became acquainted with the term on entering the EU. In Rome, for example, a former Ghanaian teacher who had crossed the central Mediterranean, describes his lack of knowledge and how he learned about the important notion of 'asylum':

[T]hey [probably someone from the government or an NGO] explained this asylum just to us after when we have already taken our fingerprint. After they have already taken our fingerprint, I think that was next day, the next day it was, yes. The next day they came to explain this issue to us, that Italy receive people, those people who are coming to seek asylum, people who are us, so that was the time I started ah, what is it? Asylum, asylum, what is this asylum?

(ROM2.08, man from Ghana, Rome)

The ways people on the move describe what it means to be an 'asylum seeker' or 'refugee' further challenge assumptions that the asylum system is under siege or in 'crisis'. Many were clearly aware of the connection between refuge and rights. For example, a Syrian man in Istanbul rejects the term refugee from the outset, stressing the importance of rights and especially work:

I don't like the word refugee. As a Syrian, whenever someone hears that someone is Syrian, they are a refugee. I am just seeking refuge in a country not looking for food and drink. I am here or to any other country, I'm leaving Syria to work. The refuge is just the place. But as a country that is hosting Syrians, the only thing that is requested is that you maintain his rights. Maintain his rights and he will work. Any place the Syrian went ... He went to Lebanon, to Turkey, to Egypt, to Europe and the Syrian is working and looking after himself. They are not a burden to the society. This is the idea. I don't like the word refugee ... I don't know why but I don't like it.

(IST2.05, man from Syria, Istanbul)

An Afghan man we spoke with in Athens also speaks about rights, stressing the humanity of the refugee, and has a distinct view of how a refugee should be treated:

Refugees should get their rights. Just the normal rights of everybody. And the balance is very important ... The balance between local people. There is no specific

Contesting protection

word for asylum seeker or refugee if you think that everybody is human. Refugees don't expect too much. They can provide for themselves, they can survive once they get the right to live in a country or in another country. After they get their right they can live themselves and they don't need any other support. They only want justice and that's it.

(IST2.08, man from Afghanistan, Istanbul)

For this man, that '*everybody is human*' means that classification as 'asylum seeker', 'refugee' or 'migrant' is somewhat irrelevant, in contrast to established distinctions between asylum seekers, refugees and migrants. Rather, '*justice*' and the right to live like everyone else is fundamental.

The quest for justice is highlighted by the Eritrean man cited above, who refers to '*economic justice, social justice*' (ROM2.12), as well as by a man from Syria who says: '*I am not asking the government of Greece to deal with me like a Greek citizen. Just justice as a human being. And as a refugee I am not asking for a hotel or apartment or a salary. If I want to rent an apartment, it's easy for me, just allow me to get a job*' (ATH2.13, man from Syria, Athens). A second Syrian man also expresses disappointment at his treatment in Greece. When asked what it means to be a 'refugee', he focuses on a lack of justice and a misperception of the reasons as to why people are forced to travel to Greece:

I feel there's no justice. There's no justice. No justice by the government, not the people. So far I've seen more justice from the people, not the government. There's injustice on the part of the governments, they don't appreciate why this person is coming, that he is tired coming here, he's not here on tourism. There's no justice, such as trying to do something for the refugees that might remedy their grievances.

(ATH2.22, man from Syrian, Athens)

These expressions of failing justice relate not only to the understanding of the meaning of asylum, or what it means to be an 'asylum seeker' or 'refugee', but also to the system itself, as suggested by ATH2.22 in his reference to the failures of government to recognise the drivers and conditions of flight. His is not a lone voice. In a thought-provoking reflection, for example, a man from Syria, who knew he was entitled to apply for asylum (and was the only person we spoke with in Greece

125

who preferred to remain there), articulates his frustration in the following terms:

> *Asylum, it's something really bad, how can I explain it to you? Asylum, it's as if someone is using you to beg. They are using us to beg and profit from us. These countries are taking us because behind us, there is money. This is what I consider asylum. Why do they receive a refugee and not an immigrant? I didn't seek refuge with you, I immigrated from my country to you. Why are you calling me a refugee and not an immigrant?*
>
> (ATH2.24, man from Syria, Athens)

When asked what he considered himself to be, he replies simply: '*A human*' (ATH2.24).

Interestingly, these assertions of humanity are indicative of Wynter's 'Man vs Human struggle', which is centred on 'the usually excluded and invisibilised situation of the category identified by Zygmunt Bauman as the "New Poor"' (Wynter, 2003: 261). Wynter (2003: 261) goes on to clarify that this category is 'defined at the global level by refugee/economic migrants stranded outside the gates of the rich countries, as the postcolonial variant of Fanon's category of les damnés …'. While postcolonial scholars, such as El-Enany, also demand that we 'work towards a language that refuses terms such as … "irregular" or "illegal/economic migrants"', amongst others (El-Enany, 2020: 228), our participants had already reached this point. In the refusal to be categorised or labelled as asylum seekers or refugees, the appeal to be treated *as humans*, and the critique of their treatment on arrival to the EU, people on the move instinctively and expertly rejected a limited, exclusionary and failing EU asylum regime that is tainted by 'the coloniality of power' (Mayblin, 2017: 178). Indeed, the testimonies of people on the move have further significance in challenging the prevalent view in the EU and its member states that people who enter without authorisation are intent on abusing the system and invoke an 'asylum crisis'. The man from Ghana cited above as asking '*Asylum, asylum, what is this asylum?*' (ROM2.08) was unaware of the possibility of applying for asylum before he arrived, and therefore could not be accused of being a 'bogus asylum seeker'. Yet more broadly, even those who were aware of the asylum process sought safety from war, personal threats and human rights violations. Rather than presenting a case for humanitarian succour, however, what the analysis in this chapter emphasises is that people on the move make diverse claims to protection on the grounds of a contestation of the inequalities and injustices that they experience not only en route, but also in the EU. That asylum processes in EU states overlook these experiences and enforce asylum in reductive terms, both legally (in the assessment of claims) and geographically (in the limited territoriality of asylum), reflects a wider policy agenda that silences the cumulative experiences of precarity in which it is implicated. Indeed, it also reflects an agenda that silences the colonial connections cutting across migratory routes (such as between Libya and Italy or between Syria, the UK and France), historical connections that are manifest in the racialised exclusion of the EU protection regime, yet nevertheless ignored in the 2015 *Agenda*.

Conclusion

This chapter has emphasised the ways that people on the move, in their ongoing search for peace and safety, contest the EU's approach to asylum and protection and its adoption of a humanitarian narrative of crisis. Drawing on our counter-archive of testimonies with people on the move across the Mediterranean during 2015 and 2016, we have shown how journeys to safety were frequently fluid or lacked pre-planning, and were fragmented with various interruptions and challenges along the way. Often, these challenges gave rise to further drivers of movement and to cumulative experiences of precarity, which we have referred to as 'intersecting drivers and conditions of flight'. Together, fluid and fragmented journeys and intersecting drivers and conditions of migration challenge the view that Europe's so-called migration crisis was unique or, indeed, a crisis. Many people had been travelling for many months – even years – and were forced to continue moving in flight from racialised and epistemic forms of violence that reflect colonial histories otherwise silenced in EU policy debates. The

Reclaiming migration

cumulative precarity experienced along the migratory journey continued to reverberate in experiences of arrival, with the limits of asylum and protection perpetuating precarity in the EU. In the words of Innes, for far too many, 'the never-ending journey within the physical space of Europe' is a lived experience or an impending reality (Innes, 2015: 511). In this context, many of those we spoke with rejected the narrow focus of EU law and policy and its framing of humanitarianism, asylum and protection, while also refusing the labels of 'asylum seeker', 'refugee' and 'migrant' (Zetter, 1991, 2007). In so doing, the cumulative experiences of precarity, faced both before and after arrival to the EU, were also contested: people on the move advanced a multiplicity of claims and demands that highlight the limits of assumptions about the need to provide them with humanitarian succour. In Chapter 5, we show how such contestations reflect a more fundamental questioning of Europe and the European Union itself.

Notes

1 See, for example, *A European Agenda on Migration*, May 2015: https://ec.europa. eu/home-affairs/sites/homeaffairs/files/what-we-do/policies/european-agenda-migration/background-information/docs/communication_on_the_european_agenda_on_migration_en.pdf (accessed 22 July 2020).
2 The EU–Turkey Statement was announced on 18 May 2016 and set out several commitments by the two countries regarding irregular travel between Turkey and the EU. Its aim was to reduce unauthorised arrivals in the EU, through financial incentives to Turkey (European Council, 2016c).
3 A limited number of Skype interviews were carried out with contacts who had passed through Malta previously. Please see Chapter 2.
4 Art 1A(2) of the Refugee Convention states that a refugee is a person who 'owing to well-founded fear of being persecuted for reasons of race, religion, nationality, membership of a particular social group or political opinion, is outside the country of his nationality and is unable or, owing to such fear, is unwilling to avail himself of the protection of that country; or who, not having a nationality and being outside the country of his former habitual residence as a result of such events, is unable or, owing to such fear, is unwilling to return to it'.

5

Questioning Europe

Well they say that they have human rights [in Europe]. *I saw that the Syrian doesn't have rights. The Syrian, the Afghan, the Iranian, these people that were sent into refuge. You're responsible for us! Merkel opened the border, ok? After a month or two months, they should have made the decision. But just after we got to Athens, the decision was taken* [to close the border]. *I would haven't left Syria! They're humiliating us with this decision, humiliating these people … We arrived at the door and you closed on our face.*

(ATH2.27, woman from Syria, Athens)

I was in Hal Far detention centre, it is a military camp … It was not a proper place for kids. For me it was ok. You know when we came from Africa we never, never expected something, so it was not as if we expected something. But they were also expectations from Europeans who are always preaching about human rights, about children's rights. And then to keep the child in a detention centre, with no sunshine at all, innocent people?

(MAL1.26, man from Ethiopia, Skype interview)[1]

Introduction

Chapter 4 examined both experiences *en route* and experiences of *arrival* to the EU, revealing how multiple intersecting drivers and conditions of flight often led to cumulative forms of precarity for people on the move. It also showed how these lived experiences served as conditions for a contestation of the limitations of European asylum and protection policies, and a problematisation of the EU's humanitarian narrative of crisis. This chapter further develops the analysis by exploring the expectations and experiences of Europe prior to and on arrival to the EU. In particular, it emphasises a contrast between the stated aspirations and values of the *European Agenda on Migration* and the experiences of people on the move across the Mediterranean in 2015 and 2016. As a central intervention in the EU's 'migrant crisis', the 2015 *Agenda* invoked the key principles and values of the EU. It was framed as aiming 'to halt the human misery' and 'to protect those in need', and called on member states to work together 'in accordance with the principles of solidarity and shared responsibility' in responding to the 'human tragedy' in the Mediterranean (European Commission, 2015b: 2; see also Introduction). As such, the European Commission presented Europe as 'a safe haven for those fleeing persecution as well as an attractive destination for the talent and entrepreneurship of students, researchers and workers' (European Commission, 2015b: 2). Critically engaging with such a claim, this chapter opens space for reflection on what we call the EU's *postcolonial present* (Bhambra, 2016: 188; see also Chapter 1). In using this term, we highlight recurring dynamics of power from the colonial past to the present, which are manifest in the racialised violence and precarity faced by people on the move today. In addition, we use the term 'postcolonial present' to suggest that a preventative policy agenda implies new forms of violence associated with colonial legacies and attitudes. Contrary to the immediate rupture suggested by dominant crisis narratives, our counter-archive thus reveals a longer temporal horizon to lived experiences of precarity (see also Conclusion).

This chapter critically interrogates assumptions about the EU as a desirable place based on shared values and principles, specifically from the perspective of those seeking a place of peace and safety. It explores the distinct challenges that people on the move encountered across different member states in 2015 and 2016, and follows the frustration of many on reaching the EU. Reflecting on people's stated expectations of Europe, the chapter highlights the EU's attraction as a place that projects itself as upholding human rights and humanitarianism for people seeking safety.[2] Contrasting this with the lived experiences of people on the move across the EU, we chronicle sub-standard living conditions, a lack of information on asylum and reception procedures, long periods of uncertainty due to opaque bureaucratic systems, as well as delays and administrative hurdles to family reunification. Instances of 'reverse smuggling' (that is, the facilitated return to often unsafe locations along the migratory route) point to people's horror and anger at reception conditions in the EU, which are often described as having severe consequences on the mental and physical health of those affected. Further problematising common understandings of Europe's so-called migrant crisis, these conditions highlight the continuity of racialised violence and precarious conditions that many people on the move face during their fluid and fragmented journeys (see Chapters 3 and 4). At the same time, we show how people on the move also reject a framing of the hardships they faced in 2015 and 2016 as a 'humanitarian crisis'. Rather than these being merely a matter of unfulfilled humanitarian needs, our analysis exposes counternarratives which make it clear that more far-reaching political questions and demands are at stake. Some, such as the Syrian woman (ATH2.27) and the Ethiopian man (MAL1.26) quoted at the beginning of this chapter, question whether Europe lives up to its self-proclaimed values of human rights when it comes to the treatment of people on the move. Others highlight the role of EU states in creating the conditions that have driven people to migrate (see Chapter 6). Indeed, the testimonies from our counter-archive throw into sharp relief the question of Europe itself, which is inseparably linked to how the EU relates to its 'others', especially people on the move in precarious conditions.

A community of values?

The EU embraces principles and values that are deemed foundational to its existence, across a range of legal and policy documents. For example, the Treaty on European Union (TEU), a core text outlining such values, reads as follows in Article 2:

> The Union is founded on the values of respect for human dignity, freedom, democracy, equality, the rule of law and respect for human

rights, including the rights of persons belonging to minorities. These values are common to the Member States in a society in which pluralism, non-discrimination, tolerance, justice, solidarity and equality between women and men prevail.

(European Union, 2007, Article 2)

Article 3 proceeds by declaring the EU's aim to be 'to promote peace, its values and the well-being of its peoples' (European Union, 2007, Article 3). The Article lists a range of other goals, including establishing an area of freedom, security and justice without internal frontiers, combating social exclusion and discrimination, promoting social justice, equality and solidarity, and the protection of the rights of the child. In addition, it notes that '[i]n its relations with the wider world, the Union shall uphold and promote its values and interests and contribute to the protection of its citizens' (European Union, 2007, Article 3). Indeed, EU treaties – including the TEU – are explicit in invoking the importance of values, both on EU territory and in the EU's relations with other states. This is reflected in EU documents on migration policy – in particular those issued by the European Parliament and the European Commission – which often invoke values such as human rights or humanitarian concerns. These values also feature strongly in the language framing the 2015 *Agenda*. A commitment 'to meet our international and ethical obligations' and to '[uphold] our international commitments and values' were named as key to the policy responses outlined in the document (European Commission, 2015b: 2). Moreover, the acceptance of and provision of assistance to legally admitted migrants was described as 'central to the values Europeans should be proud of and should project to partners worldwide' (European Commission, 2015b: 7). As such, the *Agenda*, like a range of migration policy documents at EU level, is infused with declared values and legal principles, including references to fundamental rights and the right to asylum.

Examining the EU's history more closely, Williams (2009, 2010) argues that the foundational role of human rights declared in the TEU is a myth. During the establishment of the European Economic Community in 1957, he suggests, 'human rights did not figure in the political or legal landscape constructed by the Treaty of Rome' (Williams, 2010: 110). Rather, the study of the foundation of the EU reveals a historical entanglement with colonialism and an enduring postcolonial character today. Hansen and Jonsson (2014a, 2014b) show how an intellectual, political and institutional discourse on Eurafrica emerged in the early twentieth century that understood European integration as instrumental to securing the continued European colonisation of Africa. Examining political, legal and journalistic accounts of the time, they argue that a belief prevailed that 'European integration would come about only through a coordinated exploitation of Africa, and Africa could be efficiently exploited only if European states combined their economic and political capacities' (Hansen and Jonsson, 2014b: 447). On this reading, the foundation of the European Economic Community signified an interlocking of both propositions and was perceived as the creation of Eurafrica, i.e. the securing of continued European exploitation of Africa's natural resources (Hansen and Jonsson, 2011). Importantly, Europe's colonial history continues to shape its postcolonial present today, as is reflected, for instance, in the EU Charter. The preamble to the Charter invokes the EU's 'spiritual and moral heritage', and respect for 'the diversity of the cultures and traditions *of the peoples of Europe* as well as the national identities of the Member States' (Williams, 2010; emphasis added). On this basis, Williams argues that the Charter's 'preambular language indicates a preference for promoting cultures and traditions that emanate from Europe not elsewhere, and Europe's "others" are effectively excluded within the very core of the EU's human rights creative and promotional rhetoric' (Williams, 2010: 126).

This critical reading of Europe's founding resonates with scholarship that addresses the long-standing histories of exclusion embedded within humanitarianism and a human rights framework more widely. As Mayblin (2014, 2017) shows, the human rights and refugee protection frameworks were deeply exclusionary when they were enshrined in international law, with colonising powers seeking to limit access to rights on the part of colonised peoples. Postcolonial scholars have shown how human rights are built on a notion of the 'human' shaped by European philosophers, which had historically been understood as excluding people of colour (Mignolo, 2009; see also Wynter, 2003). Despite the central role of rights claims during the Haitian Revolution, the history of human rights tends to be narrated as rooted in the French Revolution and in abolitionist movements (Kaisary, 2014). As Wall notes, this reveals much about how human rights are imagined: 'Instead of the active subjects of the slave revolts, the traditional human rights histories emphasise slavery in the context of the (British) abolitionist movement (with its international (white and middle-class) subjects rescuing poor black people)' (Wall, 2012: 21). There are thus important limits to human rights in terms of their legal history, their dominant imaginary and their philosophical grounding. Despite the universalist framing of the Universal Declaration of Human Rights and EU policy instruments invoking human rights, therefore, 'the legacies of ideas of human hierarchy … made the exclusion of millions of people from "human" rights during the late colonial era, live on' (Mayblin, Wake, Kazemi, 2020: 110).

Despite these enduring legacies, the EU largely silences its colonial past and ignores the implications of such histories in the postcolonial present. This can be seen, for instance, in the way the EU responded to the so-called migrant crisis – a 'crisis' which has been framed as emanating from outside of Europe independently of EU actions. Questioning the 'logic of innocence' that this denial of responsibility involves, Samaddar draws attention to the EU's complicity in producing the conditions that compelled many to migrate, suggesting that the 'crisis' can better be understood as a crisis of EU imperialism (Samaddar, 2016: 107; see Chapter 1). He notes, for example, that the EU worsened the situation in Syria by joining US bombings and interventions there, and contributed to further instabilities in the Middle East with its policies against Iran and Lebanon (Samaddar, 2016: 102). Similarly, Bhambra argues that the 'humiliating conditions' that drive people on the move to come to Europe have been produced in large part by inequalities that were historically created by European colonial powers

Questioning Europe

(Bhambra, 2016: 194). Following Bhambra, we contend that the failure to address Europe's own colonial history partially explains why Europe and its politicians seem 'unable to address their postcolonial present, or even recognise it as something other than an external intrusion disrupting an otherwise ordered European polity' (Bhambra, 2016: 188). Rejecting the common view of migratory 'others' as disrupting an ordered Europe, this chapter thus understands people on the move 'as constitutive of Europe's own self-understanding' rather than as disconnected from it (Bhambra, 2016: 188). As such, engaging the perspectives of people on the move in Europe is central to any endeavour to understand what Europe is – and does – today. In counterposing the relations of postcolonial Europe with its proclaimed values and principles, our migratory testimonies critically engage the notion of Europe and formulate clear demands for justice.

Expectations of Europe

The first thing I was sure about and I believe in it, was that I was coming there, and here people are being respected, there is humanitarianism. I was sure of this. That is why I chose … I did not choose a country, I chose Europe. They respected people a lot here, they respect humanity, they love humans, humanity.

(KOS1.30, man from Pakistan, Kos)

We heard that in Europe they have safe, normal lives. No one commits an injustice against another. There is no one for example who violates the rights of another. If that's your right, it's your right. Those are the things we know. And they respect human rights.

(IST2.20, woman from Syria, Istanbul)

When speaking to people on the move about their expectations of Europe, two key themes emerged: peace and safety, and human rights and humanitarianism. Notably, people travelling along the eastern Mediterranean route often had much clearer ideas of Europe prior to arrival. Many travelling on the central Mediterranean route primarily sought to escape dangerous or intolerable situations rather than intending to travel to Europe: instead of a particular place, safety was their destination (see Chapter 3). Those crossing the eastern

Mediterranean, on the other hand, tended to travel more purposefully towards the EU (see Chapter 4). The quote by the man from Pakistan above illustrates this, where he explains his decision to travel to Europe in the expectation of experiencing a humanitarian response to his situation. A Syrian man similarly describes how he decided to attempt the journey to Europe for such reasons: '*Because European society has humanitarians. Humanitarians in the real sense of the word. They speak to someone and they think "this is a human", regardless of everything*' (IST2.23, man from Syria, Istanbul). Many of those using the eastern route had heard about Europe as a place of humanitarianism before they began their journeys, as a man from Afghanistan recounts: '*When I was in Afghanistan I had heard that in Europe there is humanitarianism, that they respect humans, they respect the humanity*' (KOS1.51, man from Afghanistan, Kos). Being respected as a human being and being treated accordingly were central expectations of many when travelling to Europe: '*I was sure they would treat me as a human being*' (KOS1.04, man from Iraq, Kos); '*They* [Europeans] *respect humanity … the humans*' (KOS1.16, man from Pakistan, Kos); '*I expected to be treated as a human*' (KOS1.41, man from Syria, Kos).

In addition to understanding Europe as a place of humanitarianism, people on the move seeking a place of peace and safety on both routes also imagined Europe as adhering to human rights, or in the words of a man from Mali as '*a continent of human right*' (MALI.21, man from Mali, Malta). A woman who had not yet reached the EU elaborates on what she anticipated respect for human rights might mean in practice:

> *Maybe in Europe if you come as a refugee it's your right to eat and drink. Maybe you get a house, the state helps you with half the rent. This is a good thing for learning the language and acclimating so they gave it to them. They put their children in schools. Europe is different in this regard than any other country whether it is Turkey, or the Gulf, or the Middle East.*
> (IST2.17S, woman from Syria, Istanbul)

Without having set foot there herself, this woman viewed Europe as unique in terms of the rights she believed would be granted to refugees, and continued to emphasise in particular the importance of allowing children to go to school. Her statement illustrates that for many of those we spoke with, human rights were not an abstract ideal. Instead, people often had quite specific ideas of what arriving in a place of human rights entailed for them. Many invoked specific rights for which they were searching. Explaining her expectation of Europe, another Syrian woman invokes the right to stay in and leave EU countries, the right to family reunification, the right to basic sustenance and health care: '... *you have a residency permit you can leave on, you have family reunification that you can bring your family on, you have a monthly stipend if it's just your food and drink, you have health insurance*' (IST2.03, woman from Syria, Istanbul). Others highlight the importance of finding freedom of religion or freedom of expression in Europe: '*The most important thing to feel free, freedom*' (BER2.02, man from Syria, Berlin); '*I must live, I must express my opinion, I must live in freedom, regardless of religion*' (IST2.23, man from Syria, Istanbul). As the woman from Syria quoted at the beginning of this section indicates, hopes regarding the respect for rights in Europe include not only state behaviour, but also the expectation that European citizens will refrain from violating each other's rights, or from '*commit[ting] an injustice against another*' (IST2.20, woman from Syria, Istanbul). Europeans are described as '*respect[ing] humans and the human rights*' (KOS1.13, man from Pakistan, Kos), and as '*good people* [who] *respect humans and their rights*' (KOS1.14, man from Pakistan, Kos). Overall, our counter-archive thus points to high expectations on the part of people on the move regarding European states and citizens, both in terms of their respect for human rights and their concern for the well-being of those seeking safety.

Some juxtapose their expectation of Europe as a place of humanitarianism and human rights with their experiences across fluid and fragmented journeys, explaining why they travelled to reach safety in Europe. For example, a man from Afghanistan says: '*of course they don't pay attention to human rights in Iran and Pakistan. We Afghans are bothered and beaten* [in] *Pakistan and Iran. And we have no rights there. We think that European countries pay more attention to human rights and we think we have rights there'* (IST2.12, man from Afghanistan, Istanbul). A man from Gambia shares how he was hoping to find more humane treatment in Europe than the violence he had experienced in Libya: *'Yeah, before I left Libya, I thought that in Europe at least they understand humanity, they are not like the Libyans'* (SIC1.01, man from Gambia, Sicily). Others contrast their expectations of Europe with the insecurity they left behind when embarking on their journeys, as this man from Iraq explains: *'You treat humans like humans. There is no such thing in our country. In Europe, there is … there is humanitarianism, there is respect. But we do not have such thing. It's war, war, war all the times. We are fed up. The ISIS and the jihadists. Daesh destroyed Iraq and Syria. They destroyed Syria and Iraq.'* (KOS1.10, man from Iraq, Kos). A man from Syria similarly reflects: *'human beings matter in Europe. They have a value. It's not like in our country. Now in Syria, humans and animals are the same. You get slaughtered the way they slaughter an animal'* (KOS1.29, man from Syria, Kos). In escaping generalised instability and violence, these testimonies reflect the conviction that human beings matter and an expectation that all people are respected in Europe. As we will see in Chapter 6, the role of EU states and colonial histories in the creation of such situations is not ignored by people on the move, but the act of escape is understood as critical to the contestation of brutality and processes of dehumanisation within which these are implicated.

For many of the people we spoke with in 2015 and 2016, migration journeys involve a search for a place of peace and safety above all else: *'I didn't have any specific expectations, wherever I may go I want to be quiet and safe'* (KOS1.50, man from Afghanistan, Kos); *'I want to feel safe'* (IST2.01, man from Syria, Istanbul). Having fled multiple sources of violence, those travelling along the eastern Mediterranean route emphasised the importance of finding safety in Europe. For example, a man from Afghanistan explains:

> *What I had in mind is that I will come here and I will be safe. I would come here and bring my family … and have a better life and be safe … Because we are not safe there. No one is safe there. Everyday someone dies … Now lately,*

Questioning Europe

many have died ... children ... everybody ... This happens every day. There is
no safety, no peace ... This is why I was thinking of here [Europe].
(KOS1.31, man from Afghanistan, Kos)

Importantly, peace and safety are understood by people on the move not only as the absence of violence or war. Instead, our counter-archive shows that finding peace and safety entails a more comprehensive sense of being able to re-establish a 'normal life', as evident in the quote from the Syrian woman at the beginning of this section: *'We heard that in Europe they have safe, normal lives. No one commits an injustice against another'* (IST2.20). Yet, what this specifically means varies from person to person. For some, safety refers to legal status, as the Syrian man in Istanbul quoted above elaborates: *'At least I will have papers and insurance, I will feel safe* [in Europe]*'* (IST2.01, man from Syria, Istanbul). A sense of peace, in more concrete terms, is connected to medical care and basic sustenance by a minor from Afghanistan we spoke with: *'I was thinking that there will be peace, first of all it is going to be peaceful ... I will have food, if I get sick, I will be taken care of, there will be doctors'* (KOS1.09, male minor from Afghanistan, Kos). Concerns about resuming a 'normal life' are suggestive of the extent of disruption many experienced prior to – and during – their migratory journeys. Having felt compelled to undertake what were often complex and lengthy journeys, people on the move put their lives on hold, expressing hope for a return to normality in the near future. As the minor from Afghanistan continues to explain, for him the desire for a *'normal life'* not only involves being able to secure legal documents, food or medical care, but also requires the knowledge that the streets are safe: *'And also, the other thing that I was thinking is that if I am walking on the street here, when I am going somewhere, there will be no kamikazes, there will be no suicide attacks, I will not die ... I will be alive'* (KOS1.09, male minor from Afghanistan, Kos). Europe is thus envisaged as a place of safety and peace that will facilitate survival, and enable people to continue their lives as normally as possible. As we shall see later in this chapter, this also includes concerns to allow family members to escape unsustainable situations by means of family reunification: *'it's a safe place to stay in*

Reclaiming migration

Europe and to be able to get my family out of the danger in Syria' (BER2.02, man from Syria, Berlin).

It was by no means the case that everyone we spoke with had positive expectations of Europe. A few were sceptical after having heard of the challenges people on the move faced there. As a man from Afghanistan in Istanbul explains: '*They don't have the right to work and they are not all happy. So, it's not a very good life in Europe*' (IST2.08, man from Afghanistan, Istanbul). Moreover, a man from Syria had heard about the abuse people on the move often face in various EU states. He says: '*I have information from others that have been here, what did they go through the sea but to be welcomed with physical abuse – not only in Greece, they do this everywhere, to Syrians, also in Macedonia and Serbia and Hungary!*' (KOS1.26, man from Syria, Kos). He continues to explain that he nevertheless travelled to Europe because he had '*no other choice. I knew I would have to suffer all this.*' Such testimonies illustrate our emphasis in Chapter 3 on the predominance of migratory drivers in migratory decision-making, and the ineffectiveness of deterrence. While Europe is clearly not viewed positively in all our migratory testimonies, many who had clear expectations imagined, nevertheless, a place of humanitarianism, human rights, peace and safety: values that the EU officially embraces in its documents and treaties, as we have shown. Our counter-archive reveals that people on the move to EU states in search of peace and safety during 2015 and 2016 held onto these values, often drawing on universalist languages of human rights and humanitarianism in their claims to basic sustenance, medical care, the right to work, freedom of expression and the right to movement without fear of injury or death. The majority, however, experienced a cumulative form of precarity on arrival to the EU, as the next section further details.

Contesting precarity

I realised as we drove into detention I was like 'Oh, are we going to be imprisoned?' because I thought in the West once people apply for asylum, they have not broken

Questioning Europe

any law, they are not supposed to be imprisoned. So, I was like, 'Oh my God, it's different, it's just like Libya' where we were being detained.

(MAL2.09, woman from Somalia, Malta)

At the border with Macedonia, the services were really bad. As much as I can explain it to you, it's not enough. There were many people that collapsed psychologically and really suffered. And we were among those people that also suffered. Twenty days at the border we were waiting. Today it opens, tomorrow it opens, in the morning it opens and at 10.00 [p.m.] it closes. The border opened and I came and I entered Macedonia but because my wife doesn't have an ID card from Syria, they made us leave. They said, 'you and your daughter can enter, your wife can't'.

(ATH2.24, man from Syria, Athens)

The lived experiences of people on the move are frequently precarious; people are vulnerable to exploitation and abuse, and generally have limited access to rights, to justice, to certainty and to stability. Those we spoke with highlighted their precarity in its various forms. Many examples were provided, but in this chapter, we have selected some of the main issues that were commonly raised or that were especially grievous. Some sites had unique problems – such as the use of detention in Malta referred to by the Somalian woman quoted above (MAL2.09), or the very challenging conditions at the border between Greece and North Macedonia encountered by those trying to make their way through Europe, and described in the quote by the Syrian man above (ATH2.24). To address these multiple accounts of precarity, we further examine concerns regarding sub-standard living conditions, lack of information on asylum and reception procedures, and delays and hurdles to family reunification.

Sub-standard living conditions

Most people raised specific questions and issues about the challenges they confronted in relation to their living conditions. These concerns were voiced in every site we visited, including those in the EU. On the eastern Mediterranean route, disquiet about the lack of capacity, infrastructure and personnel was evident, particularly with regard to people's experiences of the Greek islands, which had to deal with large numbers of people arriving rapidly from Turkey. One Afghan man describes how on the island of Chios a camp had been established with poor conditions that had led to protests: '*The reason was that the food was not good and it took a long time to be distributed. There were 3,000 people in the camp and it took four and a half hours to distribute it*' (ATH2.39, man from Afghanistan, Athens). Another describes the conditions in a different camp in similar terms: '*Life was very hard in Lesvos, in Moria camp. There were many many refugees living in that camp*' (ATH2.37, man from Afghanistan, Athens). New arrivals on the Greek island of Kos in 2015 were provided with no official accommodation or services, and were consequently sleeping on the beaches, in parks and on the streets and fending for themselves, with some assistance from civil society organisations. A young Syrian woman with a husband and two children was appalled at the conditions she faced in Kos, including having to sleep outside in a tent. She explains: '*never in our life we had to sleep on the floor … We had a house in Syria … we had everything*'. Going further, she says: '*We haven't had a bath for eight days now. My husband has a bath in the sea. But I do not. And there is this tent … and there is nothing underneath it … lately we started searching for supermarkets, shops that are cheaper … Sometimes we eat a souvlaki only with potatoes because it is cheaper. And sometimes we eat only bread*' (KOS1.02A, Syrian woman, Kos).

The situation in Malta was different from the Greek islands, as people had long been travelling there by boat from North Africa – 17,000 people had arrived without authorisation between 2005 and 2015 (UNHCR, 2015).[3] Malta had been applying automatic and mandatory pre-removal detention since 2001 (Global Detention Project, 2019). This was still in place when we spoke to people in Malta during the summer of 2015, though the government subsequently introduced legislation in December 2015 to end mandatory detention.[4] While many of the people were in detention, and were therefore not exposed to the elements as in Kos, they found the conditions unpleasant and stressful. A frequent complaint was that they were sleeping close to one another in containers. The 'Initial Reception Centre', Hal Far, that one Gambian man refers to was in reality a detention centre. He says: '*Hal Far, it was ... the only thing we don't like about there, it's the way of living, it's not nice, too many people living together, eight people in one container, we all use one bathroom*' (MAL2.05). A young Somali man describes comparable feelings when asked about the conditions: '*Little bit hard at Hal Far because it was a camp and you sleep six people, no eight people in one container. So you can't sleep, someone is sleeping someone is watching television, someone is using Facebook, talking with family so it's little bit hard, it's difficult. If you know someone meet with you and you cannot find some place to sit. It was all the time busy*' (MAL2.04). Nevertheless, alternatives to detention were also described as very poor, if not worse. As a man from Mali explains: '*It was bad. Because first we were in the tent, a few weeks in the tent, and that tent when it is raining you have to sit on the bed, you cannot sleep, the water is entering the bed everywhere*' (MAL1.21, man from Mali, Malta).

As the main point of arrival in Italy, Sicily, like Malta, had also received significant numbers of people in the years preceding 2015, including from North Africa since the 2011 'Arab Spring'. As noted in Chapter 3, many of those who reached Sicily had not planned to go to a European destination, but had been forced to attempt the crossing of the Mediterranean Sea due to the extreme circumstances in Libya. A Gambian man puts it in the following terms: '*when I arrived in Libya, I thought I would have found life easier there, that I could work to make some money. I start helping people back home, mothers and brothers back home. As soon as I arrived in Libya, I found that that place was not so peaceful ... But as soon as we reach the country ... wow ... what we thought what we found there is going different*' (SIC1.01, man from Gambia, Sicily). Many of those we spoke with in Sicily were in formal reception centres, though we also spoke to people in informal reception sites and some had passed through several centres or camps. For example, an 18-year-old Ghanaian who was categorised as an unaccompanied minor on arrival had been housed in a stadium for one month and five days, a camp for ten months and finally by a SPRAR (the Protection System for Asylum Seekers and Refugees) – a centre run by one of a network of local institutions organising 'integrated reception'. He explains how minors and adults were initially mixed, but that the 'bambinos' were eventually transferred out. However, information was lacking and conditions problematic, as he describes: *'Before they told us that the underage … we will not have problem! That they will make us feel! But when we go there I don't see that! They treat us like adults in that place! They are bad people! Even clothes, they don't give us clothes! In that place'* (SIC1.3, man from Ghana, Sicily).

Mainland Europe was not significantly better than the islands. A year on in 2016, the Western Balkans route was no longer a feasible option for those hoping to reach Western Europe, with tight restrictions and documentary checks introduced by the then Former Republic of Macedonia, Slovenia, Croatia and Serbia. 'Hotspots' had also been set up on the Greek islands of Lesvos, Leros, Samos and Chios, and the EU–Turkey Statement had been agreed.[5] Those interviewed in Athens in the summer of 2016 had arrived months earlier but were unable to move on through European countries and were unwilling to turn back; their sense of frustration was evident. As an Afghan man explains: *'Greece is like a jail, like a prison and that's why we don't want to stay in Greece anymore'* (ATH2.38, man from Afghanistan, Athens). Another continues: *'It's very hard now. We cannot move from here to European countries and I haven't talked to any smugglers. I will have to wait until the border is opened. Some of my friends close to the Macedonia border and other borders are telling me that it's very hard to cross the border. I hope that if it's possible I can go legally'* (ATH2.37, man from Afghanistan, Athens). A third Afghan man says: *'There are many empty houses in Greece but why do they not prepare a place for us to live? A house. Only a house. They should do something for the refugees. Work. A company where we can start working in Greece. People here in the camp are all jobless and they are all fighting because they are jobless'* (ATH2.36, man from Afghanistan, Athens). The difficulties described here are also reflected in the experience of a rare individual granted asylum in Greece, a man from Afghanistan: *'Asylum means nothing now. I'm like other refugees. The ID, the passport, do nothing for me. Since asylum was granted and residency issued why have they not given me a house or a safe place? Or maybe they could give me my passport and some money so I can go to some other European country'* (ATH2.39, man from Afghanistan, Athens).

144

Questioning Europe

The failed realisation of people's expectations of life in the EU, and the disappointment felt, was very clear in relation to encounters with the reception system. Many were in informal camps in Athens, and although some people had greater access to food and water there were still enormous concerns:

> *Life in here is very, very hard. Let me explain. For food you have to stand in line for two hours for breakfast which is at 9am and lunch which is at 3pm. Dinner is at 9pm and the only thing to eat is boiled potatoes in water without any oil or salt on it. They bring them dry. How can you eat this? It's also very hot. And then life inside the tent ... I'm sure has a temperature higher than 45 degrees Celsius and lots of kids who one day were poisoned with the food because we all had a stomach ache in here ... It is very hard.*
> (ATH2.39, man from Afghanistan, Athens)

For some, living 'on the street' in informal camps, such as that at Pireaus Port in Athens, was considered an improvement on formal camp life:

> *This camp is not really a camp. It's on the street so we cannot call it a camp. It's not a formal camp. We are happy to be here. Like, if you go to other camps, they are formal. For example, Skaramangas, another one. Those camps are very far from the capital, from the city, and there no one cares about the refugees. We are just happy that we can travel from here to Victoria's Square, to other places, easily. So that's why we are happy in this camp.*
> (ATH2.37, man from Afghanistan, Athens)

In a similar way, a man from Pakistan, despite sleeping out in the open in Kos, is relatively positive about the lack of proper accommodation or shelter: '*I mean ... we come here ... at the forest* [park behind the Kos police station] *and we felt so calm ... Even when I was in my house sleeping in my bed, I did not feel this calm. I am here, sleeping on the streets in this forest, under these circumstances but I am calm. I feel calm*' (KOS1.13, man from Pakistan, Kos).

Italy, by contrast, had a complicated two-tier reception system in place, with regional hubs and temporary reception centres managed by the Ministry of Interior and Prefectures, and other reception facilities managed by local municipalities (Italian Interior Ministry, 2015).[6] There were also emergency centres and hotspots in existence when we carried out our research (as discussed with reference to Sicily, above). Despite this, some people we spoke to were living on the streets. In Rome, a Mauritanian man challenges the apparent failure of human rights, drawing attention to the numbers sleeping rough: '*Look there, there are five people sleeping under the tree. They can steal from them here, taking from the jackets. There's no rights, no humanity ... Do you think it is right someone to sleep* [on the street], *do you think it's respecting human rights?*' (ROM2.01, man from Mauritania, Rome). Those in camps also highlight the lack of provision of basic necessities:

> *can you believe that since I came here I've not got a single clothe like this, or a shoe, or anything ... I don't know the leaders who decided on this type of issues, not to give clothes, not to give shoes, not to give a common pair of socks, they will not give it to you. If you wish to know, I can go and bring some of the shampoo that we use to bath ... this soap that I'm talking about, after you bath all of your body will be scratching you, so what is it? Is it a crime to enter such a country or what? It's like more or less like a punishment. But I don't really know why they are doing this to us.*
>
> (ROM2.08, man from Ghana, Rome).

Many people had anticipated that conditions in Germany would be much better, but experiences were highly variable. In Berlin, hangars that had been converted into temporary accommodation at Tempelhof airport shocked one Syrian graduate we spoke with. He explains:

> *When we first entered Tempelhof, that hanger there were only tents. So it was very depressing sight. You feel yourself that you are not in a developed country. I ... when I first saw that site, I thought I'm back in Syria. It's very uncivilised, unbelievable. There were only three sockets to have your mobiles charged, and all the camp came to have their mobile charged. The bathrooms were outside. About twenty toilets for 600 people. You can't enter the toilet, you have to queue. No bathrooms, no, no shower facilities. We had to wait for about two weeks, buses came to take us to a swimming hall. Ten showers were available, you take shower with each other. I was surprised, is this Germany? They told me this is a temporary solution, and it will not be more than one month, now I've been here for nine months. Each time they promised us to be transferred to a better place. Improvements were done in the camp, but there were things, sorry to say, trivial things, for example, they bring two more shower ... two more shower facilities for 600 people.*
>
> (BER2.30, man from Syria, Berlin)

Questioning Europe

It was not unusual to hear that the prospect of a one month stay – and in some cases even one week – led to extreme disappointment. Yet the periods of stay were frequently much longer than this. An Afghan man in Tempelhof, whose wife was struggling with mental health issues, confirms that his stay, too, had extended unexpectedly into months: *'it has been eight months that we are living in this camp; you are seeing how it is. So, this is how we live here. So, the Arab singles are also living in this Heim* [reception centre]. *So, when singles or some people are just bothering us when we are sleeping then we get awake, it's scary, our hearts beat, and we are wondering what's happening'* (BER2.06, man from Afghanistan, Berlin). A 16-year-old from Afghanistan with serious medical conditions also speaks of his disappointment and the failure to realise his basic expectations of a new life:

> *[W]e had imagination that they will give us the house in here, we will go to the school and the treatment of my illness will be good. And now we are here now, we don't have any kind of house. The treatment for my illness it like, till it's not getting so dangerous, they won't help me. And I don't have a school.*
> (BER2.16B, male minor from Afghanistan, Berlin)

While many people were shocked about the circumstances they were confronted with in EU member states, and the gap between these and their expectations, there was not universal condemnation. Those who had suffered at the hands of smugglers and traffickers – largely in Libya – were often grateful that they were not facing similar violence and trauma in Europe. That said, when reflecting on the future, many were less hopeful, particularly in relation to the possibility of finding work. This was most evident for those arriving to Italy, who explain: *'I knew before I came, you cannot work because it's difficult to find a work in Italy, there is problems work now'* (ROM2.26, man from Eritrea, Rome); *'Yeah, I am happy about Italy but the problem I think I have … no work! And it is a problem … no work, nothing! That one year and four months no work, nothing, nothing. Eat pasta and sleep, eat pasta and sleep'* (SIC1.36, man from Nigeria, Sicily). Compounding the distress many were experiencing as a result of such conditions, many of the people we spoke with in 2015 and 2016 also reported a lack of information about asylum and reception procedures. We will now examine this in further detail.

Lack of information on asylum and reception procedures

Interviewer: *As long as you are here, have you received any information on how to apply for asylum in the EU?*
KOS1.05: *No, no one talked to us about this.*
Interviewer: *Did you receive any information about options available to you for shelter?*
KOS1.05: *No, no one told me if there is a place here where I can stay.*
(KOS1.05, man from Afghanistan, Kos)

This exchange in Kos is relatively typical. People arrived on the beaches after crossing in small boats from Bodrum on the Turkish coast, and it was often a matter of luck if and how they found out what to do next. As several men from Syria describe: '*When we first arrived, we were asking around where should we turn ourselves in*' (KOS1.18, man from Syria, Kos); '*We walked for almost three km … They told us that we should get registered … An organisation or I do not know what … told us that we should get registered*' (KOS1.49A, man from Syria, Kos). Many people in this situation relied on mainstream and social media, as well as information from friends. Thus, people describe how: '*I got informed by my friend that I met in Bodrum* [who was already in Kos]' (KOS1.19, man from Syria, Kos); '*I do not know* [whether I can receive refugee status in Greece or the EU] *but I have seen on TV, all refugees warn not to give fingerprints in Hungary*' (KOS1.45, man from Syria, Kos). Mostly, however, people on the move provided information to one another. This is evident in various testimonies: '*We got informed from other Syrians that were here already. They said we should go to the port at 24.00 to get registered, they will give us a number and then, after 3–4 days will receive a document and we will leave*' (KOS1.20, man from Syria, Kos); '*We have no information on anything … We have just asked the people around. We were told that we have to wait for some paper that will be provided to us so that we can go to the capital … That's all. We do not know anything else*' (KOS1.22a, man from Syria, Kos). Even when documentation was received from the police that enabled people to leave Kos for mainland

Greece, information remained scant beyond the bare minimum. A man from Syria says: '*What we know is that we will get that document and we have to leave Greece within six months*' (KOS1.18, man from Syria, Kos). As indicated in the narrative of the man from Afghanistan quoted above (KOS1.05), there was also a lack of information on basic needs, such as shelter. In response to our interview question about whether any information about shelter was offered, the same reply was repeatedly given in Kos: 'No!' Others who crossed from Turkey to Samos, Lesvos or Chios had almost identical experiences – for example, when discussing Chios, an Iraqi man states that: '*Nobody gave us any information about asylums procedures or relocation, but we have hope in God*' (BER2.10, man from Iraq, Berlin). Similarly, a young Syrian described how in Samos there was no assistance, shelter or food: '*We had to stay in a hotel and we had to pay for our own food … They give us the "khartiyat"* [Greek departure document], *put us on the bus, and ask us to go*' (BER2.24, man from Syria, Berlin). This lack of preparation and dearth of information on the Greek islands in 2015 is not unduly surprising when consideration is given to the sudden increase of arrivals and the lack of preparedness to deal with them. However, a year on in Athens, in July 2016, it did not appear that much had improved. People were still reliant on individuals and civil society organisations for advice on legal processes, as a man from Afghanistan explains: '*No one has come from an organisation … No one comes from the asylum services. It's only the volunteers. They say "you can go to this country if you have this problem, you can stay there, they will give you a house"*' (ATH2.37).

Those we spoke with in July 2016 who had reached Germany also reported failings in information provision. When asked whether anyone had explained how the asylum procedure worked in Berlin, an educated Afghan man says:

> *No, no one explained. No. But, I just, I am searching in some websites, in the websites, it's a little bit … complicated. It's complicated and con- confusing. I … I'm trying to understand how this … how it works, how I don't know. I don't know. I am trying. But still I didn't receive any interview, any Termin* [appointment] *for an interview, still I didn't receive anything.*
> (BER2.31, man from Afghanistan, Berlin)

Reclaiming migration

Another describes how he received no information about asylum on entry to Germany, but was *'questioned by one detective'* who told him *'"you are not Syrian, and you have a problem with your passport. You don't look like a Syrian, you don't sound like a Syrian."'* He continued, *'I was surprised. It was a tricky question, to know if I'm Syrian, Syrian or not'* (BER2.29, man from Syria, Berlin). In Kos, a young mother puts her finger on a key issue: complicated and non-transparent bureaucracy. She says:

> *I would ask them* [EU politicians] *to help the people that are on the streets. I would like somebody working on asylum to come just for one day, one day only, to come and see the suffering. To make it easier … to facilitate the procedure for the people living on the streets because there are sick people and young children and women* [living on the streets] *… to make the procedure easier.*
> (KOS1.02a, woman from Syria, Kos).

Similarly, on the central Mediterranean route those ending up in detention in Malta had received no government information about why they were in detention or what was likely to happen to them, as a 20-year-old Gambian man confirms:

> Interviewer: *So we were talking about information when you came and you said nobody gave you information, not reliable information; so who was the first person to give information to you, apart from the Somalis, from the Maltese government?*
> MAL2.05: *No, we don't have any information.*
> (MAL2.05, man from Gambia, Malta)

Instead, knowledge about what was likely to happen to an individual was usually passed between detainees. The same man from Gambia explains: *'When we go to detention we met the Somalis at the detention* [centre], *they told us that here is prison that you gonna spend here, you come here, if you agree to come inside, you will stay for one year six months* (MAL2.05, man from Gambia, Malta). Equally, in Sicily, many were not provided with information for some time. This Malian man's testimony is typical:

> Interviewer: *Who was at the harbour? What information did they give you?*
> SIC1.27: *There was police and doctors … the doctors checked us but no one gave us information …*
> Interviewer: *When you were transferred to CARA de Mineo, what information did they give you about what will happen, about the type of centre it was …*

Questioning Europe

SIC1.27: *No, no information …*
Interviewer: *And, before the Commission* [to hear the case], *no one gave you information about your legal condition, about your documents?*
SIC1.27: *No, I didn't receive information like that … only the day of the Commission, when I came here for the Commission in Catania.*
(SIC1.27, man from Mali, Sicily)

Shockingly, this lack of information was also evident in the case of children. An unaccompanied minor from Gambia explains that on arrival in Pozzallo (Sicily) he was not told anything, and once transferred to the unaccompanied minors' reception centre, he was only provided with minimal basic information:

> *I don't think in Pozzallo I was given information … as soon as I reach here, what I received was here is at … Centro d'accoglienza, is an emergency centre, they told me is an emergency centre. As soon as they settle they will move me to another centre. So, that was what I was told here … that's an emergency centre. They will take you to a centre where you could be paid, you have education, and all there sort of things. That were the information I was told.*
> (SIC1.01, youth from Gambia, Sicily)

To some extent, NGOs and individual lawyers across all the sites that we visited sought to fill the gaps in the provision of advice and information about asylum and legal documentation. In Malta, for example, a man from Sudan explains: '*At that time, there was a lawyer called Sarah;*[7] *she came there to tell us about the law and human protection here*' (MAL1.05, man from Sudan, Malta). In Sicily, a young Senegalese man reports that '*only my lawyer … explained me how to have documents*' (SIC1.17, man from Senegal, Sicily). In Kos, a Pakistani man confirms that he was provided with some information on claiming asylum from Medécins Sans Frontières (MSF): '*The MSF gave me an information leaflet with organisations working with migrants and refugees and offering assistance for free; medical assistance … all the organisations in Athens and Thessaloniki.*' Interpreters, too, provided assistance beyond that of interpretation, as a Syrian man explains: '*There are some people here … they are here for a long time, they know the language here. They are interpreters. They told us. They were interpreting … they could speak Urdu, Pashto, Farsi*' (KOS1.07, man from Syria, Kos).

151

Reclaiming migration

Delays and hurdles to family reunification

Perhaps one of most significant factors that led people to describe EU policy as inhumane was the delay or impossibility of family reunification. Many were in considerable distress when talking about their desperation to join family members, and reunification was often their main objective. For instance, a man from Afghanistan describes: '*I am looking for family unification. I do not want anything else. Only family unification. I do not care about citizenship and documents. I just want the rest of my family with me*' (KOS1.09, man from Afghanistan, Kos). A Syrian man in Berlin, recently married, pulled no punches:

> *I love my wife. I love my wife and I want to bring her over to Germany. And I was recently wedded. I hope I can be able to get her to Germany. I have a hope to get her to Germany. But I don't know what's going on, psychologically I'm collapsed. Wait, wait, wait. All this time, I didn't learn German. I go to the Sozialamt, I stay two days there. With the insult I get there. I sit here thinking about my wife. How could I overcome all the paper formalities, to send her money, her expenses?*
>
> (BER2.05, man from Syria, Berlin)

Continuing to explain that he has all the documents required for reunification except his wife's passport, the man says: '*My wife doesn't have a Syrian passport. How on earth could I have a Syrian passport of her when we are wanted by the regime. She cannot go back to Syria to get a Syrian passport.*'

A Syrian woman we spoke with in Athens had been separated for ten months from her 10-year-old daughter, who had been sent ahead to Germany, and had been told it could be up to a year before she was reunited with her daughter. She explains:

> *I'd like to go to any country if my daughter was with me. I don't care about the time or the place. I just want to be with my family. Really. I talked to my mother a few days ago and I said "mom, I feel for you. I feel for you. My brothers and I are far away." I'm away from my daughter and I told her "I won't be relaxed until I join my daughter. I'm tired. I can't bear it anymore." There is a lack in my life. Families dispersed with the war. The mother separated from her child, the husband from his wife. What is this war that did this? Families in ten countries.*
>
> (ATH2.33, woman from Syria, Athens)

Questioning Europe

In Istanbul, families were equally desperate to join those who have reached Europe, but found themselves trapped by the change in policy and lack of relevant Turkish documentation. A Kurdish woman from Syria with eight children explains the Kafkaesque situation she found herself in:

> *My husband went to the German government and asked for reunification. The German government then contacts the Turkish government and says "We have this refugee who wants to do family reunification." But the Turkish government says we are not here because we don't have a kimlik* [Turkish residence document]. *We don't have those names.*
>
> (IST2.19, Kurdish woman from Syria, Istanbul)

The pain and uncertainty associated with waiting led some people to consider returning to situations of danger rather than face indignity and family separation in Europe (see Squire and Touhouliotis, 2016). Others, such as a Syrian law student in Berlin, were suspicious of changes to policy and bureaucratic hurdles, suspecting that they were intended to encourage people to return. He explains:

> *Help us with family reunion, there are thousands of us stranded all over Europe, to expedite formalities. So they tell me to go to the regime, get papers, get passports, this is ridiculous. I think the policy-makers are trying to push, let's put it in other way, they are trying to push on the refugee crisis to compel, to force the refugees to go back home. Because they realised later on that they did make a mistake. Or maybe they want the refugees who are already in Europe to phone their family members and friends back home, saying, 'It's very bad in Europe, don't come'.*
>
> (BER2.05, man from Syria, Berlin)

There is no doubt that one of the most difficult issues faced by people who had reached EU countries was separation from close family members, and this was particularly marked on the eastern route. There was a lack of understanding about why family members could not join those in the EU and some cynicism about the underlying rationale. This is voiced clearly by the young Syrian cited above. Such expressions of overt suspicion regarding the motives of European policy-makers arose in various ways in the testimonies from our counter-archive. This leads us on to the final section of this chapter, in which we highlight in greater detail how people on the move were intent on

Reclaiming migration

exposing the many perceived gaps between European commitments to key values and principles and their lived experiences.

Questioning Europe

Asylum is present in their [European] *constitution and law. They follow international law. That's not because of a love for us. It's a law, one, two, three. It's a law, they follow it. If they didn't have this law, they wouldn't have received us or absorbed us. This is my opinion. The issue is a matter of the law and reputation. Reputation. Because they are the countries that respect human rights. They have to keep up their reputation, they can't distort it. If they were really humane, they won't let people go by the sea to reach them. They would have found a route with an airplane or something. A route that allows the refugees to stay alive. But they don't ... That's not humaneness. That's the law.*

(IST2.11, woman from Syria, Istanbul)

Europe just talks about human rights and things like this. If they really cared for the Syrians, they would take the people legally so that no one had to die in this sea and none of this would have happened. Where are the human rights, when someone escapes war and you shut down all the doors to his face?

(KOS1.46A, woman from Syria, Kos)

The previous sections in this chapter explored the expectations that people on the move have of Europe, and the challenging conditions experienced on arrival to EU states. Those affected were often outspoken about the frustration and anger they felt in response to poor reception conditions. As in the testimony of the Syrian woman we spoke with in Kos, quoted above (KOS1.46A), people on the move directly challenge the EU to live up to its own values, pointing to the gap between the principles it projects outwards, and the experiences people on the move are confronted with in EU countries. In Athens, another Syrian woman asks: '*Where are human rights? Europeans are the first to say that human rights are above everything else. So where are they?*' (ATH2.33, woman from Syria, Athens). This question recurs multiple times: '*Where are the human rights? We want freedom*' (ATH2.38, man from Afghanistan, Athens); '*Where is the human rights?*' (ROM2.01, man from Mauritania, Rome). By asking about human rights, people on the move directly confront the EU with its own proclaimed values. Many expressed anger about what they experienced as a harsh response by the EU. For example, the mother referred to in the previous section who was waiting to be reunified with her 10-year-old daughter asks: *'Where is the humanness? This is what I want to understand. Where is the humanness in this issue? She's ten years old and you know that I'm in Europe. You have the ability to solve this. It's a paper. They speak about humanity and humanitarianism and cooperation. Okay, but where? I didn't* [see] *any of this. Nothing. Nothing'* (ATH2.33, woman from Syria, Athens). Beyond waiting to be reunited with her daughter in Germany, this woman also shared that she was not offered accommodation for herself and her children travelling with her, and was left to sleep on the street in Athens.

In light of a similar lack of state support in Kos, a man from Afghanistan exclaims: *'Look at the situation here! We are here … under these circumstances …* [Pointing towards the beach where people on the move are sleeping in the tents, on the street] *This is how we live. How can you talk about humanitarianism or human rights here?'* (KOS1.09, man from Afghanistan, Kos). Further challenging the EU's commitment to humanitarianism, the Syrian woman we spoke with in Istanbul, quoted at the beginning of this section, analyses European behaviour towards people on the move as merely law-abiding, rather than based on *'love'* or *'humaneness'* (IST2.11, woman from Syria, Istanbul). Her analysis suggests that EU states tolerate people on the move rather than welcoming them, offering practical support only as far as required by law, if at all. Others similarly problematise Europe's refusal to open safe and legal routes, suggesting that knowingly letting people risk their lives at sea represents a failure to respect the spirit of human rights. For example, another woman from Syria claims: *'If you are calling for the human rights, then it* [Europe] *should be able to cope with the … and bring … help the refugees to come in safe way'* (BER2.12A, woman from Syria, Berlin).

Not all were critical of the EU, with some expressing appreciation of their treatment, often in contrast to their own countries or states of departure. Nevertheless, these views were relatively rare. When asked about his treatment since arriving in Europe, a Syrian minor, who had spent three months in Turkey, responded: *'Very excellent treatment*

Reclaiming migration

I got, with respect to human rights' (BER2.03, youth from Syria, Kos). A man from Ethiopia who had been granted refugee status in Malta is also generally positive: *'I have seen that one can be treated like human being, and when you are in the EU, your human rights shall be respected. And I think I have been given some rights'* (MAL1.08, man from Ethiopia, Malta). In Kos, a similar comment is made by a Syrian Kurd: *'We found our value here. Now I am talking for Greece, for these few hours that I am here. I realised I am a human being. I do not know what is going on in our countries, but now that I am here, I understood that human beings matter'* (KOS1.28, man from Syria, Kos). Others express how they have been heartened by the humanity shown: *'here I experienced something more ... I experienced and witnessed something much more than* [my life being saved] *... There are people who love humans, humanity. I witnessed that strongly'* (KOS1.30, man from Pakistan, Kos).

Nevertheless, while positive narratives exist, most of the people we spoke with were highly critical of what they perceived as the EU's failure to live up to its proclaimed values and principles. This man from Ivory Coast explains:

> *When I was in my country, the way I was expecting Europe, when I reach in Europe, I was disappointed. Totally different things in the life. What people are saying, is not true. They must work hard, you must work hard, you must suffer for the discrimination, everything. You must take care of all these things cause when they are saying human right, when they say that in Europe you have the human right, I say no. Some have, people who have the money them they are alright. They can do something what they want and nothing can happen. This is what I see in Europe. The same thing in Africa. That is the thing.*
> (MAL1.23, man from Ivory Coast, Malta)

Pointing to the prevalence of discrimination and the selectivity of human rights, this man exposes the continuation of a legacy of exclusion at the heart of human rights, while challenging Europe's projected image as a continent of equality and human rights for all. His testimony makes clear that it was his belief that Europe was a place of human rights that made the experience of living in Malta particularly disappointing. Such disappointment in the lack of human rights was also evident in Kos, where a Syrian man draws attention to the fact that the presence of children, the group considered by the EU to be most vulnerable, does not improve the quality of treatment:

> *I ask for human rights. And it has nothing to do with human right … to be sleeping on the streets, to have people kicking you. This is not* [respect for] *human rights. You do not* [respect human rights] *when someone with two little children wants and get on the bus to go somewhere and you do not let him because he has no documents.*
>
> (KOS1.11, man from Syria, Kos)

This testimony clearly highlights the disparity between the man's demand, '*I ask for human rights*', and the response to that demand, '*This is not respect for human rights*'. In a similar vein, a man from Ethiopia also identifies a comparable divergence between expectations and lived experiences: '*I thought that when you enter the EU your human rights are immediately respected … When I came here it was nothing like that*' (MAL1.03, man from Ethiopia, Malta). When asked what message he would like to convey to EU policy-makers, a young Afghan man trapped in Athens for two months following closure of the land borders in Greece was very clear in his condemnation of the rhetoric of human rights. He says: '*I would tell them that in their speeches you speak about human rights and about solidarity. But in reality, there is nothing of this. You don't do what you say*' (ATH2.07, man from Afghanistan, Athens).

In sum, the people we spoke with in 2015 and 2016 questioned the EU's adherence to human rights and humanitarian principles in practice and pointed to poor reception conditions, including sub-standard living conditions, a lack of information on asylum, opaque bureaucratic procedures and a lack of support for family reunification. While race was not usually directly referenced as a category of exclusion in relation to these issues, the observations of many expose the continued relevance of long-standing racialised violence that critical scholars have shown to be integral to the colonial histories of human rights and humanitarianism (Lester and Dussart, 2014; Mayblin, 2014, 2017). In addition, people we spoke to strongly criticised the EU's unwillingness to open safe and legal migration routes as contrary to human rights, as it leaves those seeking safety in the EU only risky and unauthorised options to do so (see also

Chapter 6). Critiquing the limits of human rights law, our migratory testimonies problematise the ways in which policies fail to engage those migrating as equals and violate the spirit of human rights when they knowingly let people die at sea. Nevertheless, the testimonies from our counter-archive do not simply emphasise the ways in which lived experiences stand in contrast to the rights and values of EU institutions and member states. Critically, they also provide a damning critique of the EU or European project more broadly, questioning its self-proclaimed identity as a normative, value-based entity. Indeed, people on the move demand justice and a right for their voices to be heard in a way that, hitherto, has been absent from EU asylum and migration policy. Such demands are summed up succinctly by a Syrian woman in Athens in the following terms: '*Give us back our country, we don't want any of Europe! Syria is amazing, Syria is paradise. We had rights. We had a house, a store, a car. It's all gone. We want security, we're looking for the opportunity to work, for a future for our kids. Is this wrong?*' (ATH2.15, woman from Syria, Athens).

Conclusion

This chapter has critically engaged with the framing of Europe as a place of rights and protection from the perspective of those seeking peace and safety, exposing the limits of the EU's commitment to human rights and humanitarianism. Indeed, our counter-archive of 'Europe's migrant crisis' holds up a mirror to the EU, which though espousing values such as freedom, security and justice, is challenged by people on the move on the basis of their lived experiences. Our counter-archive thus destabilises a European identity that involves a value-based polity, serving as a powerful reminder that the EU's treatment of its 'others' fails to live up to the universalistic foundational claims of equality and human rights on which the ideal of Europe rests. Similarly, the testimonies that we have engaged in this chapter highlight how peace and safety in a holistic sense remain unattainable for many due to prolonged separation of family members, sub-standard accommodation or uncertain legal status. Indeed, our counter-archive highlights how the preventative policy agenda – along with the politics of crisis that this implies – ultimately *produces* and perpetuates the precarity of people on the move, who find themselves living in EU states facing the threat of deportation, without access to regular health care, housing or work, and without the right to reunite with their families who often remain in dangerous situations outside the EU. As a man from Afghanistan succinctly explains: '*Human rights mean that ... they should treat refugees and residents in the same manner, not in different manner*' (BER2.31, man from Afghanistan, Berlin). This chapter has highlighted both the lived experiences of precarity and the specific demands to justice that these give rise to on the part of those affected by the preventative policy agenda. The testimonies on which it has drawn call on the EU to take seriously its commitment to non-discrimination, human rights and humanitarianism, and to rethink its treatment of people on the move in order to offer redress for the cumulative precarity so many experience. Yet, far from a simple appeal to humanitarianism and human rights, the multiple claims that this chapter has highlighted pose a direct challenge to Europe to reconsider its relations with its 'others', and to align its policies and practices in this regard with its proclaimed values and principles. As we will see in the next chapter, this involves a more fundamental challenge to the EU's postcolonial present.

Notes

1 This Skype interview was conducted from Malta with a man from Ethiopia who was located in Norway. Please see Chapter 2.
2 The people we spoke with used the terms 'Europe' and /or 'EU' without clear differentiation. When discussing their testimonies, this chapter draws as far as possible on the term that was predominantly used by the respective individuals.
3 Malta is an anomalous case in the central Mediterranean region. Only 104 people arrived without authorisation by boat in 2015 and 25 in 2016, all of whom were medical evacuees. Many of the people we spoke with had been in Malta for several years.
4 People who are apprehended on account of an unauthorised border crossing and are not subsequently authorised to stay in Malta are still detained (Global Detention Project, 2019).

5 Hotspots were introduced by the European Commission as part of its *Agenda* in May 2015 (see Introduction). They are designed for short-term stay to screen and register new arrivals. They are located on the Greek islands, in Lampedusa, Sicily and southern Italy. Following the EU–Turkey Statement, hotspots in Greece changed into sites of detention where arrivals wait until asylum applications are processed and/or they are returned to Turkey. Hotspots in Greece exceed their capacity with overcrowding and extremely poor conditions.

6 Since we carried out our research, changes have been made to the Italian reception system.

7 Not her real name.

6

Demanding justice

Don't consider us as a trade. We have a lot of good people among us.
(BER2.30, man from Syria, Berlin)

Back in time, we used to have Europeans as refugees ... I don't know what I would say [to European policy-makers]. *We expect to be treated humanely in Europe.*
(KOS1.03, man from Iraq, Kos)

Introduction

Chapter 5 emphasised the ways in which people on the move across the Mediterranean in 2015 and 2016 questioned the failure of the EU to live up to its human rights commitments and its projected image as a place of peace and safety. This chapter further extends the analysis by considering how the claims and demands advanced by people on the move provide a more far-reaching critique of the role of EU policy in *producing* the drivers and conditions of flight across various sites and along diverse migratory routes. We have already shown how the European Commission's launch of *A European Agenda on Migration* in 2015 facilitated the intensification of a preventative or deterrent approach based on a problematic form of crisis politics (see Introduction and Chapter 1). Indeed, various scholars have highlighted the ways in which 'rich democracies' attempt to 'repel' people from seeking asylum on their territory through a deterrent approach that rolls out migration controls beyond territorial borders (FitzGerald, 2019; see also Bialasiewicz, 2011; Casas-Cortes and Cobarrubias, 2019). The analysis in this book builds on such works to show how the deterrent approach failed to prevent precarious migration to the EU in 2015–16, while at the same time succeeding in rendering those travelling without prior authorisation increasingly precarious (Chapters 3–5). Importantly, we also show how people on the move *challenge* the policy agenda, such as through contestations surrounding the development of anti-smuggling measures (Chapter 3) and the limited provision of protection (Chapters 4 and 5). As we shall further see in this chapter, such a critique runs even deeper than that outlined in Chapter 5, because responsibility is often attributed to EU policies for the situations that drive migration across multiple sites, both in regions of departure and en route. Demands, such as those opening the chapter about the importance of people on the move being 'treated humanely', can be understood as contestations over more extensive injustices and the policies through which these are sustained.

This chapter focuses on the ways in which our counter-archive of migratory testimonies advances demands for justice that contest the unequal right to free movement embedded in the EU's preventative policy framework. More specifically, it examines the challenges that such testimonies pose to a policy agenda that is oriented towards resolving the 'root causes' of migration, and which addresses border security and development as interconnected concerns. After providing an overview of the various ways through which people on the move oppose the preventative policy agenda and advance demands for justice, the chapter focuses on two broad sets of demands that emerged in particularly striking terms within our counter-archive. These largely, though not perfectly, correspond to the testimonies of people travelling along the central and the eastern Mediterranean routes respectively. First, the chapter examines testimonies that advance claims about the role that the EU and its member states play in perpetuating conditions of war and conflict, which are expressed most prominently by those travelling along the eastern route. We show how such claims emerge, particularly in relation to narratives about the need to escape enforced

Demanding justice

conscription, and suggest that migration in this regard is better understood as an anti-war or 'peace movement' rather than as a security 'threat'. Second, the chapter focuses on testimonies surrounding the ongoing significance of colonial legacies as drivers and conditions of flight, which are most evident in the claims of people travelling along the central route. We draw attention to concerns about failing development initiatives and generalised conditions of instability, to show how migration can be understood as a postcolonial or 'anti-colonial movement' that rejects the continued inequalities on which the preventative policy agenda is built. Addressing such claims to justice as an opportunity for a revival of theoretical imaginations through a reclaiming of migration, the chapter concludes by arguing that our counter-archive of Europe's so-called migrant crisis opens alternative ways to address migration that cannot be ignored.

Justice, not aid

What I saw on the road, what I saw in my country, what I saw in [Europe]. *Injustice, blood. Everything bad I saw back home.*
(BER2.08, man from Iraq, Berlin)

Be fair, justice. I am not going to ask you to deal with me as one who has a nationality from your country ... I am not asking the government of Greece to deal with me like a Greek citizen. Just [for] *justice as a human being.*
(ATH2.13, man from Syria, Athens)

I am trying anyway ... anywhere, in [search of] *any justice ... I am trying to make my voice heard.*
(KOS1.17, man from Pakistan, Athens)

Our counter-archive of testimonies surrounding Europe's 'migrant crisis' brings to bear a range of claims to justice through which people on the move contest the unequal right to free movement that is embedded in the EU's preventative policy framework. As is evident in the quotes above, a sense of injustice not only characterises people's descriptions of their journeys and situations prior to and during the migratory journey, but also on arrival to the EU. Many people we

Reclaiming migration

spoke with highlight their '*awful*' living conditions (BER2.16A, woman from Afghanistan, Berlin), with '*bad food*' and without clean clothes or '*pyjamas to sleep*' (ROM2.06C, woman from Nigeria, Rome). A sense of '*frustration and exhaustion*' (ATH2.33, woman from Syria, Athens) is often evident, as people explain that the experience of '*European policy is like subjection*' (ATH2.24, man from Syria, Athens). There are various dimensions to this experience of 'subjection', with many simply emphasising the need for normality: '*we just want to go to work and to the school, live normally. And that's it*' (BER2.17, woman from Afghanistan, Berlin); '*I just want to study the language, and work and continue my life*' (ROM2.03, man from Chad, Rome). Yet, as outlined in Chapter 5, experiences of subjection also often reflected concerns about the barriers to reunifying with family members – those who were left behind, had travelled ahead or who had become separated during the journey. This was a prominent concern for those travelling along the eastern Mediterranean route, with people explaining: '*my worry is about my family, always that I get only humanitarian asylum, which will not allow for Familiennachzug* [family reunification]' (BER2.02, Kurdish man from Syria, Berlin); '*the European law doesn't allow automatic reunification for children above eighteen. If you have a child above eighteen, you might each get sent to a different country*' (ATH2.26, woman from Iraq, Athens). More broadly, concerns were frequently expressed about overly slow and bureaucratic asylum, relocation and settlement processes: '*please expedite procedures*' (BER2.10, man from Iraq, Berlin); '*open more centres … to register the refugees*' (ATH2.18, man from Syria, Athens); '*make it easier, not always paper, paper, paper, black and white, black and white*' (BER2.02, Kurdish man from Syria, Berlin). Similarly, many advanced requests for status documents to be provided: '*my documents, give me documents*' (KOS1.33, Kurdish man from Syria, Kos); '*give me passport right now*' (MAL2.03, man from Somalia, Malta); '*give me a resident permit*' (BER2.14, man from Iraq, Berlin).

Beyond these appeals to just treatment on arrival to the EU, in response to our question asking research participants what they would want to say to European policy-makers, one of the most common demands was for free movement or for the EU to '*open the borders*'

(IST2.15, man from Afghanistan, Istanbul). These claims often came from those who were held back in Turkey following the EU–Turkey Statement of March 2016 (see Chapters 4 and 5), as well as from those who were stuck in Greece after the closure of the 'Balkan route' in 2015. They were also advanced as a demand for safe and legal routes to the EU, such as in the request that people *'can travel legally and not have to leave through the route of the sea and the forests'* (IST2.05, man from Syria, Istanbul). This was sometimes associated with broader accusations: '[as well as] *Bashar al-Assad or al-Nusra Front or ISIS … you* [Europeans] *are also the cause of this. You are the cause of this because you closed the routes to them. You are forcing them to take a road in which there is death'* (IST2.05, man from Syria, Istanbul). Others argued that Europe *'should open the route for them and bring them legally … Or you should solve their main problem – the war – you should stop the war either in Iraq or Syria … So that people do not leave this way'* (KOS1.35, man from Iraq, Kos). For some, European policy-makers *'don't understand … what it is to be a migrant'*, leading to a demand that *'just as they* [policy-makers] *have rights to live in peace and security, we have those rights too because we are all human'* (ATH2.06, man from Aghanistan, Athens). Nevertheless, the claim to free movement was also one that involved a more direct attack on the Dublin Regulation, in which people are normally expected to remain in the country of first registered arrival. As one man from Afghanistan explains:

> *I would like to say something to the EU. They should not do something … people that leave Greece by plane, wants for example to go to Austria … but the plane goes to Denmark. And they have to get off in Denmark. And they take their fingerprints there and they say 'if you want to stay, you have to stay here!'. Let them go! Let them go where they want to go. If they have relatives in Austria, let them go to Austria. In Europe, anybody should go to the country they want to. Let them go. This is what I want to say.*
>
> (KOS1.09, man from Afghanistan, Kos)

Indeed, this concern to *'stay serene and stable and free'* (ROM2.09, woman from Eritrea, Rome) is one that was particularly evident on the central route. Here, many demanded that the EU *'stop fingerprinting'* (ROM2.05b, man from Eritrea, Rome), contesting the way they were *'cheat[ed]'* to provide fingerprints, in order to '*force* [us] *to stay in Italy*' (ROM2.02b, man from Eritrea, Rome).

Despite this widespread discontent about the situation that people faced both en route and on arrival to the EU in 2015 and 2016 (Chapters 4 and 5), it is nevertheless worth noting that many people also expressed gratitude to the communities that hosted them (see also Chapter 5): '*I would like to thank them for saving people's lives*' (MAL2.05, man from Gambia, Malta); '*I would like to thank them for receiving us*' (KOS1.25, man from Syria, Kos); '*I would thank Italians. I would thank them very very much, because they would help me*' (SIC1.08, woman from Eritrea, Sicily). Some focused in divisive terms on the differences between the various groups of people arriving to Europe, such as through an appeal not to be measured alongside '*Iraqis and Afghans and others*' (ATH2.16, man from Syria, Athens), or through pointing to '*some of the refugees in Europe who are not really good, who are really low in their levels of education, work, culture*' (BER2.05, man from Syria, Berlin). However, considerably more emphasised the importance of the equal treatment of those arriving, stressing that: '*I would ask them to build up better conditions for everyone coming here, not only the Syrians, the Iraqis and the others coming here*' (KOS1.06, man from Syria, Kos); '*a person who moves from country to country should have freedom, there shouldn't be conditions or restrictions. The land isn't for you or for someone else or for someone else. It should be that the activity of moving is easy*' (ATH2.18, man from Syria, Athens). Indeed, many people spoke back to the discrimination faced on arriving in the EU, expressing a wish '*to have respect*' (BER2.04, Palestinian man from Syria, Berlin), and appealing to '*please believe us, please think about us*' (ATH2.40, man from Afghanistan, Athens). Emphasising the importance of respect, people on the move also pointed to the ongoing problems of discrimination and violence that they so often faced: '*racism is hard*' (MAL1.31, man from Eritrea, Malta).

One of the most charged sets of demands that emerge from our counter-archive involve claims about the EU's complicity in the injustices that have driven people to migrate in the first place. These emerged most strongly along the eastern route, where there were various demands that the EU should take action in Syria. For example, a Syrian woman we spoke with in Athens appeals:

> *Stop the war in Syria and return us. We don't want anything else. And if you don't want to stop the war, at least let us live in security. We Syrians want to work, everyone talks about education in Syria, my husband is a mechanical engineer, an inventor we used to call him. We Syrians are not a burden.*
>
> (ATH2.15, woman from Syria, Athens)

Going further, this woman also stresses that the civil war in Syria is a *'universal war'*, in which Syrians are *'just a pawn in their hands and they are playing with us – Russia and America and Europe and Saudi Arabia and Qatar'*. Indeed, this is echoed by various Syrian men and women, who describe being *'a toy in the hands of politicians'* (ATH2.19, woman from Syria, Athens), as *'the major countries … make the decisions'* (ATH2.23, man from Syria, Athens). Such analyses lead to demands to *'stop messing with the Syrian people to get your own benefits'* (BER2.11, man from Syria, Berlin), as well as to appeals to *'help us solve the problem of our country'* (IST2.11, woman from Syria, Istanbul). In many cases *'the politics of the powerful countries'* are deemed to be accountable for *'bloodshed in Syria'* (IST2.16, woman from Syria, Istanbul), with Syrians claiming that *'what's going on in our country is all* [of] *European mak[ing]'* (BER2.09, man from Syria, Berlin). Nevertheless, it was not only Syrians who saw the EU as having a responsibility to make a difference in the countries people had travelled from in 2015 and 2016, but also Afghans and Iraqis. For instance, an Afghan man says: *'Do something for my country. First they should talk with the people who are responsible for destroying my country, Afghanistan. They should talk to them'* (ATH2.39, man from Afghanistan, Athens). International organisations, such as UN agencies, were also criticised in this context, with one couple from Afghanistan who we spoke to in Berlin describing UNHCR as *'so corrupted'* (BER2.16, couple from Afghanistan, Berlin). Going further, EU states were also criticised for benefitting from the conflicts that drive migration. For example, one man from Iraq argues that *'when they grant us asylum … they take … our share of our oil'* (BER2.14, man from Iraq, Berlin). In sum, what emerges from our counter-archive with people travelling along the eastern route is a series of demands for justice that hold the EU responsible for the conditions of conflict and instability that drive migration in the first place.

From people whose journeys were along the central Mediterranean route, a somewhat different series of demands emerged regarding the poor conditions in people's home regions. Though these were often posed in less direct and charged terms than those from along the eastern route, they also involved claims regarding the responsibility of the EU to address the injustices that drive migration. For example, a man from Ivory Coast claims that: *'Africa needs factories. If there is a factory, you have a job'* (MAL1.23, man from Ivory Coast, Malta). Along similar lines, a man from Gambia talks about the poverty and the need for a *'better life'* and *'education'* in his home country (SIC1.01, man from Gambia, Sicily). In more politicised terms, a man from Ethiopia claims the need for *'government change … But* [in the] *EU they don't want government change'* (MAL1.32A, man from Ethiopia, Malta). This sense that the EU could play a more active role in addressing various drivers and conditions of flight is more explicitly drawn out by a man from Mali, who suggests that: *'before* [European policy-makers] *focus on returning, stopping people to come and so on, does the money that they are spending to create so much stuff for nothing, waste of money … can* [they] *maybe at least try to build something for people – home – that make people stop coming?'* (MAL1.21, man from Mali, Malta).

These claims are significant in challenging the EU and its migration policy agenda. Notably, they also raise important insights regarding debates about the need to address the 'root causes of migration', which was an integral dimension of the 2015 *European Agenda on Migration* (European Commission, 2015b: 2). An emphasis on 'root causes' links development and migration issues, enabling border security concerns to be embedded in the provision of international aid and thus providing an effective way for the EU to meet its dual concern of upholding 'our international commitments and values while securing our borders' (European Commission, 2015b: 2). As such, it is worth noting that some of the demands advanced in the testimonies from our counter-archive appear to reflect an appreciation of EU development initiatives. For example, the question from the Malian man above potentially lends support to advocates of a preventative migration agenda, in particular where he asks: '*can* [they] *maybe at least try to build something for people – home*', making '*people stop coming*' (MALI.21, man from Mali, Malta). Nevertheless, we argue that a more nuanced account is required in order to appreciate the more critical dimensions of the demands for justice that such testimonies involve. This is partially hinted at in the claim by an Ethiopian man we spoke with in Malta, who said that Europe '*should make better decisions in terms of delivering aid*'. Going further, he suggests: '*Giving aid from government to government is not going to help. The government receives aid and uses it. The EU should focus on human rights issues if it's genuine about helping others*' (MALI.08, man from Ethiopia, Malta). As we shall see in the next section, the call for justice, *not* aid, is an important one that emerges from our counter-archive, because it involves more far-reaching challenges to the EU's preventative policy agenda. These demands for justice resonate with testimonies advanced along the eastern route, which similarly hold the EU responsible for migration drivers and intersecting conditions of flight. It is to such testimonies that we will now turn.

Testimonies for justice

In the last section, as well as in the preceding chapters of this book, we documented a range of demands for justice that emerge from our counter-archive of migratory testimonies with people on the move during 2015 and 2016. These range from calls for better living conditions and opportunities to work and study, through calls for family reunification and expedited asylum, relocation and settlement procedures, to calls for open borders, the freedom of movement and a life without discrimination and racism. Nevertheless, what also emerges from the analysis are two more far-reaching sets of demands that provide a direct contestation of the preventative agenda and the politics of crisis: demands for justice that highlight the EU's complicity in war and conflict across the Middle East, and demands for justice that highlight the EU's ineffective aid policies in sub-Saharan Africa. In different ways, these two sets of demands suggest that the EU is involved in producing or perpetuating the situations that drive migration, as well as in creating conditions that drive ongoing movements across multiple sites en route. By situating these claims in relation to EU attempts to address the 'root causes' of migration, what emerges from our counter-archive of Europe's so-called migrant crisis is an appreciation of how people on the move engage in more far-reaching contestations over long-standing colonial injustices and the forms of racialised violence through which these are sustained. Such contestations trouble the assumptions on which narratives of crisis rely, including perceptions of self/other in which people on the move in precarious conditions are viewed as 'threatening' criminals and/or as 'helpless' victims (see Chapters 1, 3 and 5). Specifically, this section emphasises two key ways such narratives, and the assumptions on which they rest, are challenged by people on the move: first, through testimonies that highlight the injustice of debates surrounding migration as a security 'threat' and, second, through testimonies that highlight the injustices of debates surrounding migration as a problem of humanitarian development.

Contesting securitisation

... use your brains, stop selling weapons to our country to kill ourselves ... go to Warschauer Strasse and see the pictures there. There are a big pictures ... you see pictures of war, images of war ... Very simply ... very simply stop interfering with our country, we will go back to our country. Stop bombing us. Stop the big lie which you have invented.

(BER2.26, man from Syria, Berlin)

It is because of instability in our countries that there are many illegal refugees [sic] coming into Europe. Total insecurity is pushing us to migrate. Politicians need to solve that issue. War is terrible, I have seen girls wearing bombs, I even know some of them. I left in order to not have to carry bombs and to have to blow myself up. If security issues are not solved, migration will only continue to increase. This is my message.

(ROM2.11, woman from Cameroon, Rome)

Demanding justice

The above quotes represent a direct challenge both to EU policy-makers and to securitising narratives of crisis. What is being suggested here is that, if the aim is to stop migration to Europe, then steps need to be taken to resolve warfare and conflict in the societies from which people migrate. We heard the testimony provided by the man from Syria at various times in different ways throughout our research along the eastern Mediterranean route, as those fleeing from a spiralling conflict focused attention on the role of powerful states in perpetuating warfare across the Middle East (see Samaddar, 2016). Testimonies such as that from the woman in Cameroon were heard less often, though claims regarding the role of conflict in driving migration did arise on various occasions along both the central and eastern routes. We suggest that, in the most basic sense, these statements can be interpreted as demands for peace. Whether the EU is directly targeted for its complicity and interest in perpetuating warfare in the regions people have travelled from (as indicated by the man from Syria), or called on to help solve issues of conflict (as indicated by the woman from Cameroon), such claims provide a challenge to the EU to do more to prevent (rather than perpetuate) conditions of war and conflict in the regions people flee from. Indeed, the migratory testimonies opening this section are particularly important, because they suggest that concerns regarding the potential spread of security 'threats' due to migration to the EU are both problematic *and* misplaced (see Chapter 1).

Many of the testimonies from our counter-archive along the eastern route suggest that in 2015 and 2016, continuing a longer trend, the EU ultimately 'closed its doors' to those seeking peace and safety. The following statements are indicative of the significance of this:

> *I was afraid to be taken to the army because normally the students are exempted for* [a] *temporary* [period] *to serve the army. But with my friend, they didn't allow them … so they went to the army. And I didn't want that to happen to me.* [without translation:] *I don't kill anyone.*
> (BER2.03, man from Syria, Berlin)

> *I had to serve in the army. And at the first checkpoint in the border, I will be taken away, because I, I didn't go to the army myself. I would be taken away to serve*

the army and carry the weapons to kill innocent people. I didn't want to carry the
blood in my name.

(BER2.22, man from Syria, Berlin)

I was called, summoned to the army, I didn't want to join the army. If I join the
army, I have to kill people. I don't want to kill anybody, not from inside either
[the] *opposition, or the regime. Furthermore, I wanted to do my postgraduate*
studies.

(BER2.30, man from Syria, Berlin)

This series of statements from various Syrian men interviewed in
Berlin all resonate strongly with each other in providing a clear specifica-
tion of the decision to migrate: in the face of forced conscription,
leaving Syria is deemed necessary in order that a commitment not to
kill others can be fulfilled. The first involves a direct statement – notably
without translation – that highlights the powerful conviction arising
from a refusal to kill. The second points to the threat of punishment
that occurs in the act of escaping from army forces. The third draws
attention to the ways in which forced conscription not only occurs at
the hands of the Syrian state, but also at the hands of opposition
forces. Collectively, the three testimonies represent a powerful contestation of warfare as this is advanced by both governmental and
oppositional forces in Syria. The migration of these three young men
would be defined as desertion from the perspective of the Syrian state
and, as such, would be deemed a punishable offence. Yet, from the
perspective of the young men making such statements, desertion is
better understood as a more fundamental rejection of the Syrian war
and as an act invoking the 'right to escape' (see Mezzadra, 2004).

Although migration as an act of escape from army conscription
is most directly enacted by young able-bodied men, as a gendered
process it also implicates different family members. For example,
the wife of a couple from Syria who we interviewed in Berlin
describes how the couple fled Syria together to escape her husband's
conscription:

There's something particular, which forced us to have ... to leave. We were forced
to leave Syria, because the Syrian regime wanted to call my husband to the army

*to serve the reserve. And so we had to flee as soon as possible before the ... getting
to the army, he doesn't want to kill any Syrians.*

(BER2.12, couple from Syria, Berlin)

In the context of civil war, desertion here stands as a matter of refusing
to be involved in the deaths of fellow citizens. Yet, more than simply
the affirmation of an anti-war stance, the escape of people on the
move from Syria might also be understood as 'anti-terrorist'. This is
evident in the statement of another young man we spoke with in
Berlin, who highlights as the primary reason for his decision to migrate
the risk of conscription by militant groups in conflict with the state,
as well as by the army:

> *I decided to leave because I didn't want to join the regular army, I didn't want to
> join the army at all. The city I live in, Daesh- ISIS controlled it. Their main
> objectives [are] ... to get all the young people to join them. I cannot flee to the
> regular territories which are under the control of the regime because they will take
> me [for] their army, [to] be a soldier in their army. That's why I had to flee
> Syria, to start a new life ... a new life again from the beginning.*
>
> (BER2.21, man from Syria, Berlin)

Based on these testimonies, we might understand the migration of
those fleeing warfare and terrorism as a pacifist movement, which
works against masculinist forms of military violence that emerge across
various sites and that serve as a driving force conditioning the lived
experiences of many people who take flight (see Jabri, 2013).

While many of the testimonies of escape from conscription were
advanced by people travelling along the eastern route from Syria via
Turkey and Greece, we also spoke with people along the central route
who had experiences of fleeing the army. For example, one man from
Eritrea describes how he limited his period of national service by
working as a teacher for the government, only to be punished when
he left his position:

> *I have started to working in teaching* [in Eritrea for the government] *... first
> of all* [I did] *national service and the pocket money ...* [then I was teaching,
> but the money] *... it is not enough,* [you] *cannot buy anything ... I ask to
> the government to leave the teaching to join another work, but* [I was] *not allowed
> to do another work ... Then I decided to change myself, I left teaching and I ...*

do another work, a business. Then after six years the policemen come and take me
to prison. I [was i]*n the prison two years and six months.*
(ROM2.26, man from Eritrea, Rome)

What is highlighted in this statement and across the various testimonies
in this section is that precarious migration often involves forms of escape
that challenge assumptions about the risks posed to the EU by people
on the move. While war and conflict emerge here as key drivers of
flight that are conditioned by gender in significant ways, in focusing on
forced conscription what also emerges is a sense that migration in this
context might in and of itself be understood as an 'anti-war movement'
that is grounded in the act of desertion (Squire, 2020b). The work of
Mezzadra is insightful here, in suggesting that 'desertion, as a figure of
civil disobedience, has been almost a privileged way to subjectivity, a
road to freedom and independence' (Mezzadra, 2004: 267). While the
various testimonies of people we interviewed suggest that this may be
a rather optimistic and somewhat limited view of escape, it is also worth
recalling the ambivalence of desertion as a concept and practice that
not only involves an act of abandonment, but also an act of refusal or
renouncement (Squire, 2015b). Indeed, it is precisely in terms of this
refusal that migration can be viewed as contesting a situation in which
people are forced to fight in conflicts that they do not support. Far from
posing a danger or security 'threat' to the EU, migration in this regard
involves escape to an EU that projects itself as a place of peace and
safety (see Chapters 3–5). As such, these forms of flight might be
understood as forming part of an anti-war or 'peace movement' that
precisely *rejects* the violence of conflict and warfare.

Contesting development

… many people are leaving Gambia, many youth men are coming this way, they
are coming because of problem, not because I like to go Europe, no.
(ROM2.27, man from Gambia, Rome)

Wars, people dying even now. We have been losing agriculture and there is no rain
… there is no agriculture … The women, they buy things and put [them] *in*

Demanding justice

front of their house, [I am] *told they just buy and sell, this is the life. Difficult, the life out there* [in Sudan].

(ROM2.28, man from Sudan, Rome)

While a rejection of war and conflict was most prominent in the testimonies of those travelling along the eastern route, the testimonies of those along the central Mediterranean route indicate that warfare is often not an isolated driver of migration. As the man from Sudan quoted above indicates, the decision to migrate is often the result of multiple drivers, including war and conflict, as well as poverty and environmental deterioration. Indeed, the Gambian man quoted above suggests that it is not the *pull* of Europe that is significant for many who escape regions of origin, but rather the drive of a diverse range of *'problems'* that make life untenable in various states in sub-Saharan Africa (ROM2.27; see Chapter 3). As we saw in Chapter 4, most people on the move along this route travelled from Libya or sometimes Egypt to Italy in 2015 and 2016, though the journeys that they had taken beforehand were wide-ranging, fragmented, and often lasted for months or even years. Many people had passed from one place to another in the attempt to find reprieve from their difficulties, only to experience further difficulties along the way. As we saw in the first section of this chapter, on asking our research participants what they would say to EU politicians or policy-makers if they had the chance to do so, many made claims about the need for action to be taken to improve the situation in the regions they had travelled from. Yet, while such claims might initially be viewed as a demand for the improved distribution and application of development aid from EU states, we argue that on closer consideration they appear to involve a more fundamental rejection of the colonial legacies that impact on many of those travelling along the central Mediterranean route.

Let us consider the following statement by a man from Sierra Leone. On first sight, this appears to support recent moves by the EU to enhance development aid in addressing migration. He says:

> . . . *what I think they should do is to sit down with our Head of States, try to solve, because there are some certain problems in Africa, yes, the governments must amend, yes, especially the problem of corruption, corruption is so much in Africa*

Reclaiming migration

... So the problem of corruption they should try and amend it, try hard for children to go to school. As for me I dropped out of school, yes I dropped out from school because of monetary issue, yes, so they should support education ...

(ROM2.29, man from Sierra Leone, Rome)

This claim that EU leaders need to address development problems and support efforts to educate children, in collaboration with African leaders, reflects some of the core tenets of the recent move by the EU to enhance aid and investment programmes in regions of departure, despite corruption itself being a notoriously sensitive issue. An emphasis on third country partnerships, work compacts in regions neighbouring conflict zones, investment in trust funds, and the tying of border security to development aid are all important aspects of an established migration–development agenda that has taken on a new lease of life over recent years.[1] However, if we continue reading the statement by the man from Sierra Leone directly from where we left off, it becomes clear that what is being advanced is a much more complex claim:

... yes, and help at least the people because [in] Africa we are very poor, yes, but we are rich again, in my country we are very rich, but the people are very poor, my country situation, it's a rich country, poor people, yes, because we have plenty things if we can utilise them properly our country will be good, so they need to sit down with our Head of State try to know some of our problems if possible, they solve them for us.

(ROM2.29, man from Sierra Leone, Rome)

That the people of Sierra Leone are described as poor while the country itself is described as '*rich again*' is important here, because it highlights the impacts of processes of dispossession that have a long history in colonial (and, indeed, postcolonial) governing practices. This is an issue that is directly referred to in this interview, where the man from Sierra Leone expresses his love for England and the English as his '*colonial masters*' (ROM2.29). Interestingly, what this suggests is that even if colonialism might somehow be accepted on one level, the colonial legacies that impact on those who are driven to migrate are not. Indeed, a rejection of colonial legacies is evident across a range of testimonies advanced by those travelling along the central Mediterranean route, as we shall see.

Demanding justice

While some of the people we spoke with appeared to have trust in the capacity and willingness of EU states to facilitate positive change in African states, others did not. As one man from Ivory Coast stresses:

> *I never saw a real action taken by the EU that can make really change in Africa. So if this are all problems from Africa, if the European want to solve it, I know they can solve it … Listen, if you go to my country for example, in Ivory Coast … the Europeans of those who colonise us they have a lot of organisations, or* [organisations run] *by the government by the country of Europe to cooperate with our government in my country. You know you want to help this, you want to do that, to open projects but in reality when you look at the project they open and* [at] *what they said that they are doing or* [what] *the project is for … what you will found them doing is really totally different. You know?*
>
> (MAL1.22, man from Ivory Coast, Malta)

Explicitly highlighting colonial dynamics that recur in the actions of contemporary aid organisations operating in Africa, this statement raises far-reaching questions about the role that development plays in making a change to situations that drive migration.

Strikingly, the testimony of three Nigerian women also poses a direct challenge to the contemporary inequalities and racialised dynamics that are associated with long-standing colonial legacies. On being asked whether they believed they have the right to enter EU territory, the women answer as follows:

> ROM2.06b: *To enter?*
> Interviewer: *To enter Europe, or Italy?*
> ROM2.06c: *Yeah.* [I think we have the right to enter.]
> Interviewer: *Why would you say that?*
> ROM2.06c: *White people normally go to Nigeria, they are safe, they are ok. I know that very well. So everybody I want, you know God created everybody.*
> ROM2.06a: *Everybody have equal rights.*
> ROM2.06c: *So it is the same. Everybody is free. You are free to go to Nigeria, there is your choice. So your push allows us enter Italy freely without no problem, that is what we want.*
>
> (ROM2.06, three women from Nigeria, Rome)

This exchange is critical, because the right of EU states to exclude people from migrating to their territory is explicitly denied and presented as an unequal racialised process in the testimony of these three women (see Anievas et al., 2015). Far from representing a request for the EU to provide more effective aid and support to African states, this statement can be interpreted as a contestation both of the unequal right to movement that is embedded in the EU's preventative policy framework, and of longer colonial histories and practices of dispossession that condition contemporary migratory dynamics. Acts of escape might be interpreted in this regard as forming part of a postcolonial or 'anti-colonial movement' that rejects the forms of racialised violence on which EU migration policies are built.

Reclaiming migration

The analysis in the last section suggested that the movement of people across the Mediterranean Sea in 2015 and 2016 can be understood in terms of acts of escape from enforced conscription, as well as from a range of problems attributed to the ongoing colonial legacies that condition Europe's postcolonial present (see also Chapter 5). We have suggested that migration in this regard forms a 'peace movement' and an 'anti-colonial movement', rather than representing a security 'threat' and indicator of the need for 'more development' as the 2015 *Agenda* implies. What we hope is clear from the above analysis is that the migratory testimonies from our counter-archive do not suggest that 'rich democracies' *should* intervene more effectively in regions of origin and transit in order to 'repel' people on the move. Rather, they collectively advance demands for a more fundamental transformation of the EU's policy agenda, in order that the underpinning drivers and conditions of flight are openly addressed. For some, this involves the rejection of a military industry that capitalises on warfare and conflict (BER2.26), while for others it means rejecting global injustices and situations of generalised instability (ROM2.28; ROM2.06). Ultimately, the testimonies do not suggest that people on the move want EU states to do development better, but rather that people seek justice through having the equal right to migrate (or, indeed, remain), and for those migrating under precarious conditions to be treated humanely and with respect. In other words, the testimonies do not collectively support dominant perceptions of the need to address 'root causes' or reiterate an appeal to humanitarianism, but instead advance a more far-reaching critique of the EU's preventative policy agenda in terms that reject the very assumptions on which such policies are built.

To put it another way, our counter-archive of Europe's so-called 'migrant crisis' provides an opportunity to revive imaginations surrounding migration beyond the terms in which current debates appear to be caught. In his discussion of the work of the Amazonian anthropologist, Viveiros de Castro, Skafish (2009: 10) highlights the importance of research that is appreciative of 'the theoretical imaginations of all peoples'. He suggests that this contributes to the 'permanent decolonisation of thought', by drawing out 'coordinates, values, suppositions and truths' that 'throw our own into disarray' (Skafish, 2009: 10, 18). Adapting such an insight for the purposes of this book, our analysis of Europe's so-called migrant crisis does more than simply 'rehumanise' those who are dehumanised; it also seeks to expose counter-narratives that *disrupt* dominant conceptions of what it means to 'be human' (see also Squire, 2015a, 2020a). While a strategy of 'rehumanisation' can be important in a context marked by the racialised dehumanisation of people on the move, in its humanitarian form it can also preclude an ability to 'think about how we might forge a different future' (Ticktin, 2016: 263). Such a strategy is inherently problematic if it involves humanity being granted by those in positions of privilege, rather than being 'taken' by those who claim it (see Chapter 2): this would further embed the hierarchies and injustices of a universalist conception of 'Man' (Wynter, 2003). By contrast, an analysis that is grounded in appreciation of the biographical detail, experiential expertise and political demands of people on the move provides critical opportunities for a more exhaustive revival of theoretical imaginations and, indeed, a *reclaiming* of migration from the preventative agenda that has become so dominant in the EU context. People on the move in this regard play a crucial role not only as 'experts' of migration, but also as 'theorists' of migration – and indeed of world politics – in their own right (see Chapter 2; see McLaughlin, 1996).

One example of this type of attempt to revive theoretical imaginations might be viewed in the work of Achiume, who argues that contemporary migration can be understood as a form of 'decolonisation' that emerges in response 'to the asymmetrical … structure of co-dependence' that was forged on the basis of migration from Europe during the colonial period (Achiume, 2017: 142). She points to the ways in which migration from Europe stood as an indefinite arrangement of colonial advantage, and makes the case for a 'new logic, ethics and lens' for the application of international law to global migration (Achiume, 2017: 142). Defining decolonisation as a 'geopolitical reordering of benefits of a global order defined by interdependence forged in the colonial era' (Achiume, 2017: 145), Achiume argues that individuals who 'move across international borders fleeing *or rejecting* severe political-economic conditions and the fall-out of these conditions' take an important first step towards the process of decolonisation (Achiume, 2017: 145, original emphasis). Drawing on the insights of those who contributed testimonies for our counter-archive, we go further to demonstrate in concrete terms how Achiume's argument could be said to reflect precisely a dynamic that is overlooked in wider political debates surrounding migration and development. Taking the demands of people who migrate as a starting point, in other words, points directly to the ways in which addressing people on the move as experts of migration can revive theoretical imaginations in terms that highlight and potentially move beyond the violent and hierarchical relations that are embedded in long-standing structures of colonial power (Achiume, 2017: 142). Reclaiming migration in such terms, we argue, is a critical endeavour.

Beyond Achiume's analysis, the testimonies of people on the move clarify further how to direct the decolonisation of migration policies towards *justice*. In broad terms, the testimonies examined in this chapter imply that it is not more or better aid that is required, but a more fundamental restructuring of the geopolitical scene and the injustices that render cross-border travel the privilege of primarily white global elites (see Sheller, 2016). Moreover, rather than advocating for peace-building or conflict-prevention efforts, what people on the move collectively propose is a more fundamental rejection of geopolitical investments in conflict and warfare that promote situations in which escape becomes the only option to stay alive. These are, of course, far-reaching critiques that expose dynamics that are hardly hidden, but that are nevertheless rarely connected in wider political debates surrounding migration. Although the question of how to put these changes into motion is a challenging one, what this book seeks to emphasise is that this challenge is not going to disappear simply by further rolling out preventative policies. In more modest terms, people on the move do advance a range of demands in terms that precisely suggest ways forward for migration policies that are oriented towards the promotion of justice. Developing legal migration routes rather than investing in anti-smuggling, extending qualifications for family reunification in recognition of diverse familial units, diversifying protection mechanisms in appreciation of the cumulative traumas of precarious journeys, exposing and rejecting corruption and the complicity of powerful states in situations of conflict and dispossession: these are all proposals that emerge from the testimonies of people on the move, whose theoretical imaginations offer opportunities for reclaiming migratory politics in both creative and critical terms. In sum, what the analysis in this chapter suggests is that these alternative ways to address migration simply cannot be ignored.

Conclusion

This chapter has highlighted how an approach which engages the testimonies of people on the move as a form of 'expert' knowledge brings to bear a range of demands for justice, which should be understood in the broadest sense as constituting migration as a collective movement striving towards peace and equality (see also Squire, 2020b). On the one hand, people escaping warfare and enforced conscription highlight the ways in which militarist violence infringes on a personal commitment not to kill. In appealing to EU policy-makers to '*stop selling weapons*' and '*stop bombing us*' (BER2.26, man from Syria, Berlin), the demands of people on the move are better understood as representing a 'peace movement' than as a security 'threat' as is so often assumed. On the other hand, people escaping war, conflict, poverty, environmental changes, corruption and a lack of services highlight the ways that EU states are implicated in long-standing colonial dynamics of violence and dispossession that create conditions of '*total insecurity*' (ROM2.11, woman from Cameroon, Rome). Such demands are better understood as constituting an 'anti-colonial movement' rather than a plea for development aid. Indeed, in Achiume's (2017) terms these can also be understood as forming the 'first step' towards a process of decolonisation, in which long-standing relations of racialised violence and colonial advantage are questioned and begin to be unmade. On this basis, the analysis in this chapter suggests that the testimonies of people on the move unlock opportunities for a renewal of theoretical imaginations and migratory politics in terms that throw the existing policy agenda into disarray. Far from a request for EU states to do development better, as the emphasis on 'root causes' assumes, people on the move across the Mediterranean during 2015 and 2016 advance wide-ranging demands for justice that problematise the grounds on which such policies are built (see Suliman, 2016). This poses a vital question which EU policy-makers need to respond to: will a preventative agenda, justified through the linkage of border security and humanitarian development, be pursued regardless of its impacts on people on the move, or will the relentless struggles and demands of people on the move finally be heard?

Notes

1 The UN's (2018) global compact on migration and the 2030 Agenda for Sustainable Development are key in this regard.

Conclusion: Precarity, justice, postcoloniality

This book critically reclaims the contested politics of mobility on the basis of a detailed engagement with the demands of those who are often silenced in debates surrounding migration: people directly undertaking fragmented journeys, and living first-hand the precarious experience of arriving to the EU under conditions of so-called crisis. It does so with a commitment to respecting people on the move as those who are best placed to provide insights into the effects of policy developments in the field of migration, and with an appreciation of the importance of listening and responding to the demands that emerge from the migratory struggles of people, which otherwise largely go unheard (see Chapter 2). Indeed, one of the overarching arguments advanced by *Reclaiming Migration* is that a preventative policy agenda will continue to fail so long as people on the move are excluded from debates in the field of migratory politics. Providing opportunities for people to take or claim voice, when they are otherwise ignored, is thus critical. We have consequently developed our analysis through a sustained engagement with the counter-archive of migratory testimonies that we produced with people on the move across the Mediterranean in 2015 and 2016. These testimonies collectively expose the ways current debates reflect a limitation of the scope of what can be said surrounding migration, in terms that are profoundly harmful for those who form the focus of the EU's preventative policy agenda.

Reclaiming migration

The criticality of such an approach needs to be clarified in light of what we emphasise as the *productive* nature of the EU's failing policy agenda. *Reclaiming Migration* highlights the ways in which policy failure both drives and is driven by a form of crisis politics – one which renders people on the move as precarious in both securitising *and* humanitarian terms (see Chapter 1). The book has shown how deterrence as a form of racialised violence is ultimately ineffective in meeting its aims, with attempts to prevent people from migrating ultimately missing their target (see Chapter 3). Yet, beyond highlighting the primacy of various drivers and conditions of flight and underscoring the cumulative nature of precarity arising from migration across the Mediterranean in 2015 and 2016 (see Chapter 4), our analysis also suggests that deterrence is bound up with a form of crisis politics that *thrives* on the failure to deter people from making perilous journeys across the sea by boat. Failure in this regard drives concerns about the security 'threat' that migration poses to states and their citizens, which are often manifest in the problematic and unfounded association of migration with 'terrorism' (Nail, 2016b). Failure also steers concerns about the humanitarian challenges that arise where people move en masse in what appears, from the perspective of states, to be disorderly ways – in particular where death is a frequent outcome of such journeys. Paradoxically, the very failure of a preventative policy agenda in its attempt to stop migration, which employs *both* security *and* humanitarian measures, fuels increasingly extensive (and intensive) preventative policies. As such, we argue that a politics of crisis produces and perpetuates the precarity of people on the move, whose repeated calls for justice in the face of racialised violence so often go unnoticed (see Chapters 4–6).

Based on these insights, our claim that a preventative policy agenda will continue to fail so long as people on the move are excluded from debates in the field of migratory politics needs to be qualified. Indeed, we do not suggest that migratory testimonies must be engaged in order that prevention or deterrence is made *more effective*. On the contrary, we argue that an appreciation of the claims and demands advanced by people on the move is critical because the silencing of such voices

Conclusion

reflects a form of epistemic violence that precisely relies on claims to justice remaining *hidden*. Epistemic violence, as it is understood here, is not separate from forms of violence that are structural (e.g. Davies et al., 2017) or that operate in physical and material terms (e.g. Squire, 2015a). Rather, we understand epistemic violence to be integral to long-standing legacies of violence that are bound up with recurring colonial relations and dynamics (see Chapter 2). That these legacies and their current manifestations are hidden in debates about migration policy is a critical concern, because this serves to divest the preventative agenda from its wider politics while justifying its advancement in both securitising and humanitarian terms (see Chapter 1). Our contention is that it is critical to engage people migrating as having life histories and lived experiences that need to be understood, and as having claims or demands for justice that need to be taken into account; it is only then that we can begin to overturn trajectories of racialised violence in which we are all implicated. The claims of people on the move in precarious conditions are therefore critical in rejecting – and beginning the work of undoing – Europe's postcolonial present (see Chapters 5 and 6). Our analysis of migratory testimonies is precisely oriented towards the task of engaging with those who expose the injustices of the contemporary policy agenda to advance demands for justice that move in a direction of decolonisation.

While the argument advanced here is specific to the EU context and to the so-called European migrant crisis of 2015–16, it is also of broader significance both geographically and in light of the long-standing colonial relations and racialised forms of violence that our analysis exposes. Nevertheless, there are also some critical points that we want to emphasise here in order to qualify the analysis developed in the book, which engages claims and demands that emerge directly from migratory struggles across the Mediterranean in 2015 and 2016. Reflecting the anti-crisis framework outlined in Chapter 1, these qualifying points will be developed in the remainder of this concluding chapter along the lines of three key themes that have emerged from the analysis: precarity, justice and postcoloniality. First, we emphasise precarity as a multidimensional condition, which is not only manifest in the lived experiences of those who escape to Europe but also in the experiences of those who refuse to take flight or are unable to flee. Second, we highlight how claims to justice are not simply oriented towards movement, but also need to be appreciated as claims to settlement that reject the EU's positionality as 'host' to newly arriving migrants. Finally, we reiterate our argument regarding the recurring colonial dynamics of the contemporary policy agenda, to suggest that the voices of people on the move who speak out against a postcolonial present can no longer be ignored. We will briefly examine each of these three themes in turn.

Precarity

The approach that has guided our analysis of the counter-archive engaged in this book is mapped in Chapter 1, which highlights three key insights that emerge from an anti-crisis frame of analysis. The first of these relates to the securitising narratives of the so-called crisis, in which migration is perceived as a security 'threat' to EU states and their citizens. As noted in Chapter 1, an anti-crisis approach facilitates appreciation of the violence – or what a woman from Cameroon describes as the '*total insecurity*' – that drives people to migrate (ROM2.11, woman from Cameroon, Rome). This lies in stark contrast to an approach that engages migration as a security issue from a state-centric perspective, which is significant because it enables appreciation of the ways in which violence is enacted against people on the move. For example, in Chapter 3 we considered how racialised violence is enacted against people migrating by state authorities as well as by smuggling networks, thus undermining the dichotomous logic of 'good' police versus 'bad' smugglers on which anti-smuggling is based from within a deterrence paradigm. Our analysis also highlighted the ways in which a preventative policy agenda drives people into increasingly dangerous journeys, as routes are closed despite the ongoing and cumulative nature of precarity described in Chapter 4 with reference

Conclusion

to multiple 'drivers and conditions of flight'. By focusing on the *lived experiences* of racialised bordering practices, we have thus shown how a preventative policy agenda renders migratory journeys all the more perilous. Indeed, we have shown this to be the case not only during the dangerous journey across the Mediterranean Sea, but also on arrival to the EU where many face continued challenges and harms. The analysis developed here does not advocate a shift of the referent object of security from the state to the 'refugee', as a humanitarian narrative of crisis would imply (see Chapter 1), yet it nevertheless emphasises the harms people are exposed to through the EU's rolling out of preventative policies.

Reclaiming Migration emphasises the multiple forms of precarity that people face throughout the migratory process, which not only involves mobility but also immobility as a form of 'strandedness' or 'stuckedness' (see Chapter 4). Precarity, in our analysis, can thus be understood as a multidimensional condition, which is not only manifest in situations of mobility, but also in situations of *im*mobility. Indeed, many of our testimonies indicate that precarity is not only evident in the lived experiences of those who escape to the EU, but also in the experiences of those who refuse to take flight or are unable to flee. While this book has focused primarily on the experiences of those who successfully made the journey across the Mediterranean Sea by boat, it has also considered the experiences of those stuck in Turkey who had tried and/or were contemplating making the journey to Greece. People we spoke with also often described the situation at home and referred to family members left behind. Sometimes people hinted that they would prefer to return home and face death, rather than to live without dignity in the EU (see Chapter 5). Indeed, one limitation we face is in providing a detailed analysis of testimonies about the conditions of precarity that are produced and perpetuated through policies that operate far beyond EU territory, and in the claims to immobility as well as mobility that emerge in such contexts. Nevertheless, some insights regarding these areas do emerge in this book, such as in the critique advanced by people on the move along the eastern route regarding

Reclaiming migration

the complicity of EU states in conflict situations such as that in Syria (see Chapter 6). Further research in this area remains crucial, particularly in the context of the increasing drive towards externalised policy-making as discussed in Chapter 3. What our analysis indicates is that people live through experiences of mobility and immobility that are not only physically perilous, but also socially and psychologically harmful. Far from an external security 'threat' to Europe, people on the move thus emerge from our analysis as courageous figures who experience challenges at every step of the way in their search for peace and safety.

Justice

The second key insight that emerges from our anti-crisis framework discussed in Chapter 1 relates to humanitarian narratives of crisis, in which people on the move are presented as victims in need of humanitarian succour. By distancing our analysis from one oriented towards a narrative of humanitarian crisis, we have drawn attention to the multiple demands that people on the move advance in the context of the lived experiences of precarity highlighted in the last section. As discussed in Chapter 5, distinct demands are driven by particular needs both en route and within the EU, which derive from distinct biographical trajectories and context-specific situations. Rather than advancing an analysis of claims and demands that are confined to the limited politics of asylum and protection, as discussed in Chapter 4, an anti-crisis approach thus leads us to engage the testimonies from our counter-archive in more nuanced terms, in which various claims to rights, protection and justice all come into play. Chapters 5 and 6, especially, have highlighted how a counter-archive of Europe's so-called migrant crisis brings to bear a range of claims to justice. Showing how people on the move in 2015 and 2016 contested the unequal right to free movement embedded in the EU's preventative policy framework, Chapter 6 advanced the idea that migration forms a collective movement for peace and equality that enacts a mode of decolonisation. Our counter-archive of migratory testimonies in this regard brings to bear

Conclusion

'unstated histories' (Stoler, 2002: 90), which open up the 'non-juridical justice of the archives' (Shapiro, 2013: 83) through claims advanced 'in the name of equality' (Rancière, 2004).

Despite our specific focus in this book on claims to justice that emerge in the context of migration to the EU in 2015 and 2016, it is important to emphasise that claims to justice are not simply orientated to movement, but also engage various demands related to settlement. This is evident, for example, in Chapters 4 and 5, where we highlight the ways in which people on the move claim the right to housing, work and education on arrival to the EU. It is also evident in Chapter 6, where people advance various demands regarding the need for action to be taken to mitigate the conditions that drive migration in order to facilitate resettlement in people's home regions. To put it in other terms, claims to justice do not simply emerge as claims to migration in our counter-archive, but involve multiple claims to the right of movement *and* settlement. This rests on an understanding of the EU as involved in producing or perpetuating the situations that drive migration, as well as in creating conditions that drive ongoing movements across multiple sites (see Chapter 6). This insight is significant, because it indicates that the testimonies from our counter-archive represent a collective rejection of the EU's assumed position as 'host' to newly arriving migrants. By contrast, *Reclaiming Migration* suggests that migration is engaged by people on the move as a right to be respected amidst a range of demands that are not simply about mobility, and in terms that expose long-standing relations that undermine any straightforward distinction between guest/host or self/other. The arguments raised in *Reclaiming Migration* are therefore not restricted to 2015 and 2016 and have enduring relevance to present-day migration policy. We now turn to the third theme of postcoloniality.

Postcoloniality

The third key insight that emerges from our anti-crisis approach outlined in Chapter 1 refers to the emergency framing of 'Europe's migrant crisis', which cuts across both securitising and humanitarian narratives of the situation in the Mediterranean during 2015–16. Rather than emphasising discontinuity or a moment of rupture and emergency that requires exceptional measures, an anti-crisis approach highlights elements of *continuity* that persist over time and space. This is important to the postcolonial perspective developed throughout this book, which focuses attention on the ways in which a preventative policy agenda reflects colonial legacies of a longer duration. There are various ways in which these legacies emerge from the analysis of our counter-archive of migratory testimonies. Beyond an emphasis on the epistemic violence involved in processes of silencing (see Chapter 2), *Reclaiming Migration* also points to the racialised violence of the deterrence paradigm (see Chapter 3), the colonial ties hidden in plain sight within the EU's asylum and protection regime (see Chapter 4), and the hierarchies of the 'human' that are embedded in the projection of Europe as a place of human rights, peace and safety (see Chapter 5). Indeed, we also draw attention to the key role that EU states play in producing and perpetuating the very drivers and conditions of flight (see Chapter 6). On this basis, we argue that our counter-archive presents a fundamental challenge to the colonial legacies of the European project. Not only do the migratory testimonies collectively demand that the EU honour its own values and commitments (see Chapter 5); they also form part of a broader movement that begins the crucial work of 'unmaking' the postcolonial present (see Chapter 6).

The question as to how far the policies and measures advanced through the 2015 *Agenda* can be understood to reflect a *direct* continuation of colonial dynamics remains an open one as we approach the final stages of this book. We have suggested that, beyond a simple continuation of colonial legacies, the preventative policy agenda represents a postcolonial present that involves Europe as much as it does its 'others' (Bhambra, 2016). This can be understood in terms of recurring dynamics, which involve new dimensions rather than straightforwardly representing continuity in a strict sense (see Lemberg-Pedersen, 2019). Critically, we have drawn attention to the ways in which such recurring

Conclusion

dynamics are contested by people on the move themselves, through what we have called a broader movement towards peace and equality in which acts of migration begin the work of decolonising the post-colonial present (see Achiume, 2017). Taking this movement seriously, we appreciate our own implication in the dynamics and relations that mark the postcolonial present, and as such seek to reject an extractive approach to knowledge acquisition through our own academic practice (see Tilley, 2018). This is by no means a straightforward process, as indicated in Chapter 2. However, we hope to have provided an intervention that advances critical practices of knowledge production in the fields of migration and border studies, while also contributing to wider struggles against the multiple forms of violence that the 2015 *Agenda* represents. *Reclaiming Migration* is in this regard a product of the demands and claims advanced by people on the move as much as it is an academic analysis advanced by us as authors. This reflects our appreciation of those who speak out against a postcolonial present, and whose voices we refuse to ignore.

Bibliography

Achiume, E. T. (2017) 'Reimagining international law for global migration: migration as decolonisation?', *AJIL Unbound* 111, 142–146.

Albahari, M. (2016) *Crimes of Peace: Mediterranean Migrations at the World's Deadliest Border*. Philadelphia, PA: University of Pennsylvania Press.

Amnesty International (2013) *Scapegoats of Fear: Rights of Refugees, Asylum-Seekers and Migrants Abused in Libya*, Amnesty International website, available at: www. amnestyusa.org/reports/scapegoats-of-fear-rights-of-refugees-asylum-seekers-and-migrants-abused-in-libya/ (accessed 13 June 2019).

Amnesty International (2015) *A Safer Sea: The Impact of Increased Search and Rescue Operations in the Central Mediterranean*, available at: www.amnesty.org/download/ Documents/EUR0320592015ENGLISH.pdf (accessed 23 May 2019).

Anderson, B. (2018) 'Towards a new politics of migration?', *Ethnic and Racial Studies* 40:9, 1527–1537.

Anderson, B., N. Sharma, and C. Wright (2012) '"We are all foreigners": no borders as a practical political project', in P. Nyers and K. Rygiel (eds) *Citizenship, Migrant Activism, and the Politics of Movement*. London: Routledge, pp. 73–90.

Andersson, R. (2014) *Illegality, Inc*. Oakland, CA: University of California Press.

Anievas, A., N. Manchanda and R. Shilliam (2015) 'Confronting the global colour line: an introduction', in A. Anievas, N. Manchanda and R. Shilliam (eds) *Race and Racism in International Relations: Confronting the Global Colour Line*. London and New York: Routledge, pp. 1–15.

Aradau, C. (2004) 'The perverse politics of four-letter words: risk and pity in the securitisation of human trafficking', *Millenium* 33:2, 251–277.

Bauman, Z. (2016) *Strangers at our Door*. Cambridge: Polity Press.

Benedicto, A. R. and P. Brunet (2018) *Building Walls: Fear and Securitization in the European Union*. Barcelona: Centre Delàs d'Estudis per la Pau, available at: www.tni.org/files/publication-downloads/building_walls_-_full_report_-_english. pdf (accessed 23 May 2019).

Bergold, J. and S. Thomas (2012) 'Participatory research methods: a methodological approach in motion', *Historical Social Research* 37:4, 191–222.

Bibliography

Bhambra, G. (2016) 'Whither Europe? Postcolonial versus neo-colonial cosmopolitanism', *Interventions: International Journal of Postcolonial Studies* 18:2, 187–202.

Bialasiewicz, L. (ed.) (2011) *Europe in the World: EU Geopolitics and the Making of European Space*. Farnham: Ashgate.

Bialasiewicz, L. (2012) 'Off-Shoring and out-sourcing the borders of Europe: Libya and EU border work in the Mediterranean', *Geopolitics* 17:4, 843–866.

Casas-Cortes, M. and S. Cobarrubias (2019) 'Genealogies of contention in concentric circles: remote migration control and its Eurocentric geographical imaginaries', in K. Mitchell, R. Jones, and J. Fluri (eds) *Handbook on Critical Geographies of Migration*. Cheltenham: Edward Elgar, pp. 193–205.

Chouliaraki, L. and P. Musaro (2017) 'The mediatised border: technologies and affects of migrant reception in the Greek and Italian borders', *Feminist Media Studies* 17:4, 535–549.

Chouliaraki, L. and R. Zaborowski (2017) 'Voice and community in the 2015 refugee crisis: a content analysis of news coverages in eight European countries', *International Communication Gazette* 79:6–7, 613–635.

Collyer, M. (2007) 'In-between places: trans-Saharan transit migrants in Morocco and the fragmented journey to Europe', *Antipode* 39:4, 668–690.

Collyer, M. (2010) 'Stranded migrants and the fragmented journey', *Journal of Refugee Studies* 23:3, 273–293.

Crawley, H. (2016) 'Managing the unmanageable? Understanding Europe's response to the migration "crisis"', *Human Geography* 9:2, 13–23.

Crawley, H., F. Duvell, K. Jones, S. McMahon, and N. Sigona (2017) *Unravelling Europe's Migration 'Crisis': Journeys Over Lands and Sea*. Bristol: Policy Press.

Crawley, H. and D. Skleparis (2017) 'Refugees, migrants, neither, both: categorical fetishism and the politics of bounding in Europe's "migration crisis"', *Journal of Ethnic and Migration Studies* 44:1, 48–64.

Danewid, I. (2017) 'White innocence in the Black Mediterranean: hospitality and the erasure of history', *Third World Quarterly* 38:7, 1674–1689.

Dauvergne, C. (2012) *Making People Illegal: What Globalisation means for Migration and Law*. Cambridge: Cambridge University Press.

Davies, T., A. Isakjee, and S. Dhesi (2017) 'Violent inaction: the necropolitical experience of refugees in Europe', *Antipode* 49:5, 1263–1284.

Davis Cross, M. K. (2017) *The Politics of Crisis in Europe*. Cambridge: Cambridge University Press.

De Genova, N. (2018) 'The "migrant crisis" as racial crisis: do *Black Lives Matter* in Europe?', *Ethnic and Racial Studies* 41:10, 1765–1782.

De Genova, N. and N. Peutz (eds) (2010) *The Deportation Regime: Sovereignty, Space, and the Freedom of Movement*. Durham, NC: Duke University Press.

de Haas, H. (2008) 'The myth of invasion: the inconvenient realities of African migration to Europe', *Third World Quarterly* 29:7, 1305–1322.

Derrida, J. (1995) 'Archive fever: a Freudian impression', *Diacritics* 25:2, 9–63.

Dijstelbloem, H. and A. Meijer (eds) (2011) *Migration and the New Technological Borders of Europe*. Basingstoke: Palgrave Macmillan.

Bibliography

Dines, N., N. Montana, and E. Vacchelli (2018) 'Beyond crisis talk: interrogating migration and crises in Europe', *Sociology* 52:3, 439–447.

Dotson, K. (2011) 'Tracking epistemic violence, tracking practices of silencing', *Hypatia: A Journal of Feminist Philosophy* 26:2, 236–257.

EACEA (2013) *At the Limen: The Implementation of the Return Directive in Italy, Cyprus and Spain*. Brussels: EACEA, available at: www.mugak.eu/en/documentation/at-the-limen-report-on-the-implementation-of-the-return-directive-in-spain-cyprus-and-italy (accessed 13 June 2019).

El-Enany, N. (2020) *(B)ordering Britain: Law, Race and Empire*. Manchester: Manchester University Press.

EUNAVFOR MED (2019) *About Us*, Operation Sophia website, available at: www.operationsophia.eu/about-us/ (accessed 23 May 2019).

European Commission (2011) *The Global Approach to Migration and Mobility*, Communication from the Commission to the European Parliament, the Council, the European Economic and Social Committee and the Committee of the Regions, available at: https://eur-lex.europa.eu/legal-content/EN/ALL/?uri=CELEX:52011DC0743 (accessed 18 May 2020).

European Commission (2015a) *Joint Foreign and Home Affairs Council: Ten Point Action Plan on Migration*, European Commission Press Release, available at: https://ec.europa.eu/commission/presscorner/detail/en/IP_15_4813 (accessed 21 July 2020).

European Commission (2015b) *A European Agenda on Migration*, Communication from the Commission to the European Parliament, the Council, the European Economic and Social Committee and the Committee of the Regions, 2015, available at: https://ec.europa.eu/home-affairs/sites/homeaffairs/files/what-we-do/policies/european-agenda-migration/background-information/docs/communication_on_the_european_agenda_on_migration_en.pdf (accessed 3 April 2019).

European Commission (2015c) *European Commission Makes Progress on Agenda on Migration*, European Commission Press Release, available at: https://ec.europa.eu/commission/presscorner/detail/en/IP_15_5039 (accessed 21 July 2020).

European Commission (2015d) *Refugee Crisis: European Commission Takes Decisive Action*, European Commission Press Release, available at: https://ec.europa.eu/commission/presscorner/detail/en/IP_15_5596 (accessed 21 July 2020).

European Commission (2015e) *Implementing the European Agenda on Migration: Progress Reports on Greece, Italy and the Western Balkans*, European Commission Press Release, available at: https://ec.europa.eu/commission/presscorner/detail/en/IP_15_6324 (accessed 21 July 2020).

European Commission (2015f) *Managing the Refugee Crisis: Immediate Operational, Budgetary and Legal Measures under the European Agenda on Migration*, European Commission Press Release, available at: https://ec.europa.eu/commission/presscorner/detail/en/IP_15_5700 (accessed 21 July 2020).

European Commission (2015g) 'Remarks by Commissioner Avramopoulos at the press conference in Castille Place, Malta', available at: https://ec.europa.eu/commission/presscorner/detail/fr/SPEECH_15_4840 (accessed 21 July 2020).

Bibliography

European Commission (2016a) *Enhancing Security in a World of Mobility*, available at: https://ec.europa.eu/home-affairs/sites/homeaffairs/files/what-we-do/policies/european-agenda-security/legislative-documents/docs/20160914/enhancing_security_in_a_world_of_mobility_en.pdf (accessed 21 July 2020).

European Commission (2016b) 'EU Operations in the Mediterranean Sea', Factsheet, available at: https://ec.europa.eu/home-affairs/sites/homeaffairs/files/what-we-do/policies/securing-eu-borders/fact-sheets/docs/20161006/eu_operations_in_the_mediterranean_sea_en.pdf (accessed 3 April 2019).

European Commission (2019) *Global Approach to Migration and Mobility*, Migration and Home Affairs website, available at: https://ec.europa.eu/home-affairs/what-we-do/policies/international-affairs/global-approach-to-migration_en (accessed 3 April 2019).

European Commission (2020) *European Agenda on Migration*, Migration and Home Affairs undated webpage, available at: https://ec.europa.eu/home-affairs/what-we-do/policies/european-agenda-migration_en (accessed 13 May 2020).

European Council (2016a) *EUNAVFOR MED Operation Sophia Authorised to Start Two Additional Supporting Tasks*, European Council Press Release, available at: www.statewatch.org/news/2016/aug/eu-council-sophia.pdf (accessed 23 May 2019).

European Council (2016b) *EUNAVFOR MED Operation Sophia: Mandate Extended by One Year, Two New Tasks Added*, European Council Press Release, available at: www.consilium.europa.eu/en/press/press-releases/2016/06/20/fac-eunavfor-med-sophia/ (accessed 30 June 2019).

European Council (2016c) *EU–Turkey Statement, 18 March 2016*, European Commission Press release, available at: www.consilium.europa.eu/en/press/press-releases/2016/03/18/eu-turkey-statement/ (accessed 16 September 2019).

European Union (2007) *Consolidated Version of the Treaty on European Union*, 13 December 2007, 2008/C 115/01, available at: www.refworld.org/docid/4b179f222.html (accessed 29 August 2019).

European Union (2008) *Directive 2008/115/EC of the European Parliament and of the Council of 16 December 2008 on Common Standards and Procedures in Member States for Returning Illegally Staying Third-Country Nationals*, EU Return Directive, available at: https://eur-lex.europa.eu/legal-content/EN/ALL/?uri=celex%3A32008L0115 (accessed 30 June 2019).

Fanon, F. (1967) *The Wretched of the Earth*. London: Penguin.

Fassin, D. (2012) *Humanitarian Reason: A Moral History of the Present*. Berkeley, CA: University of California Press, 2012.

Fassin, D. and M. Pandolfi (2013) *Contemporary States of Emergency: The Politics of Military and Humanitarian Interventions*. Cambridge, MA: Zone Books.

FitzGerald, D. (2019) *Refuge Beyond Reach: How Rich Democracies Repel Asylum Seekers*. Oxford: Oxford University Press.

Forensic Oceanography (2016) *Death by Rescue*, available at: https://deathbyrescue.org/report/narrative/ (accessed 3 April 2019).

Bibliography

Fricker, M. (2007) *Epistemic Injustice: Power and the Ethics of Knowing*. Oxford: Oxford University Press.

Frontex (2014) *People Smugglers: The Latter Day Slave Merchants*, Frontex website, 30 September 2014, available at: https://frontex.europa.eu/media-centre/focus/people-smugglers-the-latter-day-slave-merchants-UArKn1 (accessed 11 May 2020).

Frontex (2016) *Risk Analysis for 2016*. Warsaw: Frontex, available at: https://frontex.europa.eu/assets/Publications/Risk_Analysis/Annula_Risk_Analysis_2016.pdf (accessed 23 May 2019).

Gammeltoft-Hansen, T. (2011a) *Access to Asylum: International Refugee Law and the Globalisation of Migration Control*. Cambridge: Cambridge University Press.

Gammeltoft-Hansen, T. (2011b) 'Outsourcing asylum: the advent of protection lite', in L. Bialasiewicz (ed.) *Europe in the World: EU Geopolitics and the Making of European Space*. Farnham: Ashgate, 2011, pp. 129–152.

Gammeltoft-Hansen, T. (2014) 'International refugee law and policy: the case of deterrence', *Journal of Refugee Studies* 112:1, 574–595.

Garelli, G., A. Sciurba and M. Tazzioli (2018) 'Introduction: Mediterranean movements and the reconfiguration of the military–humanitarian border in 2015', *Antipode* 50:3, 662–672.

Garelli, G. and M. Tazzioli (2018a) 'The humanitarian war against migrant smugglers at sea', *Antipode* 50:3, 685–703.

Garelli, G. and M. Tazzioli (2018b) 'The biopolitical warfare on migrants: EU naval force and NATO operations of migration government in the Mediterranean', *Critical Military Studies* 4:2, 181–200.

Georgiou, M. and R. Zaborowski (2017) *Media Coverage of the 'Refugee Crisis': A Cross-European Perspective*, Council of Europe Report DG1, available at: https://rm.coe.int/1680706b00 (accessed 3 April 2019).

Global Detention Project (2019) *Country Report, Immigration Detention in Malta: 'Betraying' European Values?* Geneva: Global Detention Project, available at: www.globaldetentionproject.org/wp-content/uploads/2019/06/GDP-Immigration-Detention-in-Malta-June-2019.pdf (accessed 17 September 2019).

Goodwin-Gill, G. and J. McAdam (2007) *The Refugee in International Law*. Oxford: Oxford University Press.

Graham-Harrison, E. (2017) 'Africa's new slave trade: how migrants flee poverty to get sucked into a world of violent crime', *Guardian*, 14 May 2017, available at: www.theguardian.com/global-development/2017/may/13/modern-slavery-african-migrants-libya (accessed 11 May 2020).

Greussing, E. and H. Boomgaarden (2017) 'Shifting the refugee narrative? An automated frame analysis of Europe's 2015 refugee crisis', *Journal of Ethnic and Migration Studies* 43:11, 1749–1774.

Hage, G. (2005) 'A not so multi-sited ethnography of a not so imagined community', *Anthropological Theory* 5:4, 463–475.

Hage, G. (2015) 'Waiting out the crisis: on stuckedness and governmentality', in *Alter-Politics: Critical Anthropology and the Radical Imagination*. Melbourne: Melbourne University Press.

Bibliography

Hage, G. (2016) 'Etat de siège: a dying domesticating colonialism?', *American Ethnologist* 43:1, 38–49.

Hamilton, C., V. Harris, M. Pickover, G. Reid, R. Saleh, and J. Taylor (2002) 'Introduction', in C. Hamilton, V. Harris, M. Pickover, G. Reid, R. Saleh, and J. Taylor (eds) *Refiguring the Archive*. Springer: Netherlands, pp. 7–18.

Hansen, P. and S. Jonsson (2011) 'Bringing Africa as a "dowry to Europe"', *Interventions* 13:3, 443–463.

Hansen, P. and S. Jonsson (2014a) *Eurafrica*. London: Bloomsbury Academic.

Hansen, P. and S. Jonsson (2014b) 'Another colonialism: Africa in the history of European integration', *Journal of Historical Sociology* 27:3, 442–461.

Hastie, B. and F. Crépeau (2014) 'Criminalising irregular migration: the failure of the deterrence model and the need for a human rights alternative', *Immigration, Asylum, and Nationality Law* 28:3, 213–236.

Hay, C. (1999) 'Crisis and the structural transformation of the state: interrogating the process of change', *British Journal of Politics and International Relations* 1:3, 317–344.

Heller, C. and L. Pezzani (2015) *Forensic Oceanography: Report on the Left-to-Die Boat Case*, available at: www.fidh.org/IMG/pdf/fo-report.pdf (accessed 21 July 2020).

Holmes, S. and H. Castaneda (2016) 'Representing the European "refugee crisis" in Germany and beyond: deservingness and difference, life and death', *American Ethnologist* 43:1, 12–24.

Human Rights Watch (2015) *The Mediterranean Migration Crisis: Why People Flee, What the EU Should Do*, available at: www.hrw.org/report/2015/06/19/mediterranean-migration-crisis/why-people-flee-what-eu-should-do# (accessed 21 July 2020).

Huysmans, J. (2006) *The Politics of Security: Fear, Migration and Asylum in the EU*. London: Routledge.

Innes, A. (2015) 'The never-ending journey? Exclusive jurisdictions and migrant mobility in Europe', *Journal of Contemporary European Studies* 23:4, 500–513.

IOM (International Organization for Migration) (2014) *Fatal Journeys: Tracking Lives Lost during Migration*. Geneva: IOM, available at: www.iom.int/files/live/sites/iom/files/pbn/docs/Fatal-Journeys-Tracking-Lives-Lost-during-Migration-2014.pdf (accessed 14 January 2019).

IOM (International Organization for Migration) (2017) *Missing Migrants: Tracking Deaths along Migratory Routes*, available at: https://missingmigrants.iom.int (accessed 23 May 2019).

Isin, E. and B. Nielson (eds) (2008) *Acts of Citizenship*. London: Zed Books.

Italian Interior Ministry (2015) *Rapporto sull'accoglienza di migranti e rifugiati in Italia: Aspetti, procedure, problemi*, available at: www.libertaciviliimmigrazione.dlci.interno. gov.it/it/documentazione/pubblicazioni/rapporto-accoglienza-2015-migranti-e-rifugiati-italia-aspetti-procedure (accessed 21 July 2020).

Jabri, V. (2013) *The Postcolonial Subject*. London: Routledge.

Jarvis, L. (2018) 'Toward a vernacular security studies: origins, interlocutors, contributions, and challenges', *International Studies Review* 21:1, 107–126.

Bibliography

Johnson, H. L. (2012) 'Listening to migrant stories', in M. Salter and C. Mutlu (eds) *Research Methods in Critical Security Studies: An Introduction*. London: Routledge, pp. 67–71.

Johnson, H. L. (2016) 'Narrating entanglements: rethinking the global/local divide in ethnographic migration research', *International Political Sociology* 10:4, 383–397.

Jones, R. (2016) *Violent Borders: Refugees and the Right to Move*. London: Verso.

Kaisary, P. (2014) *The Haitian Revolution in the Literary Imagination: Radical Horizons, Conservative Constraints*. Charlottesville, VA: University of Virginia Press.

Kaminski, M. (2015) 'All the terrorists are migrants', *Politico*, 23 November, available at: www.politico.eu/article/viktor-orban-interview-terrorists-migrants-eu-russia-putin-borders-schengen/ (accessed 7 May 2019).

Khosravi, S. (2011) *'Illegal' Traveller: An Auto-Ethnography of Borders*. Basingstoke: Palgrave Macmillan.

King, N. (2016) *No Borders: The Politics of Immigration Control and Resistance*. London: Zed Books.

Koselleck, R. (2006) 'Crisis', *Journal of the History of Ideas* 67:2, 357–400.

Krastev, I. (2017) *After Europe*. Philadelphia, PA: University of Pennsylvania Press.

Krzyzanowski, M., A. Triandafyllidou, and R. Wodak (2018) 'The mediatisation and the politicisation of the "refugee crisis" in Europe', *Journal of Immigrant and Refugee Studies* 16:1–2, 1–14.

Lemberg-Pedersen, M. (2019) 'Manufacturing displacement: externalisation and postcoloniality in European migration control', *Global Affairs* 5:3, 247–271.

Lester, A. and F. Dussart (2014) *Colonization and the Origins of Humanitarian Government: Protecting Aborigines across the Nineteenth-Century British Empire*. Cambridge: Cambridge University Press.

Leurs, K. and S. Ponzanesi (2018) 'Connected migrants: encapsulation and cosmopolitanisation', *Popular Communication: The International Journal of Media and Culture* 16:1, 4–20.

Little, A. and N. Vaughan-Williams (2017) 'Stopping boats, saving lives, securing subjects: humanitarian borders in Europe and Australia', *European Journal of International Relations* 23:3, 533–556.

Mainwaring, C. (2016) 'Migrant agency: negotiating borders and migration controls', *Migration Studies* 4:3, 289–308.

Mainwaring, C. and N. Brigden (2016) 'Beyond the border: clandestine migration journeys', *Geopolitics* 21:2, 243–262.

Malkki, L. (1996) 'Speechless emissaries: refugees, humanitarianism and dehistoricisation', *Cultural Anthropology* 11:3, 377–404.

Mavelli, L. (2017) 'Governing populations through the humanitarian government of refugees: biopolitical care and racism in the European refugee crisis', *Review of International Studies* 43:5, 809–832.

Mayblin, L. (2014) 'Colonialism, decolonisation, and the right to be human: Britain and the 1951 Geneva Convention on the Status of Refugees', *Journal of Historical Sociology* 27:3, 423–441.

Bibliography

Mayblin, L. (2017) *Asylum After Empire: Colonial Legacies in the Politics of Asylum Seeking.* London: Rowman and Littlefield.

Mayblin, L., M. Wake, and M. Kazemi (2020) 'Necropolitics and the slow violence of the everyday: asylum seeker welfare in the postcolonial present', *Sociology* 54:1, 107–123.

Mbembe, A. (2002) 'The power of the archive and its limits', in C. Hamilton, V. Harris, M. Pickover, G. Reid, R. Saleh, and J. Taylor (eds) *Refiguring the Archive.* Springer: Netherlands, pp. 19–27.

Mbembe, A. (2003) 'Necropolitics', *Public Culture* 15:1, 11–40.

M'charek, A. and J. Black (2019) 'Engaging bodies as matters of care: counting and accounting for death during migration', in P. Cuttitta and T. Last (eds) *Border Deaths: Causes, Dynamics and Consequences of Migration-Related Mortality.* Amsterdam: Amsterdam University Press, pp. 85–102.

McLaughlin, T. (1996) *Street Smarts and Critical Theory: Listening to the Vernacular.* Madison, WI: University of Wisconsin Press.

McMahon, S. and N. Sigona (2018) 'Navigating the central Mediterranean in a time of "crisis": disentangling migration governance and migrant journeys', *Sociology* 52:3, 497–514.

McNevin, A. (2013) 'Ambivalence and citizenship: theorising the political claims of irregular migrants', *Millennium: Journal of International Studies* 41:2, 182–200.

Mezzadra, S. (2004) 'The right to escape', *Ephemera* 4:3, 267–275.

Mezzadra, S. and B. Neilson (2013) *Border as Method, or, The Multiplication of Labour.* Durham, NC: Duke University Press.

Michael, M. (2019) 'Migrants stranded in Libya endure sewage, maggots, disease', *AP News* website, 30 June, available at: www.apnews.com/43eb47c8ce6b4946 a91f8c37f41c7cbe?utm_source=IOM+External+Mailing+List&utm_campaign =864feof7f9-EMAIL_CAMPAIGN_2019_07_01_03_27&utm_medium =email&utm_term=0_9968056566-864feof7f9-43634221 (accessed 16 September 2019).

Mignolo, W. D. (2009) 'Who speaks for the "human" in human rights?', *Hispanic Issues On Line* 5:1, 7–24.

Milstein, B. (2015) 'Thinking politically about crisis: a pragmatist perspective', *European Journal of Political Theory* 14:2, 141–160.

Missing Migrants (2019) *Methodology,* Missing Migrants website, available at: https:// missingmigrants.iom.int/methodology (accessed 30 April 2019).

Motha, S. and H. van Rijswijk (2016) 'Introduction: a counter-archival sense', in S. Motha and H. van Rijswijk (eds) *Law, Memory, Violence: Uncovering the Counter-Archive.* London: Routledge, pp. 1–15.

Mounck, Y. (2018) *The People vs. Democracy: Why Our Freedom is in Danger and How to Save It.* Cambridge, MA: Harvard University Press.

MSF (Médecins Sans Frontières) (2015) *Turning a Blind Eye: How Europe Ignores the Consequences of Outsourced Migration Management.* Barcelona: MSF, available at: www.msf.org.uk/sites/uk/files/turning-a-blind-eye.pdf (accessed 23 May 2019).

Nail, T. (2016a) *Theory of the Border.* Oxford: Oxford University Press.

Bibliography

Nail, T. (2016b) 'A tale of two crises: migration and terrorism after the Paris attacks', *Studies in Ethnicity and Nationalism* 16:1, 158–167.

Nieuwenhuys, C. and A. Pécoud (2007) 'Human trafficking, information campaigns, and strategies of migration control', *American Behavioural Scientist* 50:12, 1674–1695.

Nyers, P. and K. Rygiel (2012) 'Introduction: citizenship, migrant activism, and the politics of movement', in P. Nyers and K. Rygiel (eds) *Citizenship, Migrant Activism, and the Politics of Movement*. London: Routledge, pp. 1–19.

Pain, R. and P. Francis (2003) 'Reflections on participatory research', *Area* 35:1, 45–64.

Pallister-Wilkins, P. (2017) 'Humanitarian rescue/sovereign capture and the policing of possible responses to violent borders', *Global Policy* 8:1, 19–24.

Papadopoulos, D., N. Stephenson, and V. Tsianos (2008) *Escape Routes: Control and Subversion in the Twenty-first Century*. New York: Pluto Press.

Papoutsi, A., J. Painter, E. Papada, and A. Vradis (2018) 'The EC hotspot approach in Greece: creating liminal EU territory', *Journal of Ethnic and Migration Studies* 45:12, 2200–2212.

Pedwell, C. (2014) *Affective Relations: The Transnational Politics of Empathy*. Basingstoke: Palgrave Macmillan.

Pedwell, C. (2016) 'Decolonising empathy: thinking affect transnationally', *Samyukta: A Journal of Women's Studies* 16:1, 27–49.

Perkowski, N. and V. Squire (2019) 'The anti-policy of European anti-smuggling as a site of contestation in the Mediterranean migration "crisis"', *Journal of Ethnic and Migration Studies* 45:12, 2167–2184.

Pirro, A., P. Taggart, and S. van Kessel (2018) 'The populist politics of Euroscepticism in times of crisis: comparative conclusions', *Politics* 38:3, 378–390.

Pro Asyl (2012) *'I Came Here for Peace': The Systemic Ill-Treatment of Migrants and Refugees by State Agents in Patras*. Frankfurt: Pro Asyl in co-operation with the Greek Council for Refugees, available at: www.proasyl.de/en/material/i-came-here-for-peace-the-systematic-ill-treatment-of-migrants-and-refugees-by-state-agents-in-patras/ (accessed 13 June 2019).

Qasmiyeh, Y. M. (2019) 'To embroider the voice with its own needle', *Refugee Hosts Blog*, 16 January, available at: https://refugeehosts.org/2019/01/16/to-embroider-the-voice-with-its-own-needle/ (accessed 30 April 2019).

Rancière, J. (2004) *Disagreement*. Minneapolis, MN: University of Minnesota Press.

Ratcliffe, K. (2005) *Rhetorical Listening: Identification, Gender, Whiteness*. Carbondale: Southern Illinois University Press.

Roitman, J. (2014) *Anti-Crisis*. London: Duke University Press.

Samaddar, R. (2016) *A Post-Colonial Enquiry into Europe's Debt and Migration Crisis*. New York: Springer.

Saucier, P. K. and T. P. Woods (2014) 'Ex aqua: the Mediterranean basin, Africans on the move, and the politics of policing', *Theoria* 61:141, 55–75.

Schapendonk, J. (2012) 'Migrants' im/mobilities on their way to the EU: lost in transit?', *Tijdschrift Voor Economische en Sociale Geografie* 103:5, 577–583.

Bibliography

Scheel, S. (2019) *Autonomy of Migration?: Appropriating Mobility within Biometric Border Regimes*. London: Routledge.

Scheel, S. and V. Squire (2014) 'Forced migrants as "illegal" migrants', in E. Fiddian-Qasmiyeh, G. Loescher, K. Long, and N. Sigona (eds) *The Oxford Handbook of Refugee and Forced Migration Studies*. Oxford: Oxford University Press, pp. 188–199.

Schmitt, C. (2005) [1922] *Political Theology: Four Chapters on the Concept of Sovereignty*. Chicago, IL: University of Chicago Press.

Schwarz, I. (2018) 'Migrants moving through mobility regimes: The trajectory approach as a tool to reveal migratory processes', *Geoforum*, https://doi.org/10.1016/j.geoforum.2018.03.007.

Scott, J. W. (2020) 'Hungarian border politics as an anti-politics of the European Union', *Geopolitics* 25:3, 658–677.

Shapiro, M. (2013) *Studies in Trans-Disciplinary Method: After the Aesthetic Turn*. London: Routledge.

Sharpe, C. (2016) *In the Wake: On Blackness and Being*. Durham: Duke University Press.

Sheller, M. (2016) 'Uneven mobility futures: a Foucauldian approach', *Journal of Mobilities* 11:1, 15–31.

Sigona, N. (2018) 'The contested politics of naming in Europe's "refugee crisis"', *Ethnic and Racial Studies* 41:3, 456–460.

Skafish, P. (2009) 'Introduction', in E. Viveiros de Castro, *Cannibal Metaphysics*. Mineapolis: Univocal Publishing, pp. 9–33.

Sossi, F. (2013) 'Migrations and militant research: some brief considerations', *Postcolonial Studies* 16:3, 269–278.

Spivak, G. C. (1988) 'Can the subaltern speak?', in C. Nelson and L. Grossberg (eds) *Marxism and the Interpretation of Culture*. Champaign, IL: University of Illinois Press, pp. 271–313.

Squire, V. (2009) *The Exclusionary Politics of Asylum*. Basingstoke: Palgrave Macmillan.

Squire, V. (2011) 'The contested politics of mobility: politicising mobility, mobilising politics', in V. Squire (ed.) *The Contested Politics of Mobility: Borderzones and Irregularity*. Basingstoke: Palgrave Macmillan, pp. 1–26.

Squire, V. (2015a) *Post/Humanitarian Border Politics Between Mexico and the US*. Basingstoke: Palgrave Macmillan.

Squire, V. (2015b) 'Acts of desertion: the ambiguities of abandonment and renouncement across the Sonoran borderzone', *Antipode* 47:2, 500–516.

Squire, V. (2017) 'Governing migration through death in Europe and the US: identification, burial, and the crisis of modern humanism', *European Journal of International Relations* 23:3, 513–532.

Squire, V. (2018) 'Researching precarious migrations: qualitative strategies toward a positive transformation of the politics of migration', *British Journal of Politics and International Relations* 20:2, 441–458.

Squire, V. (2020a) *Europe's Migration Crisis: Border Deaths and Human Dignity*. Cambridge: Cambridge University Press.

Bibliography

Squire, V. (2020b) 'Hidden geographies of the "Mediterranean migration crisis"', *Environment and Planning C: Politics and Space*, https://doi.org/10.1177/2399654420935904.

Squire, V., A. Dimitriadi, N. Perkowski, M. Pisani, D. Stevens, and N. Vaughan-Williams (2017) *Crossing the Mediterranean Sea by Boat: Mapping and Documenting Migratory Journeys and Experiences*, Final Project Report, 4 May 2017, available at: www.warwick.ac.uk/crossingthemed (accessed 3 April 2019).

Squire, V. and V. Touhouliotis (2016) *Fleeing Europe?*, openDemocracy website, 3 August, available at: www.opendemocracy.net/en/5050/fleeing-europe/ (accessed 29 August 2019).

Steedman, C. (2001) *Dust: The Archive and Cultural History*. New Jersey: Rutgers University Press.

Steinhilper, E. and R. Gruijters (2017) 'Border deaths in the Mediterranean: what we can learn from the latest data', *Border Criminologies Blog*, 8 March, available at: www.law.ox.ac.uk/research-subject-groups/centre-criminology/centreborder-criminologies/blog/2017/03/border-deaths (accessed 3 April 2019).

Stevens, D. (2004) *UK Asylum Law and Policy: Historical and Contemporary Perspectives*. London: Sweet and Maxwell.

Stevens, D. and A. Dimitriadi (2019) 'Crossing the Eastern Mediterranean Sea in search of "protection"', *Journal of Immigrant & Refugee Studies* 17:3, 261–278.

Stierl, M. (2016) 'A sea of struggle: activist border interventions in the Mediterranean Sea', *Citizenship Studies* 20:5, 561–578.

Stoler, A. L. (2002) 'Colonial archives and the arts of government: on the content in the form', in C. Hamilton, V. Harris, M. Pickover, G. Reid, R. Saleh, and J. Taylor (eds) *Refiguring the Archive*. Netherlands: Springer, pp. 83–102.

Stoler, A. L. (2009) *Along the Archival Grain: Epistemic Anxieties and Colonial Common Sense*. Princeton, NJ: Princeton University Press.

Suliman, S. (2016) 'Mobility and the kinetic politics of development', *Review of International Studies* 42:4, 702–723.

Ticktin, M. (2016) 'Thinking beyond humanitarian borders', *Social Research* 83:2, 255–271.

Tilley, L. (2018) *Interview – Lisa Tilley*, E-International Relations website, 19 July, available at: www.e-ir.info/2018/07/19/interview-lisa-tilley/ (accessed 29 August 2019).

Triulzi, A. and R. McKenzie (2013) *Long Journeys: African Migrants on the Road*. Leiden: Brill.

Tudor, A. (2018) 'Cross-fadings of racialisation and migratisation: the postcolonial turn in Western European gender and migration studies', *Gender, Place and Culture: A Journal of Feminist Geography* 25:7, 1057–1072.

UN (2018) *Global Compact for Safe, Orderly and Regular Migration, final draft*, available at: www.un.org/pga/72/wp-content/uploads/sites/51/2018/07/migration.pdf (accessed 19 March 2019).

UN General Assembly (1951) Convention Relating to the Status of Refugees, 28 July 1951, United Nations, Treaty Series, Vol. 189, p. 137.

Bibliography

UN General Assembly (2013) *Regional Study: Management of the External Borders of the EU and its Impact on the Human Rights Of Migrants*, available at: www.ohchr.org/Documents/HRBodies/HRCouncil/RegularSession/Session23/A.HRC.23.46_en.pdf (accessed 13 June 2019).

UNHCR (2015) *Malta Asylum Trends 2005–2015*, available at: www.unhcr.org/mt/wp-content/uploads/sites/54/2018/05/8_2005-2015_fs.pdf.pdf (accessed 21 July 2020).

UNHCR (2017) *Operational Portal, Refugee Situations: Mediterranean Situation*, available at: https://data2.unhcr.org/en/situations/mediterranean (accessed 5 April 2017).

van Munster, R. (2009) *Securitising Immigration: The Politics of Risk in the EU*. Basingstoke: Palgrave Macmillan.

Vaughan-Williams, N. (2015) *Europe's Border Crisis: Biopolitical Security and Beyond*. Oxford: Oxford University Press.

Vaughan-Williams, N. and M. Pisani (2020) 'Migrating borders, bordering lives: Everyday geographies of ontological security and insecurity in Malta', *Social and Cultural Geography* 21:5, 651–673.

Vaughan-Williams, N. and D. Stevens (2016) 'Vernacular theories of everyday (in)security: the disruptive potential of non-elite knowledge', *Security Dialogue* 47:1, 40–58.

Wall, I. (2012) *Human Rights and Constituent Power: Without Model or Warranty*. Abingdon: Routledge, 2012.

Walters, W. (2002) 'Mapping Schengenland: denaturalising the border', *Environment and Planning D: Society and Space* 20:5, 564–580.

White, H. (1987) *The Content of the Form: Narrative Discourse and Historical Representation*. Baltimore: Johns Hopkins University Press.

Whyte, K. (2018) 'Indigenous science (fiction) for the Anthropocene: ancestral dystopias and fantasies of climate change crises', *Environment and Planning E: Nature and Space* 1:1–2, 224–242.

Williams, A. T. (2009) 'Taking values seriously: towards a philosophy of EU law', *Oxford Journal of Legal Studies* 29:3, 549–577.

Williams, A. T. (2010) *The Ethos of Europe*. Cambridge: Cambridge University Press.

Withnall, A. (2016) 'Nato orders fleet to deploy in Aegean Sea "to help end Europe's refugee crisis"', *Independent*, 11 February, available at: www.independent.co.uk/news/world/europe/nato-orders-fleet-to-deploy-in-aegean-sea-to-help-end-europes-refugee-crisis-a6867076.html (accessed 30 June 2019).

Woods, T. P. and P. K. Saucier, (2015) *Slavery's Afterlife in the Euro-Mediterranean Basin*, openDemocracy website, 19 June, available at: www.opendemocracy.net/en/beyond-trafficking-and-slavery/slaverys-afterlife-in-euromediterranean-basin/ (accessed 11 May 2020).

Wynter, S. (2003) 'Unsettling the coloniality of being/power/truth/freedom: towards the human, after man, its overrepresentation – an argument', *New Centennial Review* 3:3, 257–237.

Youngs, R. (2017) *New Directions for the EU: Europe Reset*. London: IB Tauris.

Bibliography

Zetter, R. (1991) 'Labelling refugees: forming and transforming a bureaucratic identity', *Journal of Refugee Studies* 4:1, 39–62.

Zetter, R. (2007) 'More labels, fewer refugees: remaking the refugee label in an era of globalization', *Journal of Refugee Studies* 20:2, 172–192.

Zetter, R. and G. Benezer (2014) 'Searching for directions: conceptual and methodological challenges in researching refugee journeys', *Journal of Refugee Studies* 28:1, 297–318.

Zhang, X. and L. Hellmueller (2017) 'Visual framing of the European refugee crisis in *Der Spiegel* and *CNN International*: global journalism in news photographs', *International Communication Gazette* 79:5, 483–510.

Index

Index

criminalisation of migration 73–76, 98–100

crisis narratives 20–34, 38–41, 44–45, 73–78, 100, 107, 127, 130, 134, 139
  academic 27–33
  see also migration crisis

crisis politics 1–5, 9–13, 17, 52, 102–103, 158–161, 169, 183–184, 189–190

critical research 13–14, 51, 53

deaths
  documentation of 52
  at sea 4, 12–13, 21, 23, 26–33, 39–40, 45, 52–53, 82–83, 107, 158

decolonisation 122, 182, 185, 188, 191

De Genova, N. 34

dehumanisation and rehumanisation 179

deportation 14, 71, 77–80

Derrida, J. 51–54

destinations of migrants 86, 118

detention facilities 78

deterrence of migration 1–2, 5–15, 18, 21, 47, 51, 70–84, 87, 97–100, 111, 161–162, 179–187, 190
  harmful effects of 102
  ineffectiveness of 70–71, 76–77, 83, 100, 140, 183–4

development programmes 176–177, 182

Dines, N. 29

discrimination and discriminatory attitudes 49, 156

displaced persons 103

dominant groups 49

Dotson, K. 47, 49, 59

'drivers and conditions of flight' 112–121, 127, 129, 184–190

drivers of migration generally 77, 83–85, 97–98, 140, 170, 174–175, 178

Dublin Regulation 43, 77–78, 165

economic migrants 24, 32
  problematisation of the term 10

Education, Audiovisual and Culture Executive Agency (EACEA) 78

empathy 32

'enacted' borders 40–41

equal treatment of migrants 18, 166

escape from war zones 85, 138–139, 172–174, 178, 181–182

ethnography 53

Eurafrica 133

Eurocentrism 22, 28, 33, 38

A European Agenda on Migration (2015) 2–7, 23, 27, 31, 67, 70–80, 87, 92, 99, 102–103, 121, 127, 130, 132, 161, 168, 178, 190–191

European Asylum Support Office (EASO) 52

European Border and Coast Guard Agency 24
  see also Frontex

European Commission 2–3, 22–31, 34–35, 40

European Union (EU) 20, 75–76, 127
  Action Plan Against Migrant Smuggling 7, 87
  Charter 133
  critical moment for addressing migration issues 3, 5
  documents and treaties of 140
  failure to live up commitments 161, 167–168
  policy agenda 15–18, 57, 127, 168–169, 178–179, 182, 184
  values 130–132, 135, 157–159, 190

Euroscepticism 28

expectations of migrants about Europe 111, 135–140, 145–147

expertise' of migrants themselves 9, 12, 14, 54–59, 77, 179–183

extortion 93

Facebook 82

family reunification 152–154, 164, 181

Fanon, F. 36, 126

Fassin, D. 32–33

fences, construction of 27

Index

Index

Index

Index

EU authorised representative for GPSR:
Easy Access System Europe, Mustamäe tee 50,
10621 Tallinn, Estonia
gpsr.requests@easproject.com

www.ingramcontent.com/pod-product-compliance
Lightning Source LLC
Chambersburg PA
CBHW052004270326
41929CB00015B/2781